THE LAKE POWELL BOATER'S GUIDE

BY
DENNIS NETOFF
GARY LADD
SUSAN LAMB
CHARLES W. WOOD
JAMES S. HOLLAND

Illustrated by
Berniece A. Andersen
Elizabeth Morales-Denney
Pamela G. Frazier
Dennis Netoff

Photography by
Tom Bean
Gary Ladd
Dennis Netoff

The illustrations of the wood rat on page 143, the badger, black-tailed jackrabbit, porcupine, striped skunk, long-tailed weasel, and beaver on page 144, and the bobcat, desert bighorn, mule deer, coyote and gray fox on page 145 are from *Mammal Finder* by Ron Russo and Pam Olhausen, copyright 1987 by Nature Study Guild, and are used by permission of Nature Study Guild.

Edited by Sandra Scott, Ruth Reitmeier
Designed by Robert Mott & Associates, San Diego
Production Coordination: Cynthia A. Zimmerli
Editorial Advisory: Dave Pape

GLEN CANYON

Natural History Association

Published by
Glen Canyon Natural History Association
and
Grand Canyon Natural History Association
© Copyright Glen Canyon Natural
History Association, Page, Arizona 1989

ISBN 0-9622233-1-X
Library of Congress Catalogue No. 89-084049

TABLE OF
CONTENTS

MAP OF LAKE POWELL REGION

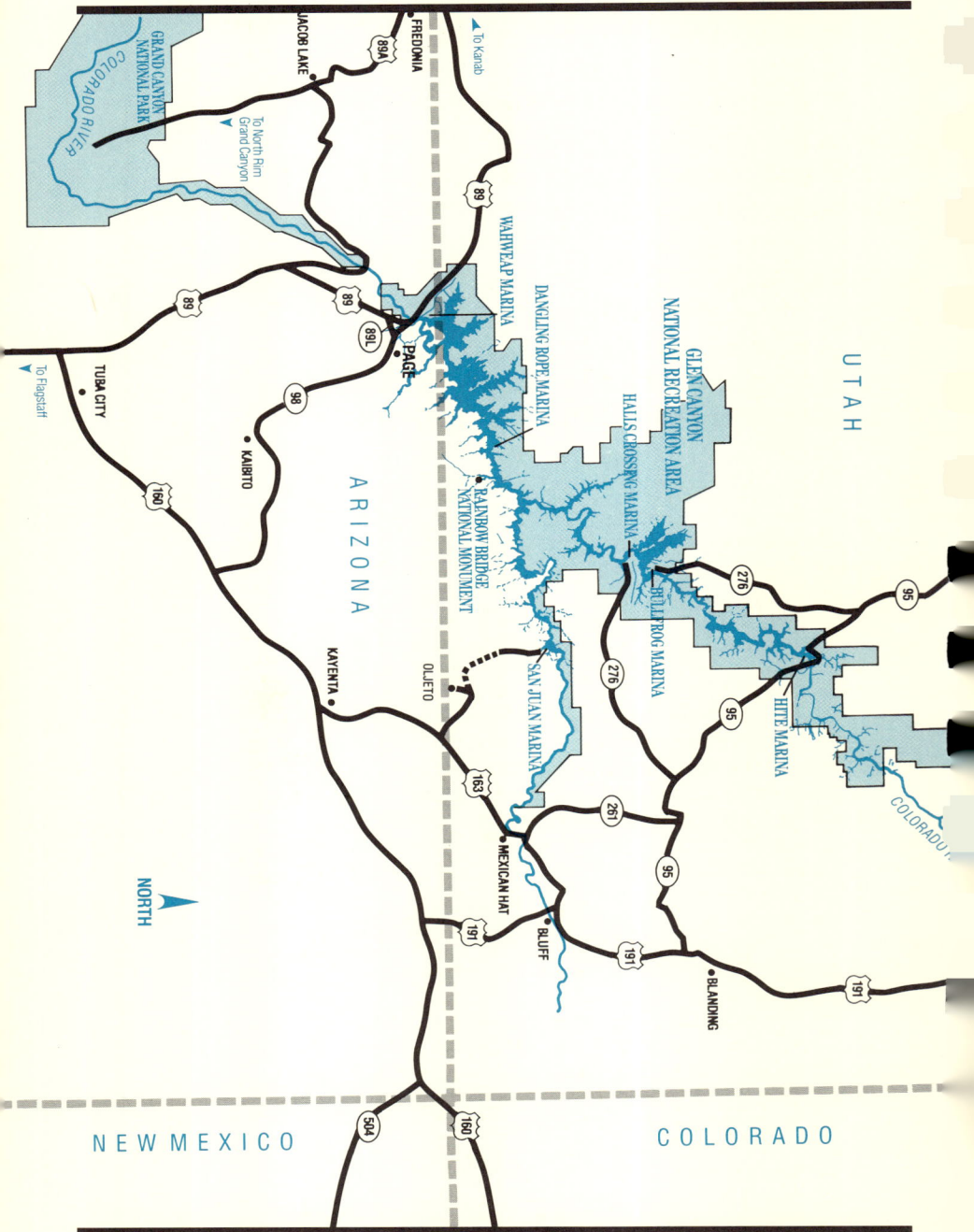

GRAND CANYON NATIONAL PARK

COLORADO RIVER

JACOB LAKE

FREDONIA

89A

To Kanab

To North Rim Grand Canyon

89

89

89L

PAGE

98

WAHWEAP MARINA

DANGLING ROPE MARINA

GLEN CANYON NATIONAL RECREATION AREA

HALLS CROSSING MARINA

U T A H

To Flagstaff

TUBA CITY

KAIBITO

160

A R I Z O N A

RAINBOW BRIDGE NATIONAL MONUMENT

BULLFROG MARINA

276

95

276

HITE MARINA

95

COLORADO

KAYENTA

OLJETO

SAN JUAN MARINA

NORTH

163

261

95

MEXICAN HAT

191

BLUFF

191

BLANDING

191

N E W   M E X I C O

504

160

C O L O R A D O

Perhaps the first and most lasting impression is of the immensity of it all: the land, the sky, the lake itself.

You can marvel at a horizon a hundred miles distant, or wedge yourself between narrow sandstone walls, the sky a blue shoelace hundreds of feet above.

Some visitors have termed this region a part of the last great wilderness of the forty-eight contiguous states, and with good reason. One can lose one's self here, both philosophically and physically, and in a seemingly endless variety of environments.

This site, administered by the National Park Service, is among the youngest of the categories of park areas, those known as national park recreation areas, and is distinguished by being perhaps the fastest growing in terms of popularity.

Lake Powell, created by the construction of Glen Canyon Dam, extends across the Arizona-Utah boundary for a distance equivalent to that between New York and Baltimore. It is the second largest man-made lake in the nation. Its corrugated shoreline extends for 1,960 miles, greater than the entire West Coast shoreline. It has ninety-six major canyons, any one of which offers adventure and discovery.

Certainly Lake Powell is the best-known and most popular attraction of Glen Canyon National Recreation Area and it is there that the Park Service and concessionaires have concentrated most of their staff and physical facilities. Yet the lake represents only 13 percent of the two thousand square mile surface area of the park and the casual visitor who confines his interest to the lake alone does himself a grave injustice. Beyond the lake shore are countless resources.

Centuries before men even dreamed of taming the Colorado with giant dams, there was a civilization here in this desert Southwest. It was a primitive culture, to be sure, and our knowledge of it is limited. Yet we know with certainty that the people who dwelled here made their homes in south-facing alcoves that offered winter sun and summer shade, harvested crops in small plots along the streams below, and maintained some degree of communication and social interchange by complex pathways along and above the canyons.

INTRODUCTION

Visitors can yet see some of their crude shelters and speculate that scores, perhaps hundreds, more of the ruins remain hidden away in remote canyons or on plateaus far from the casual tourist path. Modern visitors can see — even touch — the mysterious figures of gods, men, animals and symbols that these early canyon residents carved or painted on rock panels, and wonder at their meaning.

One can follow the path of the Franciscan Fathers Dominguez and Escalante, who were here even as our Constitution was being drafted in Philadelphia. Thwarted in their quest for a trade route to California, the Fathers left for later generations a remarkable log of their journey, a ford of the Colorado River still called Crossing of the Fathers, and their names — one for a splendid river and canyon, the other for a tall butte that stands sentinel-like in Padre Bay.

One can still see and feel the presence of Major John Wesley Powell, for whom the lake is named; the quixotic John D. Lee who gave his name to a ferry and a political boundary crucial to the water interests of seven states; and the 250 men, women and children who comprised the Hole-in-the-Rock party that challenged seemingly impossible odds — and won!

All of these are a part of the history of this remarkable area we know as Glen Canyon National Recreation Area.

These historic resources comprise a fascinating and well-documented record, a testimonial authored by men and women of bygone times.

The unparalleled scenic riches of this place are the product of time and the elements.

Lake Powell, of course, is the result of a single dam whose concrete crest extends nearly one-third mile across the sandstone rim of Glen Canyon itself.

The lake's blue waters, more than five hundred feet deep in places, come from a score of rivers draining from the Upper Basin states of Colorado, Wyoming, Utah and New Mexico. From Glen Canyon, waters released through the dam pass southward through Marble Canyon, the Grand Canyon, along the Arizona-California boundary and on through Mexico. The Colorado scarcely exists at all by the time it reaches the Gulf of California, 763 miles downstream from Glen Canyon Dam. It is a totally consumed river, its waters drawn away through canals and aqueducts for irrigation and to serve such metropolitan areas as Los Angeles.

Here in these bays and canyons, however, Glen Canyon Dam impounds precious water that offers year-round recreation for millions.

To accommodate those impressive numbers, the National Park Service, the park's principal concessioner, and the Navajo Nation have spent many millions of dollars on marinas and visitor facilities, including food service, lodging, boat and automotive repair, and campgrounds. There are six marinas presently on the lake, one of them operated by the Navajo Nation on the San Juan River. The Navajos also intend to build and operate another at Antelope Point near Page, Arizona.

Even with these developments, however, visitor demands continue for expanded levels of service throughout the lake at a time of limited funding and the pursuit of a balanced national budget. To answer this dilemma, the National Park Service and the concessioner in 1986 undertook an innovative approach known as the Set Aside Program. By contractual agreement, it provides for the concessioner to establish a special account funded by 5 percent of gross receipts at the five concessioner-operated marinas on Lake Powell. Through the year 1990, the Set Aside Program is expected to yield some $8 million for such facilities as water and sewer improvements, utility services, boat pumpout and comfort stations, launch ramps and parking to accommodate this growing public demand. The legislative charter of the National Park Service, enacted by the Congress in 1916, requires that we provide for the public's use and enjoyment of these special areas that are part of the National Park system. The developments funded by the Set Aside Program are an expression of that commitment.

But we also have another obligation, one that you, the visitor, must help to fulfill. That is the protection and preservation of the parklands and their resources. You may help us in several ways.

Here in Glen Canyon National Recreation Area, the visitor is in the heartland of what may be the richest area in all the United States in numbers and density of sites that tell the stories of earlier civilizations. Prime archaeologic sites abound. These fragile sites and their resources form a significant part of our national heritage. They are protected by law. Under no circumstances should visitors disturb any of these sites, or change or remove anything found there. We ask your help by treading respectfully, by taking only photographs and leaving only footprints.

Also, we invite visitors to assume a direct responsibility for Glen Canyon National Recreation Area with our Adopt A Canyon program. Daily during the height of the season, visitors by the thousands are dispersed in all manner of watercraft throughout Lake Powell. If you are among them, we invite you to Adopt a Canyon and spend some brief time during your visit collecting any litter that you might find in a particular canyon of your choice. Adopt A Canyon was begun in 1985 as a means of enlisting the public's aid in keeping the area as clean and natural as possible. If you are interested, stop by any ranger office and sign up. A ranger will suggest a canyon for you, provide you with trash bags, and arrange for you to receive a special certificate when you depart.

INTRODUCTION

Third, we ask that you be safety conscious while here at Glen Canyon. Your safety and that of others in your party are paramount. Visitors perish here each year—by drowning, boat accidents, propeller cuts, in auto accidents. We want to stop these tragedies, and we urgently seek your support in accomplishing that goal.

Finally, whether here at Glen Canyon or elsewhere in the National Park system, we encourage you to learn as much as possible about these special places. Each park area was added to the system because of some unique or exceptional historic, cultural, natural or recreational feature. Without exception, there is much more to a park area than first meets the eye.

Stop at the Visitor Center, view the exhibits, attend interpretive presentations. Read a variety of books and publications about the area. Talk with our rangers; hike the trails; and pause to absorb and reflect. You will rejoice with a sense of discovery, and you will emerge with an intimate sense of sharing in the stewardship of these priceless areas that comprise the National Park System.

—Jim Harpster, *National Park Service*

photo by Tom Bean

Lake Powell is the second largest man-made reservoir in the United States with a capacity of over twenty-seven million acre feet of water. Only Lake Mead is larger. At high pool the lake is 186 miles long from the dam to the rapids at the head of navigation, and has nearly two thousand miles of shoreline, more than the entire west coast of the conterminous United States.

WEATHER AND CLIMATE

T he major source of Lake Powell's water is inflow from the Colorado River, which supplies about ten million to thirteen million acre feet of water in an average year. The San Juan River, the second largest donor, supplies about 500,000 to 750,000 acre feet annually. The contributions of the other streams that feed the lake are relatively minor.

The dramatic seasonal changes in volume of flow from tributaries affect the lake level and the clarity of the water. Normally, peak flows occur during May and June as they are fed primarily from snowmelt in the high Rockies. Low inflow occurs during the fall and winter months.

Average surface water temperatures of the lake typically are at a minimum of the mid-40s in January or February, and around 80°F in July or August. Cloudy skies, cool air and strong winds can lower surface temperatures several degrees in a few hours. Cooler surface temperatures may also occur where the Colorado and San Juan rivers discharge chilly waters into the lake.

Subsurface temperatures are much cooler and show far less daily and seasonal fluctuation in temperature.

The water inflow from the Colorado and San Juan rivers, especially during times of high discharge, creates murky waters that may continue for miles into the lake. Even the smaller tributaries such as the Escalante, Dirty Devil, and Dark Canyon can cause considerable murkiness during peak flow. If the waters that enter the lake from the tributaries are cold and therefore fairly dense, then they tend to sink to the bottom of the lake, leaving the water downlake relatively clear.

Temperatures

Warm to hot summer months and cool to mild winters are the norm for the Recreation Area, although short-term temperature variations may be drastic. Ninety and hundred degree days may be followed by evening temperatures of 50° or 60°F from spring to fall. Passing summer thunderstorms can drop the air temperature twenty degrees or more in a few minutes. During the cooler season, the passage of a cold front may drop the temperature thirty degrees in a few hours. At Wahweap, July maximum temperatures average 97°F and January minimums average 24°F.

Humidity and Precipitation

Sparse precipitation and clear skies are trademarks of the Canyonlands. It has been estimated that places such as Hite Marina have cloudless skies for about two hundred days a year, with less than forty days a year receiving measurable rain.

Precipitation, like temperature, varies with elevation, averaging five to eight inches in the Recreation Area. Much of the rain comes in the form of mid-afternoon thunderstorms during the summer months. These storms usually last only a few minutes but may be very intense. Winter storms last longer but are not as intense.

High summer temperatures seem more comfortable because of the low humidities and the effects of the wind. At mid-day humidity is frequently less than 20 percent. A slight breeze will also help cool the skin, and the shade of a canyon wall can make even the hottest summer day seem tolerable, as geologist Herbert Gregory stated in his account of the San Juan Country in 1938:

> *To escape the discomfort of the hottest days spent traversing bare ledges and sand-floored washes, it is only necessary to seek the shade of a rock. The edge of a shadow is the dividing line between heat and delightful coolness.*

Winds

The prevailing winds are from the southwest, although south and southeast winds are also common, especially in the summer. Topography greatly influences local winds. They swirl around buttes and mesas, blow up and down canyons, and even reverse directions on a day-night basis in some locations. Larger mountains, such as Navajo Mountain and the Henry Mountains adjacent to the lake, are so influential that they can cause "standing waves" of wind to develop in the lee of the mountain, often producing lens-shaped, or lenticular, clouds in the sky.

During the warmer months, there is usually a fairly consistent daytime breeze with little or no wind at night. Afternoons can be gusty. Hot summer days can also produce active thermals that may become small "twisters" or dust devils. Occasional severe winds, such as the ones that damaged several mobile homes and flipped boats at Wahweap during the spring of 1983, are usually associated with thunderstorms or squall lines. Severe winter winds are less common, but can occur, particularly during the passage of fronts.

Clouds and Weather Disturbances

Clouds are a condensed form of atmospheric water and signify that some kind of cooling process has occurred to cause them. Since most clouds form due to cooling from expansion that accompanies uplift of air, they tell something of the dynamics of the atmosphere. Clouds that form on the windward side of mountains and plateaus illustrate the cooling effect of air being uplifted.

During the warmer months, the overheated ground can cause air above it to rise, resulting in the formation of small, cottonball-shaped cumulus clouds. By mid-afternoon these may grow higher and wider, forming ominous, towering cumulonimbus clouds that bring thunder, lightning, heavy rains and gusty winds. Once formed, they tend to generate more clouds, sometimes dominating the entire sky for a few hours before dissipating in the evening hours. Thunderstorms reach peak activity during the "mini-monsoon" season, when for a few weeks in the late summer moist air masses are brought inland from the subtropical ocean areas.

During the cooler season, air masses from higher latitudes occasionally penetrate the Lake Powell region. The collision of these cool air masses with warmer ones to the south creates a front. The cold air acts like a wedge, forcing the warmer air aloft and creating an extensive cloud deck in the process. Rain or snow may accompany a frontal passage. Although no single cloud type can predict an approaching front, there is typically a sequential development of clouds through time, beginning with high, thin clouds which later lower and become progressively more dense.

The lenticular clouds that form at the crests of the standing wind waves on the leeward side of mountains may also foretell the day's weather. These disc-shaped clouds are often accompanied on the surface by warm, dry, gusty Chinook winds.

Clouds and cliffs near Friendship Cove

photo by Tom Bean

BOATING

Excellent launch ramps are available at all marinas except Dangling Rope. Dry storage is available at most marinas for those wanting to leave their boats at the lake.

Rental boats are available at all marinas except Dangling Rope. They range from small skiffs and bass boats to houseboats. Houseboat reservations should be made as far in advance as possible, especially during the summer season.

Boat camping is unrestricted along Lake Powell's shoreline, except near marinas, swim beaches and within a mile of developed areas. Lakeside camping is wild (no running water or toilets), free, and limited to fourteen days per visit.

Marinas and Facilities

Mileages from Marina to Marina

	Bullfrog	Dangling Rope	Halls Crossing	Hite	Rainbow Bridge	San Juan Marina	Wahweap
Bullfrog Marina	0	55	3	47	53	88	80
Dangling Rope Marina	55	0	52	97	10	69	27
Halls Crossing Marina	3	52	0	46	50	86	77
Hite Marina	47	97	46	0	93	131	123
Rainbow Bridge	53	10	50	93	0	61	34
San Juan Marina	88	69	86	131	61	0	87
Wahweap Marina	80	27	77	123	34	87	0

Equipment Checklist

Develop your own checklist in advance of your trip. The following contains suggested equipment and some helpful hints:

Safety Equipment
- ☐ Flotation devices for all on board
- ☐ First-aid kit, including sunburn medication
- ☐ Fire extinguisher

Emergency Equipment
- ☐ Distress signals (flares, lanterns)
- ☐ Flashlights and extra batteries
- ☐ Radiotelephone

Navigational Equipment
- ☐ Maps and charts—No true navigational charts are available for Lake Powell at this time. The maps included in this chapter are adequate for most purposes and are based on a variety of sources.
- ☐ Compass *(Caution: Metal objects on boat may deflect needle.)*
- ☐ Depth sounder

13

BOATING

Boat Equipment
☐ Extra prop, shear pin
☐ Anchor
☐ Extra line
☐ Tools
☐ Fuel

Provisions
☐ Food
☐ Water
☐ Beverages
☐ Ice

Personal and Recreational Equipment
☐ Suitable clothing (including hat, sunglasses, deck/ tennis shoes, foul weather gear, hiking shoes, etc.). Resist over packing.
☐ Suntan oil, sun screen *(lots!)*
☐ Games, radio-tape player, cards, literature

Helpful Hints
☐ Make sure all on board know safety rules, docking procedures, etc.
☐ Know your destination and mileage. It is a long way from one marina to the next on Lake Powell.
☐ Be familiar with rules of the road, buoy system, etc. Much of this is explained later in this chapter.
☐ Have a second person on board capable of piloting boat in case main pilot becomes incapacitated.

Check Before Leaving the Dock
☐ Engine and steering mechanism
☐ Anchor lights and running lights
☐ Horn in working order
☐ Bilge fumes and water

NOTE: Additional literature and maps may be purchased from the Glen Canyon Natural History Association bookstore located in the Carl Hayden Visitor Center. For pre-trip ordering or for a publications list contact them at P.O. Box 581, Page, Arizona 86040.

Glen Canyon Dam and Carl Haden Visitor Center are located five miles south of Wahweap Marina on Highway 89. Carl Haden Visitor Center has information services, audio visual presentations, exhibits of the dam, tours of the dam, gift shop, and the Glen Canyon Natural History Association bookstore.

The modern town of Page, Arizona, is the only community of any size adjacent to the lake. Page is a full-service community with all expected facilities and services of a community with a population of approximately 8,000. The National Park Service Headquarters for Glen Canyon National Recreation Area are located in Page.

BOATING

BULLFROG MARINA

Fuel dock — *regular, mixed, and diesel*
Stores
Boat rental
Pump-out station for boats
RV park
Launch ramp
Fish-cleaning station
Picnic area
Ranger station
RV pump-out
Laundry and shower
Post Office
Clinic
Boat tours
Lodge and Restaurant, Gift shop
Visitor center
Dry storage
Launch and retrieval
Service station
Boat repair
Camping

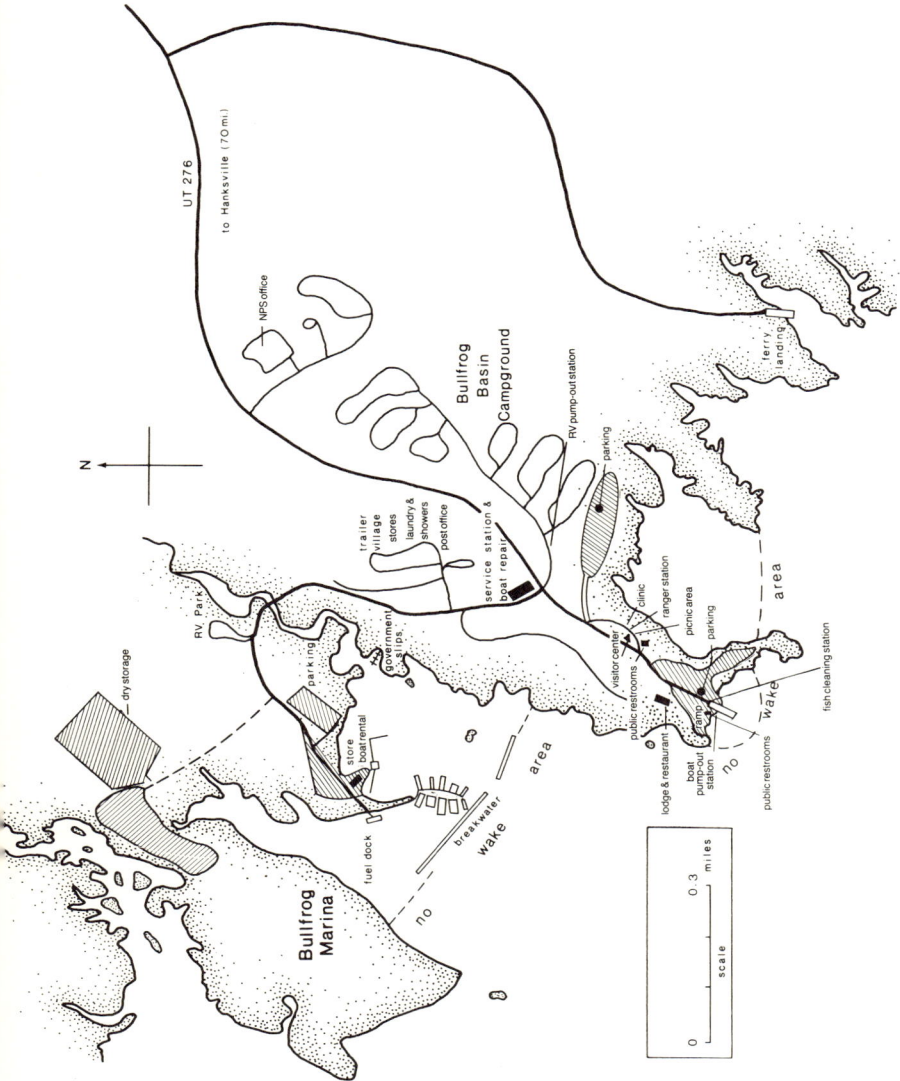

Map of Bullfrog Marina area. Labels include: UT 276, to Hanksville (70 mi.), NPS office, Bullfrog Basin Campground, RV pump-out station, trailer village, stores, laundry & showers, post office, service station & boat repair, parking, RV Park, government slips, store, boat rental, dry storage, fuel dock, Bullfrog Marina, breakwater, no wake area, visitor center, public restrooms, clinic, ranger station, picnic area, parking, lodge & restaurant, boat pump-out station, ramp, public restrooms, no wake area, fish-cleaning station, ferry landing. Scale: 0 / 0.3 miles. Compass: N.

BOATING

DANGLING ROPE MARINA — *(Accessible by boat only)*

Fuel dock — *regular, mixed, and supreme*
Store
Trash deposits
Restrooms
Pump-out station
Ranger station
Emergency boat towing and minor repair
Emergency radio communications with Wahweap

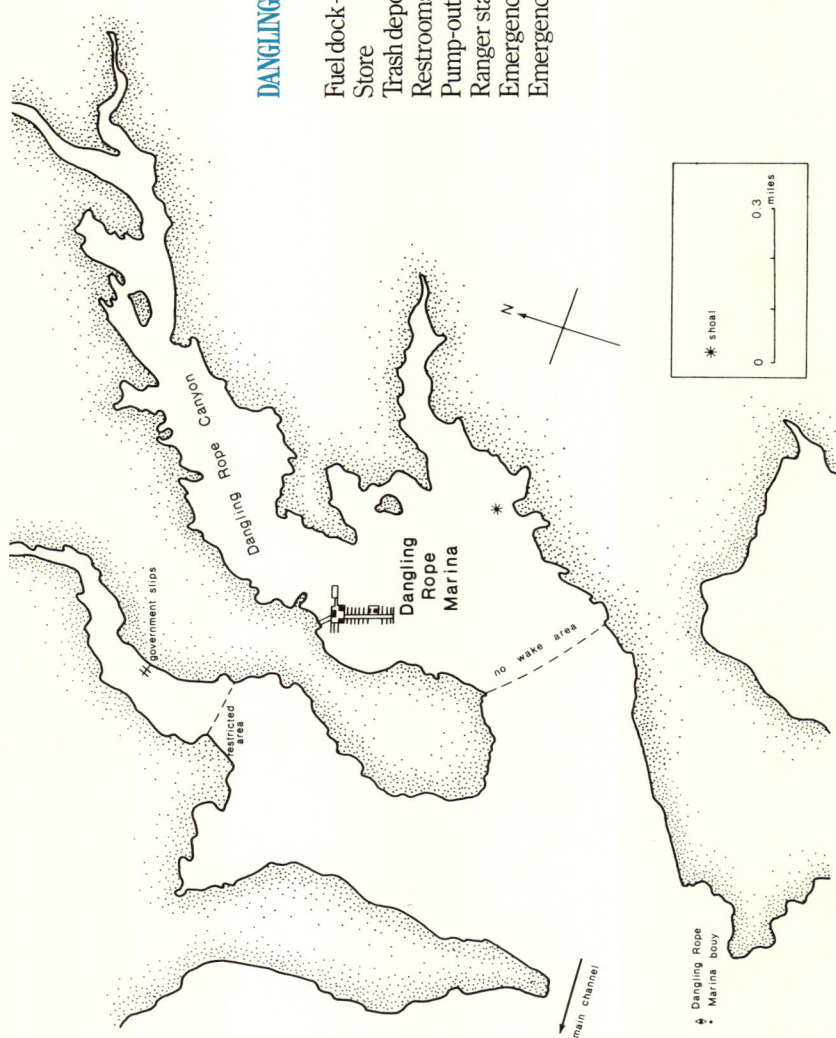

Dangling Rope Canyon

Dangling
Rope
Marina

government slips

no wake area

restricted
area

N

shoal

0   0.3
          miles

main channel

Dangling Rope
Marina bouy

BOATING

HALLS CROSSING MARINA

Fuel—*regular, mixed, and diesel*
Pump-out stations; boat and RV
Ranger station
Shower and laundry
Dry storage
Store
Launch ramp
Boat repair
Boat rental
Service station

Housekeeping units
Gravel airstrip
Boat launching and retrieval
Campground/RV park
Courtesy dock
Restrooms

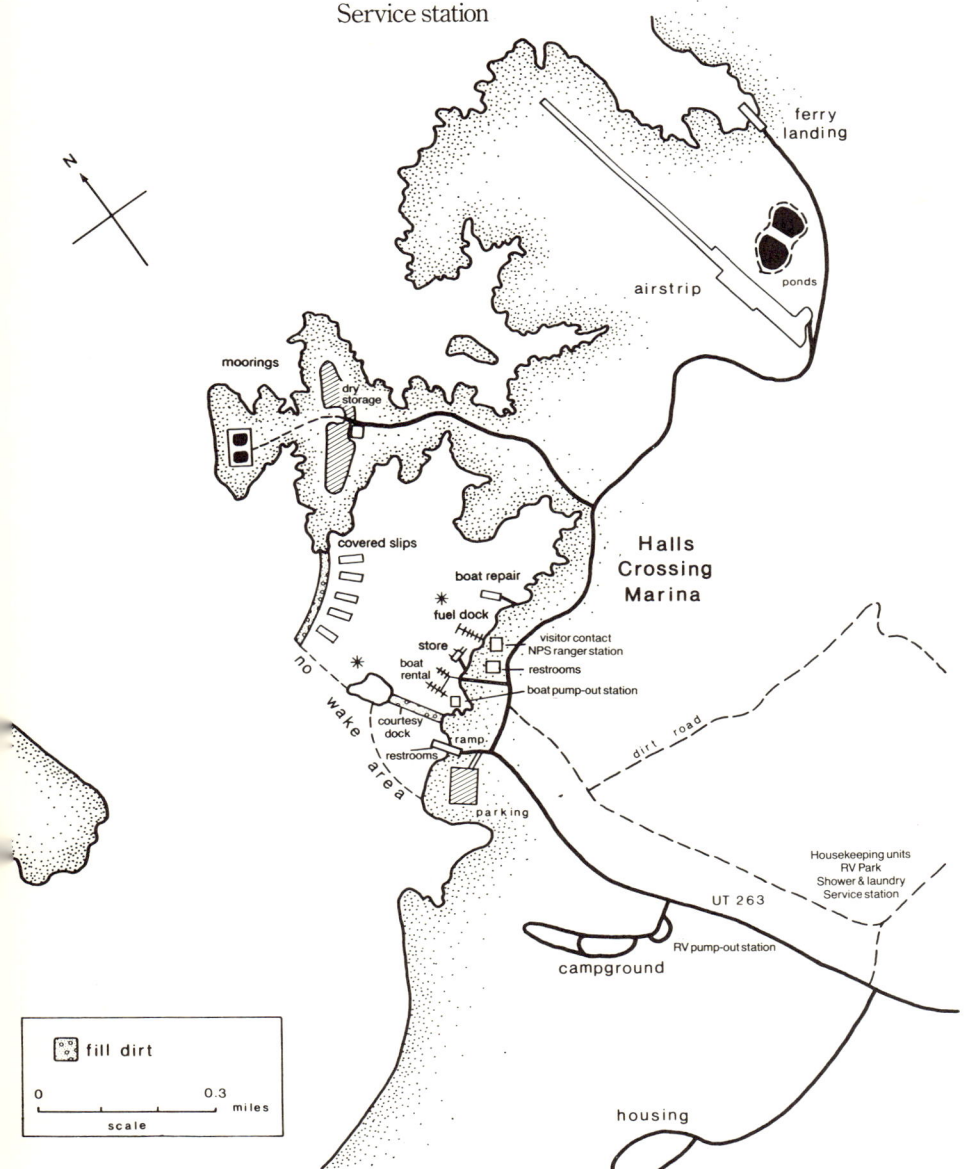

N

ferry
landing

airstrip

ponds

moorings

dry
storage

covered slips

Halls
Crossing
Marina

boat repair

fuel dock

store

visitor contact
NPS ranger station

boat
rental

restrooms

n o
w a k e

a r e a

courtesy
dock

boat pump-out station

ramp

restrooms

dirt road

parking

UT 263

Housekeeping units
RV Park
Shower & laundry
Service station

RV pump-out station

campground

housing

fill dirt

0   0.3
                    miles
      scale

BOATING

HITE MARINA AND VICINITY

Fuel dock — *regular and mixed*
Stores
Pump-out station RV
Restroom
Trash deposit
Boat rentals — *limited*
Housekeeping units
Service station

Dry storage
Launch ramp
Camping — *primitive*
Ranger station
Service station

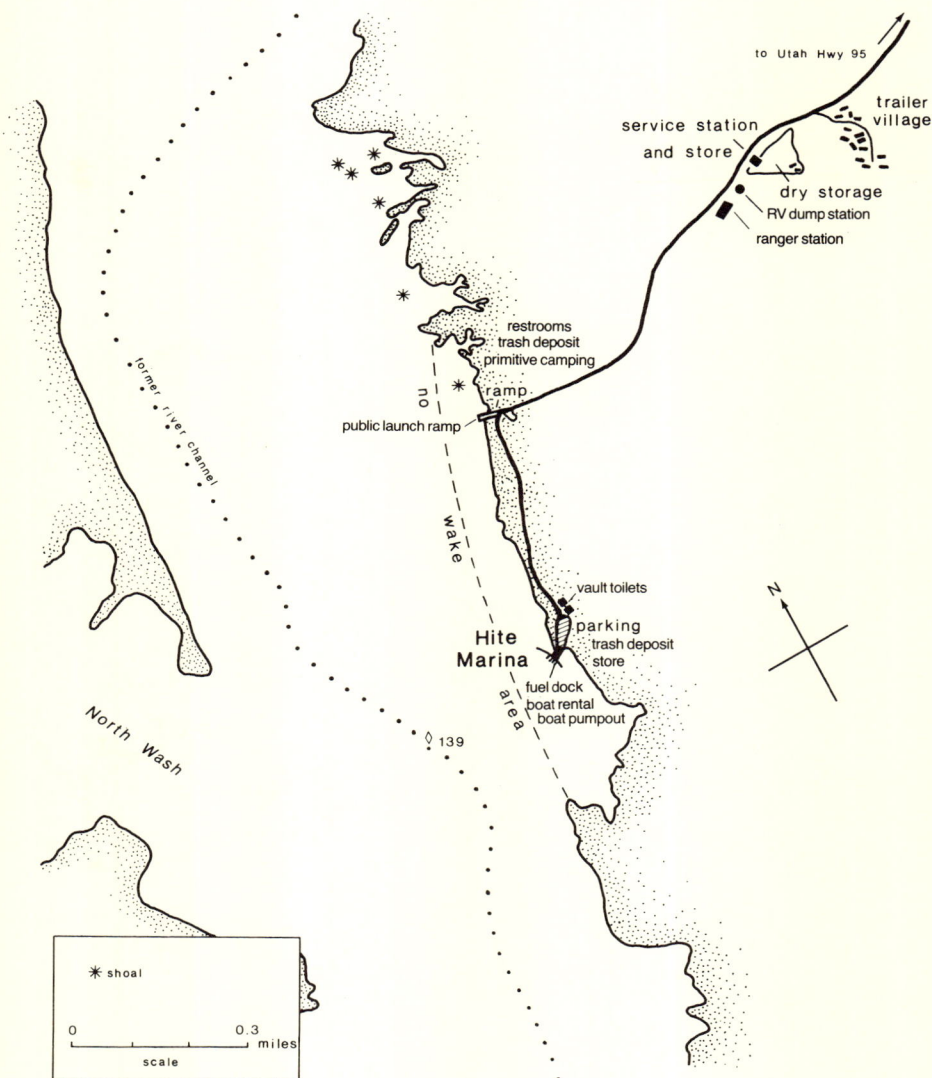

to Utah Hwy 95

trailer village

service station and store

dry storage

RV dump station

ranger station

restrooms
trash deposit
primitive camping

former river channel

no wake

ramp

public launch ramp

vault toilets

Hite Marina

parking
trash deposit
store

fuel dock
boat rental
boat pumpout

area

◊ 139

North Wash

N

* shoal

0   0.3
         miles
     scale

SAN JUAN MARINA

PUBLISHER'S NOTE:
Please note that the
San Juan marina no
longer exists, and
plan your fuel usage
accordingly while on
the San Juan River arm.

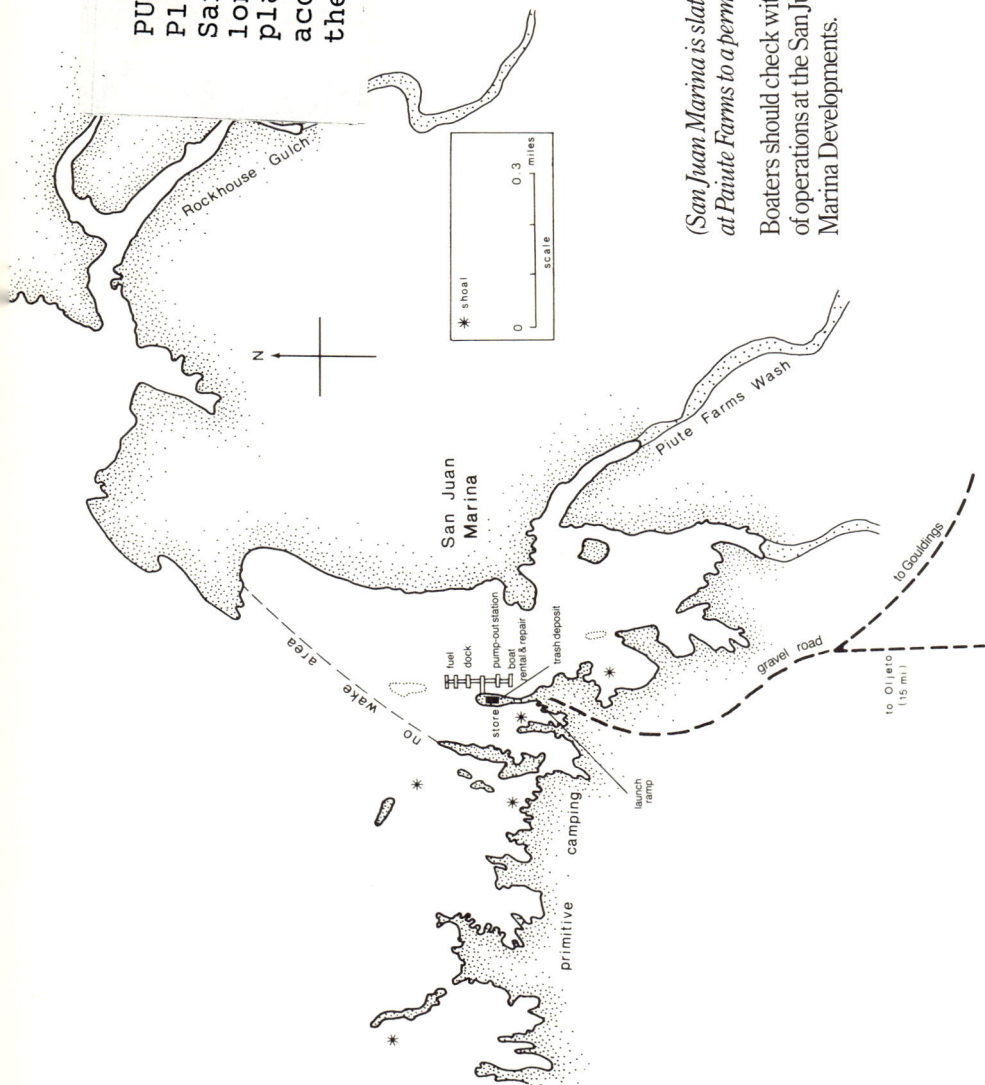

(San Juan Marina is slated to be moved from a temporary site at Paiute Farms to a permanent site at Cooper Canyon).

Boaters should check with Park Service officials as to status of operations at the San Juan Paiute Farms/Copper Canyon Marina Developments.

Rockhouse Gulch

N

scale

0   0   3   miles

* shoal

San Juan Marina

Piute Farms Wash

to Gouldings

gravel road

to Oljeto (15 mi.)

fuel dock
store
pump-out station
boat rental & repair
trash deposit

launch ramp

no wake area

camping

primitive

19

BOATING

WAHWEAP MARINA

Launch ramp
Dry storage
Boat rental
Boat and camping supplies
Pump-out stations; boat and RV
Fuel dock — *regular, mixed,*
 and diesel
Boat repair

Campgrounds/RV park
Fish-cleaning station
L.P. Gas Service
Shower and laundry
 facilities
Water toy and fishing
 gear rentals
Restaurants
Fast food outlet
Visitor contact station
Ranger station
Motel/Lodge
Boat tours
Service stations
*We have no designated
 swim beaches!*

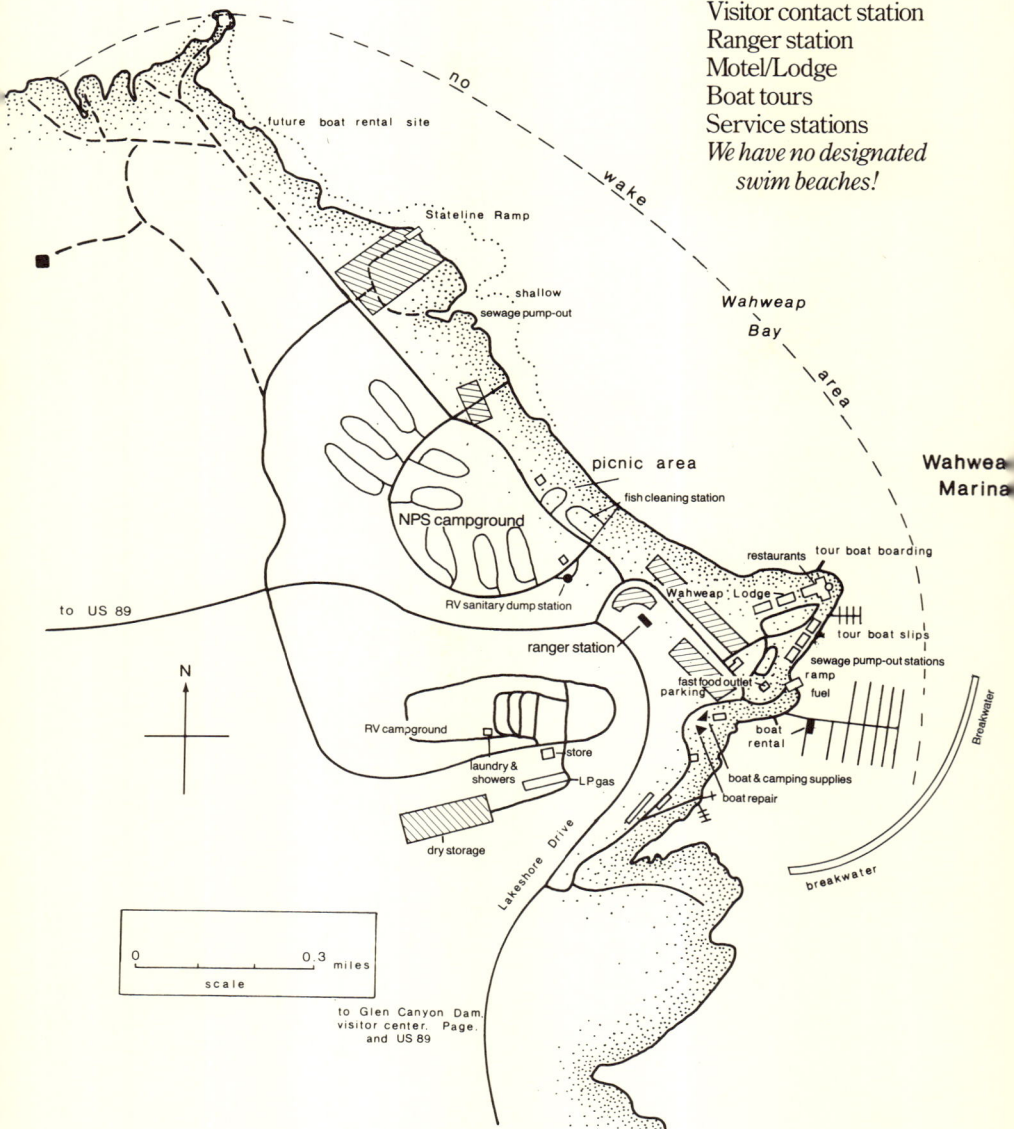

no
wake
area

future boat rental site

Stateline Ramp

shallow
sewage pump-out

Wahweap
Bay

picnic area
fish cleaning station

NPS campground

restaurants
tour boat boarding

Wahwea
Marina

Wahweap Lodge

RV sanitary dump station

tour boat slips

to US 89

ranger station

sewage pump-out stations
ramp
fuel

N

fast food outlet
parking

boat
rental

RV campground

store
laundry &
showers
LP gas

boat & camping supplies
boat repair

Breakwater

dry storage

Lakeshore Drive

breakwater

0   0.3 miles
scale

to Glen Canyon Dam,
visitor center, Page,
and US 89

BOATING

Navigating Safety Precautions and Boating Hazards

Location: Monitor your location at all times on the lake. If an emergency arises, you will need to give your exact location in order to receive help quickly. Plotting your course on maps such as the ones found in the later part of this book is recommended. A magnetic compass is useful, especially where there are no buoys. Magnetic compasses must compensate for magnetic declination, which is approximately 15 degrees east for the lake region.

Distress signals: In case of emergency, several distress signals may be used, including:
- slow and repeated raising and lowering arms outstretched to the side;
- a square flag with a ball above or below it;
- three flares at night; three fires on beach;
- a "mayday" signal. Marine VHF channel 16 is monitored during the daytime by the National Park Service. "Mayday, mayday, mayday" for serious or life-threatening situations; "Pan, pan, pan" for need of help but not as serious (need fuel, etc.);
- five short blasts of the horn;
- a U.S. flag flown upside down;
- at night, a bright white light, flashing fifty to seventy times per minute.

Weather: Keep an eye on the weather. Boating in the main channel or in open bays during thunderstorms or strong winds is not advised. Most summer squalls come out of the southwest and can be seen approaching. Shelter can usually be found along the shoreline. During the colder months, frontal passages often bring dramatic temperature changes, gusty winds, and prolonged bad weather. NOAA operates a 24-hour weather station located on Navajo Mountain which can be monitored on radio frequency 162.500 or Marine Band Weather 1.

Obstructions: Because of fluctuating water levels and the irregular bottom configuration of Lake Powell, small islands and shoals are numerous and extremely hazardous. At certain lake levels some of the larger ones are marked with buoys (along the main channel only), and many are indicated in the maps in this book. Countless others, however, are unmarked. In clear water, changes in water depth can usually be foreseen by changes in the water color, especially through polarized glasses. In muddy waters there may be no signs of obstructions, and speed should be reduced and caution exercised. Driftwood may be a problem, especially in the upper lake and the upper San Juan Arm during times of high river discharge.

BOATING

Speed: The safe speed of a boat is determined by many factors, most of which are common sense. Wakeless speeds are required in harbors, marinas, near waterskiers and swimmers in the water, and within 150 feet of another boat. Other factors that affect safe speed include visibility, traffic density, vessel maneuverability, state of the wind and water, and water depth.

Waterskiing: Boats towing skiers must have at least two people on board, an operator and an observer. An orange flag must be displayed when a skier is down in the water.

Bow riding: Bow riding is prohibited unless the bow is equipped with seats designed for carrying passengers.

Alcohol: Driving a boat under the influence of alcohol is prohibited. Many accidents on the lake are alcohol related.

Projectiles: Throwing or launching of projectiles, such as water balloons, at other boats is prohibited.

Explosive vapors: Sniff the bilge before starting the engine to make sure explosive vapors are dispersed, especially if the boat has been sitting for a time.

Capsizing: In the case of a capsized boat, it is generally advised to put on your life jacket and stay with the boat, especially in cold water or heavy traffic. In remote areas where the water temperature is tolerable, however, it may be safe to swim ashore, wearing a life jacket.

Anchorages: In some regions of the lake, anchorages are very sparse. Give yourself ample time to find a suitable spot and make sure that anchor lines are securely set.

Buoys: Know the buoy system (described under "Aids to Navigation").

Navigational Rules and Recommendations

Certain rules apply to all vessels on inland waterways in the same way driving and parking rules apply to automobiles on the road. These are often referred to as "rules of the road," and are available in complete form through the U.S. Coast Guard. This chapter contains selected topics that are especially pertinent to Lake Powell boaters, but is far from comprehensive.

Horn signals are often useful in areas of heavy traffic or restricted visibility. A series of short or long blasts have the following meanings: * = short; — = long;

    *Turning to starboard (right)
    **Turning to port (left)
    ***Going astern (backward)
    —Leaving dock
*****Danger

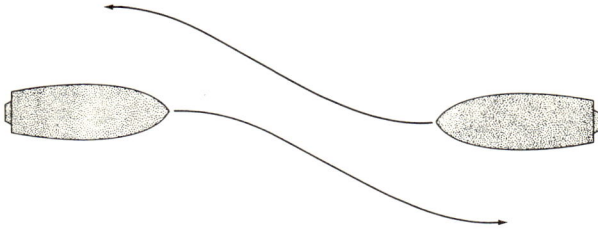

Figure 1. All vessels must use any available means to avoid collisions with other boats. If it appears that an approaching boat risks collision, action should be taken as soon as possible. Change in course should be large enough to be obvious to the approaching boat. It may be necessary to reduce speed or stop by reversing the engines. If passage is safe, each boat should turn to the starboard (right), providing there is room in the channel.

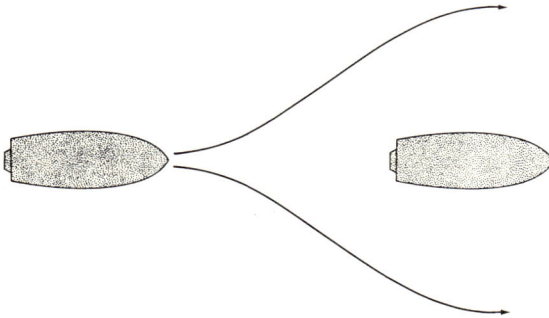

Figure 2. Overtaking another boat requires that the boat passing has the responsibility of keeping out of the way of the boat being passed. Passage on either side is permitted, assuming there is enough space in the channel. It is common courtesy to pass with enough distance so that the wake does not upset the boat being passed.

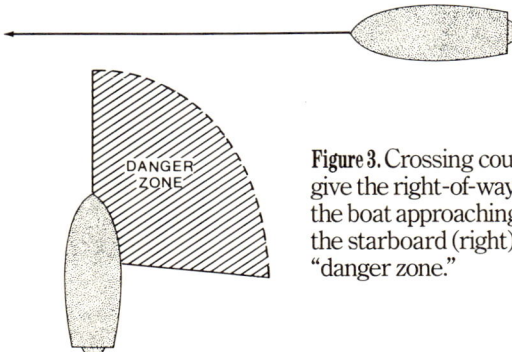

DANGER ZONE

Figure 3. Crossing courses — give the right-of-way to the boat approaching from the starboard (right) in the "danger zone."

BOATING

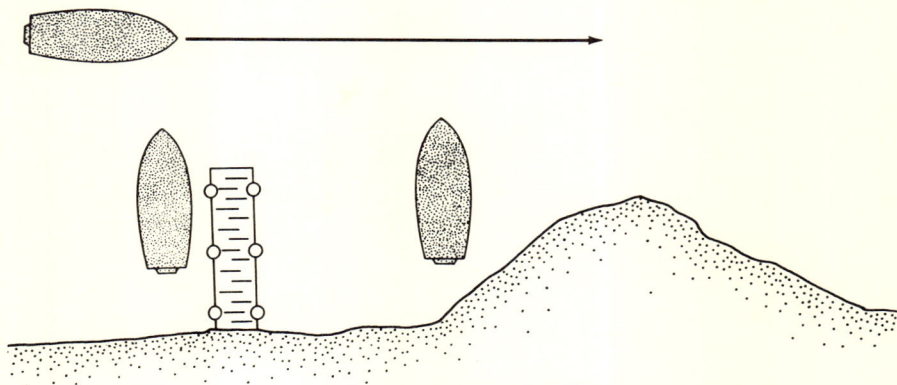

Figure 4. A boat leaving a dock, anchorage, or shoreline must give right-of-way to boats already underway. Right-of-way is also given to vessels unable to maneuver or restricted in maneuverability, vessels not under power, vessels engaged in fishing, and vessels restricted to certain minimum water depths.

Docking and Anchoring

Maneuvering a boat in limited space can be tricky, especially in adverse weather conditions. Boats are somewhat sluggish in responding to steering and lose maneuverability without power. Keeping a boat under control requires that the engine be running and that the boat remain in gear throughout most of the docking or anchoring procedure, and that the motor be left running until maneuvering is finished and the line or anchor set. Size up a situation before you are in it, including wind, currents, available space and traffic. When operating houseboats in close quarters, it is helpful to have people fore and aft to act as pilot aids since visibility is somewhat restricted on these vessels.

Docking: Under ideal conditions landing at a pier is a relatively simple procedure. With the propeller still engaged, speed should be reduced to a minimum several boat lengths prior to contact. Reverse thrust may be used at any time if speed is judged excessive. Passengers should be ready to help and should be given advance notice as to what they are to do.

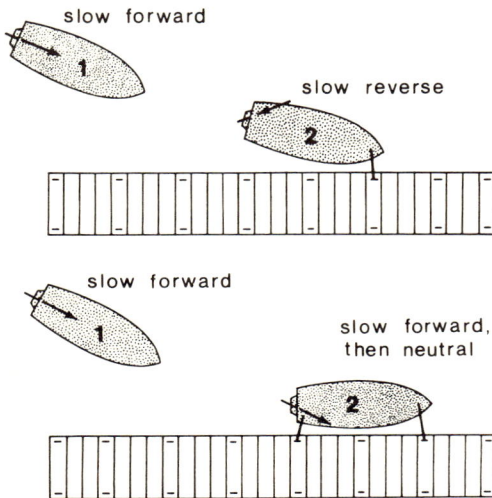

Figure 5: Under conditions of no wind, the operator generally approaches the pier or wharf at a slight angle, then brings the stern alongside by either steering slightly away from the pier just before contact, or reversing engines and steering into the pier. The bow line should be tied off first, then the stern line as the boat is brought alongside.

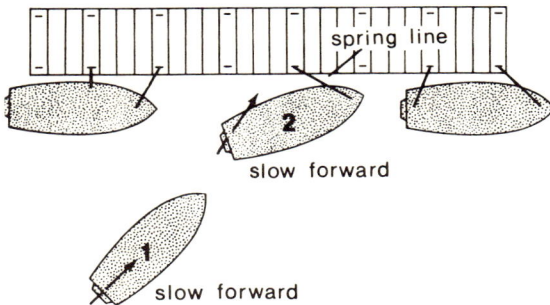

Figure 6: Docking under crowded conditions, which is typical at most of the larger marinas at Lake Powell in the summer season, will require that the approach be made at a much greater angle. As the pier is neared, a person on the bow must board the pier and quickly throw a turn or two of a spring line around a cleat on the pier so that the forward progress of the boat can be controlled. The stern is then brought toward the dock by steering away from the pier with the engine providing forward thrust.

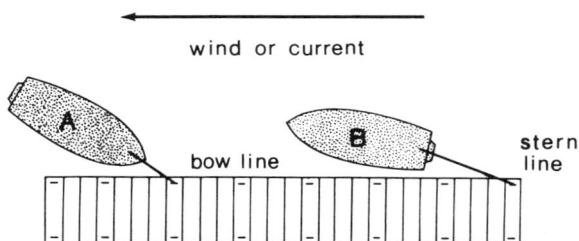

Figure 7: It is always advisable to head into a current or wind blowing parallel to the pier (boat A), keeping forward power as needed to compensate for the strength and direction of the wind and currents. This will allow control of the boat. If the pier is approached with the wind blowing toward it (boat B), control depends on reverse gear, and mechanical failures or misjudgments may be costly. If you must land with the wind blowing toward the pier, approach the pier slowly and set the stern line as soon as forward motion is checked. The wind should bring the bow alongside. The danger in setting the bow line first is the risk of the boat turning end-for-end if the stern line is not set immediately afterward.

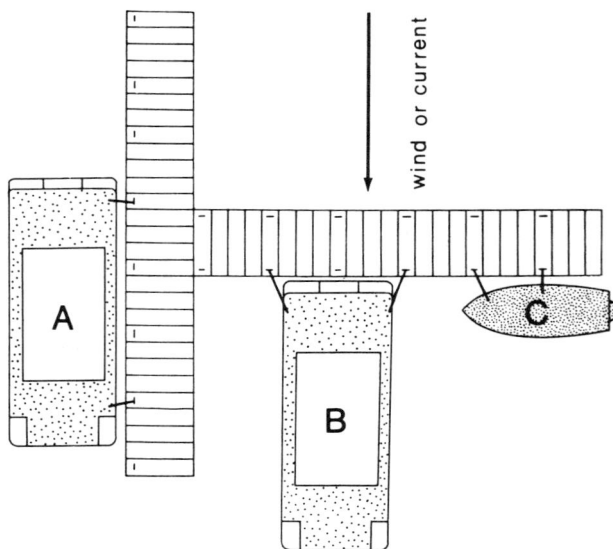

Figure 8: Docking into the wind is advised when approaching a T-shaped pier. Houseboats may choose to land bow-first and tie down using two bow lines.

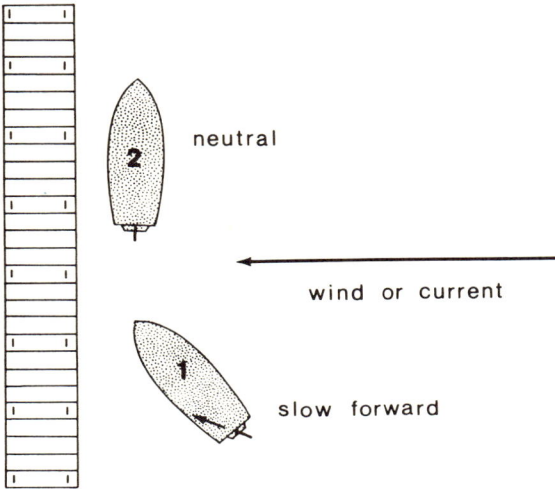

Figure 9: If the current or wind is blowing toward the pier, the boat may approach at a normal angle but move parallel to the pier, stopping several feet away and allowing the wind to bring the boat alongside. Fenders will help absorb the shock when contact is made.

photo by Gary Ladd   27

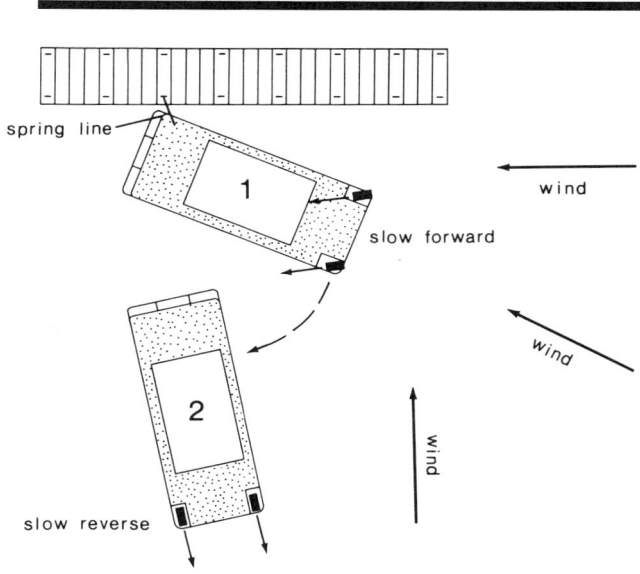

Figure 10: Leaving the pier is usually much simpler than landing. For light boats, a push-off is generally all that is needed to clear the boat and get underway. Larger boats may be more difficult to clear, especially with winds blowing toward the pier or stern. A spring line on the bow combined with a slow forward movement will move the stern out. Fenders may be needed at the pivot point. The engines are then reversed and the bow line freed.

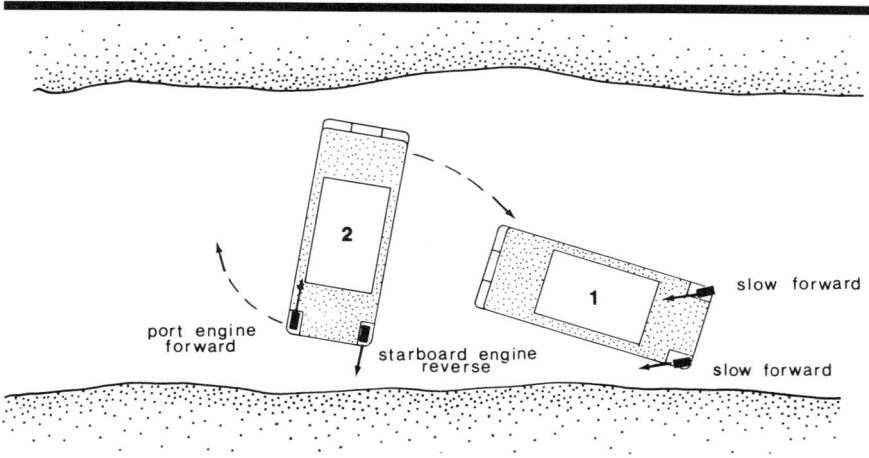

Figure 11: Twin-engine boats have an added advantage that can be useful in close quarters such as marinas and narrow canyons. Steering may be done using the throttles

only, with one engine going forward and the other in reverse. With a little practice a boat can be turned in its own length.

Anchoring: Countless good anchorages exist on Lake Powell. Most are found near the shore or along the shore, because the water is generally too deep offshore. Since most boaters on the lake prefer anchorages in soft bottoms or on sandy beaches, a "burying anchor" is most practical. The Danforth lightweight anchor and other similar types are most frequently used. Once the anchor bites into the soft bottom, further tension on the line will bury it deeper.

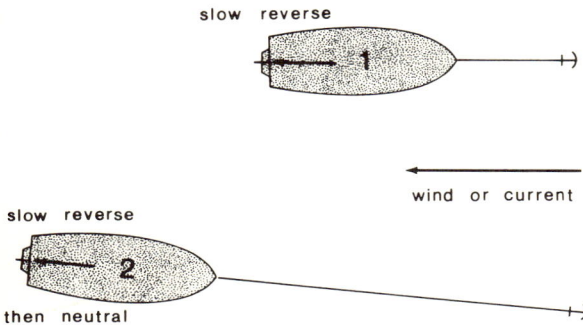

slow   reverse

wind   or   current

slow   reverse

then   neutral

Figure 12: In offshore anchoring, the first step is to find a suitable spot. Lake Powell's waters are usually clear enough so that a soft bottom can be clearly seen at depths ranging from about ten feet to over twenty-five feet. Approach the anchorage site slowly and throw the boat into reverse to check forward progress when the site is reached. Have someone ready to lower the anchor, but do not release the anchor until the boat is slowly backing. Pay out enough line so that its length is three times the depth of the water under the boat, a 5:1 scope. More scope may be required, depending on weather conditions and type of anchor used. Once the proper scope has been paid out, the anchor can be set by tying off the line and continuing reverse power until it holds. Be sure the anchor is not dragging.

When anchoring close to other boats, keep in mind that a 360 degree swing around the anchor is possible, and with the types of wind eddies in many of the Lake Powell canyons, two boats that were initially far apart may be brought into contact. If a tight situation exists, remember that the boat first anchored has priority and it is the responsibility of the boat arriving later to allow space and, if possible, some seclusion.

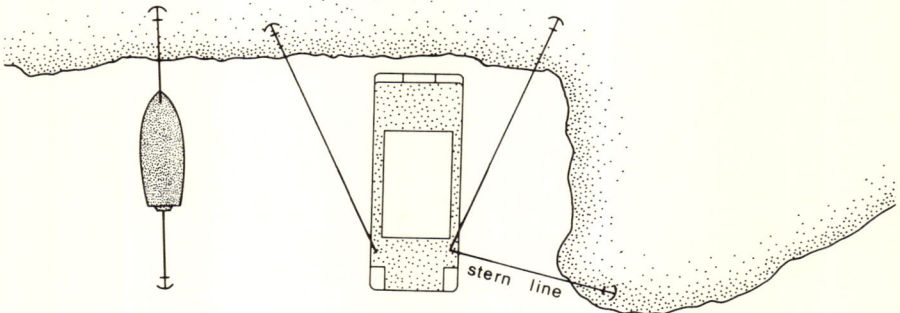

Figure 13: Beach anchorages should be approached into the wind if possible. Owners of fiberglass-hulled boats may wish to set a shore anchor and an offshore anchor to minimize damage from sand or rock abrasion. Houseboats often anchor right on the beach, and need to approach the shore slowly and squarely. When both pontoons are in contact with the beach, an added forward thrust will drive the boat slightly onto the beach face, preventing some of the obnoxious pounding that may occur as waves or boat wakes pass. With the engine still running and in forward gear at fast idle, the anchor lines should be set at an angle, preferably tied off to the stern. Additional stern lines may be needed to secure the boat under windy conditions. Cut the engines after all lines are set.

Aids to Navigation

Most navigating on Lake Powell is actually "piloting," which is the guiding of a vessel from one place to another using visual reference points. On a lake where the shoreline can always be easily seen, this should be a simple task. Lake Powell piloting is complicated, however, by the vastness of the lake, the similarities in many of the lakeside landforms, and by the fact that there are nearly one hundred tributaries to the main channel. Lake Powell is easy to get lost in, and the marinas are far enough apart (generally thirty to fifty miles) so that any errors can result in embarrassing situations. The Coast Guard and the National Park Service maintain a system of buoys and markers. The maps contained in this book show the position of these navigational aids at the time of this writing. It should be emphasized that these are not true navigational charts, and should not be used as such. Buoys can be moved from their original positions by storms. Some buoys are only present at specific lake levels. Fluctuating lake levels make it difficult to show all reefs and shoals, and caution should be taken when boating in areas where safe courses are not marked by buoys. The maps in this book are based on several sources, including U.S.G.S.

topographic maps, National Park Service maps, aerial photos, and on-site observation.

Figure 14: The aids-to-navigation system on Lake Powell is meant to indicate position and warn boaters of dangers such as reefs, shoals, and areas where there are restrictions on boating. Swimming areas, for example, are marked to prohibit boat passage, and marinas and harbors are marked with wakeless speeds.

Buoy coverage on Lake Powell marks the main channel, generally following the former river bed, from Glen Canyon Dam to Hite Marina. Many of the major side canyon entrances are also marked, and a few, such as the Escalante Arm, have several buoys within them. The general policy of the National Park Service, however, is not to mark reefs and shoals in side canyons, and travel there is at the boater's risk. At low lake levels, additional buoys are placed in heavily traveled areas. The areas around Gregory Butte, Rock Creek, and Castle Rock will have to be closed off if the lake elevation falls below 3626 feet.

The primary function of navigational aids is to warn the boat operator of some danger, obstruction, change in channel contours, or to delineate channels leading to various destinations, so dangers may be avoided and the course continued safely. **A word of caution:** *buoys and other floating aids to navigation should not be regarded as immovable objects. They may have burned-out lights, be missing, adrift, or off their proper position due to heavy storms, unusual lake elevations, collisions, or simple vandalism. Even buoys that are on their proper location should be passed at a reasonable distance, since they may be necessarily located close to shoals, reefs, or obstructions they mark.*

The aids-to-navigation system on Lake Powell uses the Lateral and Uniform State Waterway Marking System. The size, shape, position, coloring and lights all have special significance.

Red buoys are nun-shaped with red reflective tape at the top and have even numbers that indicate the approximate number of miles they are from the dam. Green buoys are can-shaped with green reflective tape and odd numbers. Running uplake away from the dam, a boat should pass between red buoys to starboard (right) and green buoys to port (left).

Mid-channel buoys are ball shaped with red and white vertical stripes and have letters in alphabetical order running uplake. Mid-channel buoys may be passed on either side.

Nighttime boating is hazardous and should be avoided. In emergency situations between Wahweap and Forgotten Canyon/Rainbow Bridge Junction there are four shore lights and eighteen lighted buoys. Their purpose is to mark a safe channel for emergency boat operations at night. Shore lights are set on shore at a higher elevation than lighted buoys so they can be seen from a greater distance. Shore lights on the starboard (right) are red with triangular daymark and even numbers; to port (left) they are green with square daymark and odd numbers. Lighted buoys, which are lower and bob around in the water, are closer together than shore lights and are seen from a shorter distance. Some marinas are marked with flashing 360 degree shore lights, lighted buoys, or lighted breakwaters. For example, Halls Crossing has a shore light; at Bullfrog, the public ramp has a lighted breakwater just offshore; and Dangling Rope Marina has a lighted buoy.

Regulatory buoys and markers include information such as natural hazards, zoned areas, directions, and distances. All regulatory markers are orange and white.

Reefs and shoals are marked with cylindrical or round buoys with an orange diamond and with words such as "reef" or "shoal" marked on them. These should be passed at considerable distance because they may mark an extensive underwater obstruction.

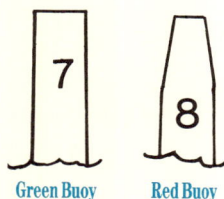

Green Buoy   Red Buoy

Mid-Channel Buoy

Red Shore Light

Green Shore Light

Regulatory Markers

BOATING

An orange circle on a regulatory buoy signifies zoning or control, such as "no skiing" or "wakeless speed."

A diamond with a cross inside marks areas where boats are not allowed.

A square or rectangular shape is used to give information such as the entrance to a bay or canyon. These indicate the canyon's name and may have additional information on the back side.

Boaters are encouraged to report any problems with the buoy system to the Park Service or Coast Guard officials.

Dangling Rope Marina

photo by Tom Bean

W hen Lake Powell reaches 3700 feet in elevation above sea level it is considered full. This level is normally approached during the summer months. In winter the lake surface falls, often to elevations of about 3670 to 3680. This guidebook has been prepared using a range of lake levels of about 3670 to 3700 feet, Lake Powell's most common surface elevations.

The guide describes side canyon features as they would be noted by a boater entering the canyon from the main channel and proceeding to the lake's end in the side canyon. Thus "left" refers to the boater's left as the canyon is traversed from the main channel through its entrance and on to its most distant upstream end.

Instructions

The following simple waste disposal rules have been formulated by the National Park Service:

GARBAGE: Bag it and drop it off at marina disposal sites.

HUMAN WASTE: The best system is to carry a portable toilet or other container designed for such purposes. Alternatively, human waste and toilet paper must be buried in a hole twelve to eighteen inches deep located at least one hundred feet from Lake Powell's full pool or high water mark. Because of the danger of wildfire, toilet paper should not be burned. Use care when selecting a location for the hole, it should be well away from any potential campsite.

Waste Disposal

photo by Tom Bean

35

CANYON BY CANYON

SUGGESTIONS FOR SHORT TRIPS

There is much to see on Lake Powell. For those who have only a day or two, consider the following locations:

Starting from Wahweap Marina.

1. Rainbow Bridge: Try a dawn or dusk visit to avoid the crowds.
2. Sandy beaches: Near Wahweap — Warm Creek Bay or the northern canyons of Padre Bay. Closer to Rainbow Bridge — Dungeon, Cornerstone, Secret or the north end of Rock Creek.
3. Narrow canyons: Twilight, Oak, right fork of Driftwood, the end of Mountain Sheep.
4. Anasazi ruins: right fork of Reflection.
5. Shady alcoves for floating lunches: left fork of Rainbow Bridge Canyon, Music Temple.

Starting from Bullfrog or Halls Crossing Marinas.

1. Rainbow Bridge: Try a dawn or dusk visit to avoid the crowds.
2. Sandy beaches: Near the marinas — northern end of Bullfrog Bay. Closer to Rainbow Bridge — Cottonwood Canyon and on the main channel between Llewellyn Gulch and the San Juan Arm.
3. Narrow Canyons: Anasazi, Twilight, Oak, Smith Fork.
4. Anasazi ruins: Three Roof Ruin, on Escalante Arm between Willow and Explorer canyons; Widow's Ledge, in Slick Rock Canyon; Defiance House, in Forgotten Canyon.
5. Shady alcoves for floating lunches: Music Temple, Indian and Clear Creek branches on the Escalante Arm, right fork of Annies, left fork of Rainbow Bridge Canyon.

Mileages from Marina to Marina

	Bullfrog	Dangling Rope	Halls Crossing	Hite	Rainbow Bridge	San Juan Marina	Wahweap
Bullfrog Marina	0	55	3	47	53	88	80
Dangling Rope Marina	55	0	52	97	10	69	27
Halls Crossing Marina	3	52	0	46	50	86	77
Hite Marina	47	97	46	0	93	131	123
Rainbow Bridge	53	10	50	93	0	61	34
San Juan Marina	88	69	86	131	61	0	87
Wahweap Marina	80	27	77	123	34	87	0

Campsite Types

Campsites on Lake Powell come in many varieties. The following terms are used in this guidebook to describe the nature of the campsite locations.

Sand—the best there is. Easiest on craft, fun to play in, attractive, adds flavor to food on windy days. Camping beaches range in size from yard-wide pockets to strips hundreds of feet long.

Slickrock—bare, gently sloping sandstone. Poor for speedboats, acceptable for some houseboats. Works best when the lake is free of boat- or wind-generated waves.

Talus—steep, boulder-strewn slope, usually at the base of a cliff. Not generally desirable but not necessarily a poor choice when alternatives are few. Some sections of Lake Powell have nothing better to offer than talus slopes. Damaging to speedboats but marginally acceptable for houseboats if utilized with care and with calm lake conditions. DO NOT CAMP ON SHALE OR TALUS SLOPES WHERE SIGNS OF SLUMPING OR ROCKFALLS EXIST.

Ledgy—mostly bare rock but lacking the convenient slopes of slickrock. Not good for speedboats. Marginally acceptable for some houseboats if used carefully.

Shaly—composed of often sticky, claylike particles of disintegrating rock. Easy on all boat hulls and pontoons but often present slopes so shallow that the craft's bow fails to reach shore. Some shaly sites are "mushy," especially those composed of Chinle shale. DO NOT CAMP ON SHALE OR TALUS SLOPES WHERE SIGNS OF SLUMPING AND ROCKFALLS EXIST.

Gravelly—punishing to most speedboat hulls but can be used with great care under absolutely calm conditions. Generally acceptable for houseboat pontoons even when the lake is rough.

Camping near Dangling Rope Canyon   *photo by Tom Bean*

37

CANYON BY CANYON

ALCOVE CANYON

Alcove Canyon and Iceberg Canyon are in some ways similar. They both have small streams, both lie close to the Hole-in-the-Rock road and both are rimmed with Navajo Sandstone. Now, make a guess, how far away are campers in Iceberg Canyon? The answer: two miles in straight-line distance. If you detect the aroma of a fine dinner on a neighboring camper's stove and shrewdly plan a friendly visit, the neighbor may be preparing dinner in Iceberg Canyon.

CAMPING: Here is where the Alcove-Iceberg similarities end. Camps are nearly impossible to establish in Alcove. Try the nameless inlets west and south of Alcove Canyon's entrance. They sometimes shelter small sandy pockets and ledge camps.

ANNIES CANYON

Annies Canyon lies at the foot of the southern end of the Waterpocket Fold, the long north-south rock layer flexure and primary feature of Capitol Reef National Park.

The right or north fork is the most interesting. Sheer walls lead to a broad flooded amphitheater. The chamber's north cliff overhangs both the lake and an adjoining strip of talus. A canyon enters on the other side, its bed suspended, ready to pour storm waters directly into Lake Powell — it would be a grand sight viewed from the protected slope across the way. Houseboats could anchor on this roofed talus slope.

CAMPING: Camping is tough in Annies. Normally, only a couple of marginal talus slope anchorages for houseboats are possible.

The left fork enters from the south and is free of campsite possibilities. It ends in a bowl of very deep water with a flooded slot at its head.

The middle fork is the main drainage in Annies Canyon. One might be able to use the talus at the end of the lake for a camp at some lake levels. Also, just north of where the left and middle forks join, a talus anchorage might be possible on the right or west side of the channel.

CANYON BY CANYON

ANTELOPE CANYON

Antelope Canyon is the drainage closest to Glen Canyon Dam on the east shore of Lake Powell. Its left shoreline is sometimes accessible by car. The mesa top above the right shoreline is the site of Page, Arizona.

Antelope Point, east of Antelope Canyon, may be developed into a marina in the future.

Silt is accumulating in Antelope's upper reaches at a rapid pace. If hikers can cross these unstable deposits, Antelope's normally dry bed can be followed most of the way to Arizona Route 98. Spectacular, convoluted corridors in distant sections of upper Antelope Canyon are most easily approached from the highway.

CAMPING: Slickrock sites exist on the left near the entrance. Beyond this point the cliffs rise sheer from shoreline. Alternatively, long strands of beach can be found on both sides of the main channel outside and just north of Antelope Canyon's mouth.

BALANCED ROCK CANYON

A gallery of balanced cobbles once stood on a terrace above the Colorado River here. The rocks were ancient stream cobbles but were not large. Many rested on tripods of pedestal legs, trivets displaying the polished rocks to their best advantage. It was an enchanting niche of Glen Canyon whose description became attached to the nearby canyon. Lake Powell is edged with low walls and sloping slickrock in today's Balanced Rock Canyon.

Beware of shallows on the left of Balanced Rock's wide entrance.

CAMPING: Sandy beaches are scarce. One combination slickrock and sandy pocket camp lies on the immediate left of the entrance. A few potential slickrock camps are located on the right at mid-canyon. And a pair of slickrock sites can sometimes be found on the left just before the waterway narrows to a slot.

BALD ROCK CANYON

A single channel branching from the San Juan leads to both Nasja Canyon (on the right) and Bald Rock Canyon (on the left). Bald Rock Canyon only infrequently contains a stream.

Hikers can gain the hanging bed of Bald Rock Canyon by climbing the ledges to the left of the lake-ending cliff.

CAMPING: Sites are unlikely. Talus offers houseboaters a chance of success and, at some lake surface elevations, a small sandy beach appears.

CANYON BY CANYON

BLUE NOTCH CANYON

Blue Notch Canyon, a tributary of Red Canyon, features extraordinarily colorful surroundings and an intricate shoreline. The canyon takes its name from a pass at its head.

Like many canyons that are surrounded by Chinle deposits, surprise shallows are a threat to props in Blue Notch Canyon.

CAMPING: Camps are usually possible. Sand is unlikely, but shaly pockets, ledges and gravel beaches are to be expected.

BOWNS CANYON

Bowns Canyon is a tributary of Long Canyon. This finger of Lake Powell is short but the canyon beyond can be hiked for miles often with a trickle of water in the bed.

CAMPING: Camping is not possible except when the lake approaches full, a strip of sand may be accessible at the very end. This site, however, lies in the watercourse and is vulnerable to flash floods. Consider the weather when using this campsite.

BULLFROG BAY

Nearly five miles long, Bullfrog Bay has it all: marina, ferryboat, lake side RV camping, miles of beaches, and views of the Henry Mountains.

Extensive shallows pervade the head of the bay, be cautious.

A dirt road, branching from the Burr Trail, reaches lake shore on the east side of Bullfrog's upper reach. It is a popular RV camping beach.

CAMPING: It is simpler to list where camping is NOT possible: within three hundred feet of Bullfrog Marina and along the cliff-bordered west shoreline of Bullfrog's southern end. Elsewhere, miles of beaches await. Some of these, however, are of gentle gradient sometimes making it difficult to beach a boat.

CASCADE CANYON

The entrance to Cascade Canyon is obscure. Look for a modest desert varnish display just to the left of some prominent island domes near the north shore. Cascade is narrow and sheer-walled for its entire length. It is an excellent canyon to visit in hot weather when shade is at a premium.

CAMPING: Hardly a prayer of a chance. The only hope: a slickrock site a few hundred feet into the canyon on the left, but only at higher lake levels.

CASTLE CREEK

Castle Creek flows along the flank of Nokai Dome, a swell of rock responsible for the sharply-dipping rock strata west of the canyon's entrance.

Be alert to surprise shallows.

CAMPING: A prime strip of sandy beach extends into the canyon's mouth on the left. Beyond, shaly beaches, often with mushy personalities, abound on both shores.

CATHEDRAL CANYON

Cathedral Canyon once possessed a wonderful series of alcove undercuts along its bed; one in particular was notable for its extreme depth. Its lofty, overhanging walls endowed it with the atmosphere of an ancient cathedral. Today, a modest bay is prelude to a narrow channel tapering into shadowy slots.

Watch for surprise shoals at mid-entrance. Above the west shore Cathedral Butte towers over thirteen hundred feet. Tour boats frequently enter Cathedral Canyon to allow passengers a peek at one of Powell's narrow waterways.

CAMPING: Even small pockets of sand are nearly absent in Cathedral. Viable slickrock sites, however, are sometimes possible on the left, mostly at high lake levels in the first third of the canyon. Sheer walls in the last half of the canyon preclude camping.

CEDAR CANYON

Cedar Canyon drains distant uplands of Mancos Mesa. Like nearby Knowles Canyon, Cedar's course encounters the rising strata of Kayenta Sandstone.

CAMPING: Also like Knowles Canyon, Cedar is beach poor. Limited talus, little sand and few ledge sites define Cedar's camping potential. Alternatively, try the coves just upstream of Warm Spring Canyon; they're ledgy with some sand and shale pockets.

CHA CANYON

Cha means "beaver" in the Navajo language.

CAMPING: Cha possesses a talus shoreline. Normally only a few pocket beaches of shale and gravel are to be found.

CANYON BY CANYON

CHAOL CANYON

When Lake Powell rises to its highest levels it extends into Chaol Canyon, a tributary of Navajo Canyon. An unusual waterfall is situated in Chaol about two miles above the confluence. As recently as 1983 the lake lapped at the foot of Chaol Falls. Unfortunately, flash floods carrying huge volumes of sand have buried about three-quarters of the falls and have pushed lake's edge far down-canyon. Even so, Chaol Falls and a nearby set of dinosaur footprints are worth the short hike should silt and lake levels allow.

It is believed the Escalante Expedition, heading south, crossed Navajo Canyon at the mouth of Chaol Canyon.

About a mile beyond the confluence watch for a sheep trail entering the canyon from the right. Beyond the sheep trail the canyon turns sharply left. Two dead-end drainages join Chaol Canyon from the right wall at this bend. They cut through the sandstone cliffs and disperse on a wide rock bench. Dinosaur footprints roughly a foot in length can be found in the gray bedrock of the bench at the end of the second drainage

Perennial Kaibito Creek extends for miles beyond the waterfall. Numerous Anasazi rock art sites decorate its cliffs and help make it an excellent hike.

CAMPING: Normally, camping is not feasible unless dry silt banks are available and flash flood danger is absent.

CLEAR CREEK CANYON

Boaters gliding through Clear Creek Canyon sometimes miss the narrow corridor continuing beyond lake's apparent end. It was here, where the canyon narrows to fifteen feet, that Cathedral in the Desert once enchanted hikers. The narrows was then a skylight a hundred feet above the floor of a lovely flaring chamber. A trickling waterfall fed a pool and ferns spread from seeping cracks.

Today's boaters ruffle the lake surface and patterns of brilliant reflected sunlight dance on the dark walls at midday. Only a few people consider the once-remarkable cathedral below.

Hikers can continue beyond lake's end for another quarter mile or so. The canyon boxes at a quiet pool.

CAMPING: Camping is impossible unless low water reveals a thin strip of talus or unusually high water reaches a beach at lake's end. As an alternative, the cove across from the entrance to Clear Creek may offer a slickrock site or two.

CANYON BY CANYON

CONFLUENCE COVE

Confluence Cove lies at the historic junction of the San Juan and Colorado rivers. It offers a series of fine sand beaches and quick access to both the main channel and the San Juan Arm of the lake.

A couple of rock arches lie in the vicinity of Confluence Cove; one is easily accessible and the other is not. Close to head of the bay, Lake Powell at full pool nearly reaches under Jack's Arch at the base of the eastern cliff. This arch can be reached on foot by hiking along the beaches to where the lake comes closest to the cliff. The second, Anteater Arch, must be admired from afar. It lies near the rim of the eastern cliff roughly above Jack's Arch. It can be seen in silhouette against the sky from some positions on the main channel just north of the San Juan and west of Confluence Cove. It is a slender curve of rock shaped and angled like the snout of an anteater.

CAMPING: There are many campsites, all of them located along lengthy strips of orange sand. However, the many campsites and central location of Confluence Cove are secrets no more — it normally shelters many craft on summer nights.

North from this point, sandy campsites are common along the main channel. Southwest from here, down the main channel, sandy campsites are nearly nonexistent. And eastward, up the San Juan Arm, campsites are scattered.

Most of the beaches in Confluence Cove offer the summer camper extended morning shade. Escape from the afternoon sun, however, does not come early.

COPPER CANYON

Copper Canyon takes its name from the deposits found in its distant upstream sections. Around the turn of the century mining men commonly followed the canyon's sandy bed to gain the San Juan.

The new San Juan Marina will be located in Copper Canyon sometime after 1989.

CAMPING: Sheer cliffs of Shinarump Conglomerate member of the Chinle Formation normally prohibit camping except at its entrance.

CORNERSTONE CANYON

River runners drifting down the Colorado River named this canyon after a distinctive cliff. The canyon is short but provides excellent afternoon shade to summer campers.

Watch for surprise shoals offshore between Cornerstone and Dangling Rope.

CAMPING: A fine strip of beach lines the left shore just inside the entrance. A number of ledgy and shaly sites may be available on the right shore and toward the end of the lake, especially with high lake elevations. Also, more sites with pockets of sand but vulnerable to high waves on windy days may be found east of the mouth of Cornerstone.

43

CANYON BY CANYON

COTTONWOOD CANYON

Cottonwood Canyon provided the exit route for the Hole-in-the-Rock pioneers. Traces of wagon road can be found by hiking about a mile from the end of the lake. The head of the canyon is still accessible by a rugged road backtracking the approximate alignment of the Mormon trail.

At canyon's northwestern end a sheer-walled gap frames a view of Hole-in-the-Rock. At high lake levels the gap provides a second connection to the main channel. Rolling eastward through this notch in 1880 the Mormon wagons first entered Cottonwood Canyon. Several of the pioneers carved their names in the hard-won gateway on what became known as the Register Rocks. The inscriptions along with the lower portions of the Register Rocks were submerged by Lake Powell.

Look for Triple Arch on the north wall; it is visible from some angles a short distance east of Register Rocks. Slickrock-smart hikers can visit Triple Arch by beginning just north of Register Rocks in a tiny bay off the main channel.

CAMPING: Cottonwood is an excellent camping canyon frequented by knowledgeable boaters. Sandy beaches are numerous. At higher lake levels the steep beaches of the stubby tributary to the north are also available.

COW CANYON AND FENCE CANYON

The shared entrance to Cow and Fence canyons sometimes goes unrecognized. It can be found to the right of the prominent fractured pinnacle close to lake's end. If Lake Powell is near full, the meandering channel soon leads to a fork. Cow Canyon goes left, Fence goes right.

Both canyons can be hiked if silt deposits are crossed successfully.

CAMPING: In-canyon campsites are scarce. The best bet is the sandy beach by the pinnacle at the canyon's entrance.

CRYSTAL SPRINGS CANYON

Crystal Springs twists gently into a slickrock desert. California Bar, one of the canyon's richest placer gold deposits, lies submerged just north of the mouth of Crystal Springs Canyon.

A boulder wedged between converging walls hangs just above Lake Powell's end in Crystal Springs Canyon at high water.

CAMPING: Sites are scarce. At some lake levels a slickrock camp or two are possible on the left near canyon's entrance. Farther on, marginal talus sites might work for houseboaters. An alcove-protected camp is possible at some lake levels on the right near canyon's end.

DANGLING ROPE
CANYON

River runners named the canyon after a rope was found dangling from a cliff not far from the Colorado River. Miners may have placed the rope and chopped the adjoining toeholds. The right fork of Dangling Rope Canyon now shelters a marina, replacing the floating marina once located in Forbidding Canyon.

Beware of shallows a few hundred feet from shore between Dangling Rope Canyon and Cornerstone Canyon.

CAMPING: There are a few possibilities. Beyond the marina, slickrock and sand sites are possible at some lake levels. The rear portion of the middle fork is closed to entry except for Park Service craft but a couple of marginal slickrock sites might be possible before the marina boundary is crossed. Also, a minor indentation in the left shoreline of the middle fork sometimes contains a small sandy site. The left fork can reveal a small beach on the left about mid-canyon and a slickrock site on the right near lake's end. Left fork camps boast early afternoon shade in mid-summer. One last possibility lies outside of Dangling Rope Canyon and across the lake: check the two small inlets west of the mouth of Mountain Sheep Canyon. They sometimes offer slickrock and small sand landings.

DAVIS GULCH

Davis Gulch corkscrews past imposing La Gorce Arch and, beyond Lake Powell's end, leads to Bement Arch. Everett Ruess, twenty-one-year-old explorer, artist and poet, mysteriously vanished from this canyon on a solo trip in 1934. To this day his fate remains unknown.

When the lake falls below elevation 3685, look for a series of Anasazi toeholds ascending the nose of rock immediately opposite the upstream face of La Gorce Arch.

Hikers may continue for miles beyond lake's end. When I hiked this stretch to Bement Arch, an annoyed beaver with a menacing tail presented me with a face full of muddy water.

CAMPING: Slickrock campsites are sometimes possible just inside the entrance, but busy summer boat traffic can be a problem. Talus slopes located up- and downstream of La Gorce Arch are a temptation but signs of recent slumps and landslides are enough to discourage wise boaters. Still farther, an obvious alcove on the right often shelters a sandy beach at lake levels of less than maximum. It was in this alcove that an extraordinary panel of thousand-year-old pictographs was located. Sadly, high lake levels have all but obliterated the ancient artwork. As Lake Powell fluctuates, more camps are sometimes possible farther up canyon.

CANYON BY CANYON

DEEP CANYON

Deep Canyon is not deep, but its walls are sheer and increase in height to the south.

CAMPING: Camping is not possible except perhaps on the less-than-endearing silt flats at lake's end. If flash floods are possible then even this camp should not be considered.

DESHA CANYON

Desha Canyon heads on a minor peak on the flank of Navajo Mountain. The peak is called "Navajo Begay" which means "Son of Navajo."

If hikers can cross the silt deposits at lake's end, a fine stream lined with cottonwoods and willows lies beyond —a hike well worth an hour or two.

CAMPING: Sheer walls prevent camping unless a normally unfriendly silt bank at canyon's end inexplicably reforms. Do not camp on the silt bank if a flash flood is possible.

DIRTY DEVIL CANYON

In 1869 Powell's men, planning to gather drinking water at the mouth of this canyon, recorded their disappointment by leaving the name "Dirty Devil" on the map. The river falls from the high plateaus to the northwest. The Dirty Devil's mouth marks the beginning of Glen Canyon and the end of Narrow Canyon.

CAMPING: The mouth of the canyon offers the best opportunities, usually in the form of slickrock with some sandy pockets. The east side of the mouth is accessible from Utah Route 95. Pleasant campsites up canyon are in short supply.

LaGorce Arch, Escalante Canyon

photo by Tom Bean

DOVE CANYON

Knowledgeable river runners often stopped at Dove Canyon to enter its difficult, muck-filled entrance and the darkened chambers beyond. Later, the rising waters of Lake Powell swept the tiny canyon from view and its name soon fell into obscurity. Not surprisingly, few modern boaters have heard of Dove Canyon.

Beware of shallows, especially between Dove and West canyons; the gently sloping rock layers sometimes extend far into the lake at little depth.

CAMPING: The entire margin of the lake in Dove Canyon is composed of sand or gentle slopes of slickrock and shale. Because the canyon is poorly defined by cliffs, boaters often fail to recognize its camping potential. Two or three fine beaches are tucked into its lobes, camouflaged by distance. Be sure to look carefully. Check farther north along the left shore for more, mostly marginal campsites of sand and shale. This last area is located at the head of a minuscule canyon some knew as Little Dungeon. All these sites offer fine views of distant mesas but are unprotected from the afternoon sun in summer.

DRIFTWOOD CANYON

River-running visitors to this tributary were not welcomed—driftwood jammed at its entrance made entry difficult. Today, the only obstacles take the form of improbably located shallows. Watch for them at high lake levels while approaching Driftwood's entrance.

Don't miss the series of steps chopped into the sloping slickrock immediately left of Driftwood's entrance. It lies at or just above lake level. These stairs once were part of a trail that descended hundreds of feet to Klondike Bar on the Colorado. Mining men constructed the Klondike Trail at the turn of the century when Glen Canyon was awash with gold miners.

The end of the right fork of Driftwood is unusually straight, narrow and confined—a cool spot even in mid-summer. However, gridlock is guaranteed if more than one boat attempts exploration.

CAMPING: Beaches are not likely. Slickrock camps are possible, however, on the right in a small bay just before the watercourse forks. The right fork is the longer of the two and it sometimes affords slickrock and ledge camping on the right along a wide stretch. The left fork sometimes allows a single small slickrock camp on the right just beyond the fork if the lake is near full.

47

CANYON BY CANYON

DRY ROCK CREEK CANYON

Dry Rock Creek Canyon is the right fork of a trio of canyons that merged into a single chasm before joining the Colorado. All three canyons drain the southwest face of the Kaiparowits Plateau.

Four features to look for: (1) the large balanced rock on the right skyline at the end of the main arm. (2) the detached sliver of rock at water's edge, left side of the channel along a sheer cliff just west of the left fork. Some folks call it "Mack the Knife." (3) the multitude of holes in the Entrada Sandstone cliffs. The holes form along pockets of poorly-cemented sand grains. Only small differences in the quantity of cement are needed to produce such unusual displays of cavernous weathering. It is absolutely false that nesting stonepeckers cut the numerous holes. (4) desert bighorn sheep close to the end of both forks. I have seen as many as eight here. Scan the shale slopes carefully.

CAMPING: A series of coves line the right shore, two or three of which provide small sandy sites with little chance of neighboring campers. The end of the channel allows more campsites, usually on sand or shale beaches. One final worthwhile possibility can be found in a left fork of Dry Rock Creek Canyon, a tributary entering close to the end of the main arm. It usually contains one or more sand or shale campsites.

DUNGEON CANYON

It is not difficult to guess the origin of this canyon's name. Hikers found here a gloomy, haunting chamber with undulating and overhanging walls. Some believed Dungeon Canyon to be the premier feature of Glen Canyon.

Dungeon Canyon is the westernmost of a series of canyons on Powell's south shore that cut deep into Cummings Mesa. But unlike the other defiles, Dungeon hosts a sheep trail leading to the mesa top. The trail lies about two miles beyond lake's end at the extreme head of the canyon.

CAMPING: Plentiful is the proper term. Beginning at the entrance, shale and ledge campsites line both shores. Long strips of excellent beaches appear at mid-canyon and extend to lake's end.

ESCALANTE CANYONS

The heart of the slickrock wilderness unfolds along Lake Powell's Escalante Arm. The stabilized Anasazi Three Roof Ruin can be visited on the main stem of the Escalante between Willow and Explorer canyons. A steep toehold trail leads up a low cliff to the ruin.

Stevens Arch and enchanting Coyote Gulch lie beyond Lake Powell's end. Hiking to these matchless spots is usually made difficult, if not impossible, by unstable silt deposits. Only during very high lake levels is the challenge reduced.

The Escalante Arm in summer is a favorite haunt. In mid-winter it is seldom visited. The Escalante in January often features snowy side canyons, falling icicles and waterways frozen solid for hundreds of feet.

CAMPING: Although the side canyons hold a number of campsites, the main stem's sheer walls preclude camping for most of its length. Beyond Explorer Canyon's entrance, however, extensive beaches appear on the left shoreline. At some lake levels, a few more beach and ledge possibilities may await farther up canyon beyond Fence Canyon.

Three Roof Ruin   photo by Tom Bean

EXPLORER CANYON

Explorer Canyon begins opposite a large sheer-walled island.

Beyond Lake Powell, a rough trail leads hikers through oak groves along a trickle of spring water.

CAMPING: The last half of Explorer offers some talus sites some of which may hold pockets of sand. Higher lake levels allow access to slickrock camps. A beach or two may be available at lake's end at some lake levels.

CANYON BY CANYON

FACE CANYON

Spacious and grand, perhaps as in no other corner of Lake Powell, are the views from Face Canyon. Empty expanses of desert punctuated with monuments and mesas extend in every direction. The pyramidal peak, called Boundary Butte, mid-canyon on the right shore, stands on the Arizona-Utah state line.

An obvious lead to the right near lake's end terminates in spooky narrows with overhanging walls. If lake and silt levels dictate, swimming is required to reach the end.

With the lake at its highest elevations the main channel splits just prior to ending. The left fork can be hiked for some distance. The right fork necessitates climbing a chain of potholes. Look for a Navajo sheep trail descending the right wall immediately down canyon from this split in the waterway.

Be alert for shoals in the wider sections of the canyon's upper reaches and near some stretches of the right shore below the big sand dune.

CAMPING: A couple of Powell's finest beaches line Face Canyon's right shore. They begin near the canyon's entrance. Farther on, smaller strips of sand can be found in a inlet below the high sand dune visible from across lake. Still more small sandy sites and a couple of slickrock camps may be found before the canyon narrows to a slot.

FARLEY CANYON

A short dirt road comes from Highway 95 near Hite to the head of Farley Canyon making it a popular RV camping spot.

Once, while camped near Farley Canyon, I awoke to the sound of my metal sierra cup bouncing over the rocks. A flashlight revealed a pack rat coaxing the cup toward a crevice. To the rascal's disappointment, I, dressed in my underwear, intercepted.

CAMPING: Many shale and gravel beaches line the shore of Farley Canyon at most water levels. More possibilities are located in the main channel coves just north of the mouth.

FIFTYMILE CANYON

The head of Fiftymile Canyon crosses the Hole-in-the-Rock Road about fifty miles from Escalante, Utah. Before the creation of Lake Powell, Gregory Natural Bridge spanned the canyon close to its mouth. When the lake covered the bridge Gregory's name was transferred to the island butte at the mouth of West Canyon. Herbert E. Gregory was a geologist who did extensive work in southern Utah and northern Arizona.

Be alert for shallows and be wary of any anchorage at the foot of steep talus slopes showing signs of slides or slumps.

Hikers can follow the canyon beyond Lake Powell along a cobble-strewn streambed. The canyon is passable all the way to the Hole-in-the-Rock Road.

CAMPING: Steep talus slopes, usually on the left, are most likely. Sandy sites are occasionally possible at mid-canyon in lower water and at lake's end. When lake level is low an alcove on the left just inside the entrance may allow camping. A nearby smaller alcove may offer shelter at higher lake levels.

FLYING EAGLE COVE

Flying Eagle Arch stands high on the mesa southwest of the cove. The arch forms an entrance to a recess below the rim. It may be reached on foot by beginning on the left shore of Flying Eagle Cove and ascending the long rock ramp — actually a portion of the Waterpocket Fold — to the base of the arch.

CAMPING: Talus and sheer cliffs make camping unlikely.

Houseboat in Middle Rock Bay

photo by Tom Bean

CANYON BY CANYON

FORBIDDING CANYON

Charles L. Bernheimer and John Wetherill named this canyon in 1921 after their failure to utilize it as part of an elusive western route to Rainbow Bridge. The following year their persistence was rewarded with the discovery of Redbud Pass and the resulting new trail to Rainbow Bridge.

Lake Powell follows a sinuous course in Forbidding Canyon. One or two blind alleys, short but convincing, branch from the main watercourse upstream from the mouth of Rainbow Bridge Canyon. Imposing Cummings Mesa looms on the western horizon above Forbidding's confusing twists and turns.

Aztec Creek still flows serenely in the upper reaches of Forbidding Canyon. However, the creek drains the entire west slope of Navajo Mountain and is therefore subject to frequent, sudden and significant flash floods. Friends of mine, camping in Forbidding and sleeping on their boat, were once swept down-canyon as Aztec Creek gushed into Lake Powell. Quick action and good fortune prevented injury but several hours of sleeplessness followed as the lake surged with flood waters rich with sand, juniper berries, driftwood and soupy matter of unknown origin.

Hiking the bed of Forbidding Canyon beyond Lake Powell is possible for several miles if one or two minor obstacles can be surmounted. Turning left into Cliff Canyon will eventually lead to Redbud Pass, Redbud Canyon and Rainbow Bridge for a full day's loop hike. Stable silt deposits at lake's end in Forbidding Canyon and a topographic map are essentials for this hike.

CAMPING: Overnight accommodations are few. A tiny inlet immediately inside the entrance on the left will sometimes allow slickrock camping. About midway between Forbidding's entrance and the turnoff to Rainbow Bridge, an abandoned meander also on the left will accept guests at lake levels up to about 3688 feet. Beyond the mouth of Rainbow Bridge Canyon the chances of lodging diminish further. Ledge and slickrock sites are unlikely but still possible at some intermediate lake levels. Accumulating silt has made camping at lake's end equally unpromising. Only unusually low lake elevations will reveal more camps in upper Forbidding Canyon.

FORGOTTEN CANYON

This canyon was once inadvertently left off a survey map. River runners discovered the omission and gave the canyon its name. Equally appropriate is the name of a restored Anasazi ruin, Defiance House, located in the main fork of Forgotten Canyon. Three striking pictographs, apparently representing armed warriors, hover on the cliff above the ruin. A short trail leads to Defiance House from the edge of the lake. Visitors are welcome, but please do not camp within the ruin.

The main fork may be hiked for long distances between ledges of Kayenta Formation capped with Navajo Sandstone.

On the main channel south of Forgotten's entrance look for a series of Anasazi toeholds ascending the cliff below a dip in the canyon rim. The route once allowed Indians and later miners access to California Bar on the Colorado River.

CAMPING: In the main fork of Forgotten Canyon, many beaches line the shore beginning in the vicinity of Defiance House and extending to water's end. The left fork is mostly sheer walled although a site might be possible at the end when flash flood danger is absent. The short right fork does not normally allow camping.

FOURMILE CANYON

Fourmile Canyon is located four miles down-river from the site of Dandy Crossing. Mount Ellsworth, eight miles distant, can be seen from the canyon's entrance.

Cliffs of Wingate Sandstone and younger rocks cap the Chinle Formation slopes that rise from lake level.

CAMPING: The Chinle Formation is uncharacteristically hospitable to campers in Fourmile. Many shaly beaches, some gravel beaches and perhaps even a sandy pocket or slickrock bench are possible.

FRIENDSHIP COVE

High cliffs protect this canyon from early morning and late afternoon sun, a welcome attribute in hot weather.

CAMPING: A magnificent fan of beach sand spills into the lake near lake's end on the left. A few more small beaches can usually be found at the rear of the canyon. And sometimes small beaches appear close to Friendship's entrance on the left where talus hills meet shoreline.

CANYON BY CANYON

GOOD HOPE BAY

The character of Good Hope Bay, wide and rimmed with broken rock, is largely dictated by the Chinle Formation that occupies most of its shoreline. South of Good Hope Bay, younger and harder rocks, mostly sandstones, dip to lake level. Because of the width of the bay, swells and waves occur most of the year.

CAMPING: Innumerable viable sites await. The eastern shore offers the most choice, usually shaly beaches between talus slopes. At the southeastern corner of the bay, however, some large sandy beaches are available at most lake levels. The western shore is mostly rough talus. Be sure to avoid locations where signs of landslides and slumps are evident.

GROTTO CANYON

Grotto Canyon's name came from a cavernous hollow that lay close to the river along the streambed.

CAMPING: Grotto Canyon is stingy with campsites. A couple of slickrock and ledge sites might be available near the entrance on the left. Another may be found about mid-canyon, also on the left. Alternative campsites are located nearby in Dungeon and Cornerstone canyons.

GUNSIGHT CANYON

Named after the butte that rises a thousand feet above the lake, Gunsight Canyon is the westernmost finger of Padre Bay.

Gunsight Pass, a boat-width slim, pokes through the narrow ridge a mile north of Gunsight Butte. The floor of the pass lies at about elevation 3680 making the short cut to Padre Canyon usable only at higher lake elevations.

CAMPING: Shaly and sandy beaches lie in abundance in the many coves of Gunsight. The sandy beaches are more common deep in the canyon.

Gunsight Butte

photo by Tom Bean

HALLS CREEK BAY

Halls Creek honors the memory of pioneer Charley Hall who built the Hole-in-the-Rock ferryboat in 1880 and shortly thereafter established a ferry at what came to be known as "Halls Crossing."

Keep alert as you enter the mouth of Halls Creek Bay; surprise shallows sometimes await inattentive pilots. Running close to either shore line is especially hazardous. Beyond the entryway, Halls Creek Bay broadens dramatically. The left shore follows the base of the Waterpocket Fold, primary feature of Capitol Reef National Park nearby to the north. The right shore parallels a ridge that separates Halls Creek Bay from Bullfrog Bay. This ridge is breached at mid-canyon when Lake Powell is within thirty feet of full, allowing a boater's short cut to Bullfrog Marina.

Seemingly endless expanses of shallow water occupy the Halls Creek Bay's northern end. Be alert for surprise shoals off of the western shore.

CAMPING: Campsites too numerous to count line the shores of Halls Creek Bay. A labyrinth of sandy coves is located on the north end of the western shore, and long stretches of beach lie on the east shore. Shaly sites are most common closer to the mouth of Halls Creek Bay.

HANSEN CREEK CANYON

A wagon road once descended this canyon to gold mining operations at Smith Bar on the Colorado River.

CAMPING: Long sandy beaches occupy Hansen's upper end, mostly on the left shore. Slickrock campsites can often be established along the right shoreline in the lower canyon.

HIDDEN PASSAGE

Hidden Passage was once one of the finest of Glen Canyon's tributaries. Its narrow entrance was obscured by heavy vegetation and it angled sharply upstream. Passing boaters might miss seeing its screened entrance. River runners often stopped to hike its confined corridors although a pour-over and plunge pool prohibited many from penetrating to its upper levels.

The short tributary crack on the left at mid-canyon is worth visiting with its muted light and tilting walls. The canyon ends in a cleft draining the benchlands above.

The main channel of the canyon splits into a pair of short branches. Both end in steep, sculptured cracks.

CAMPING: It is a challenge. Desperation sites sometimes emerge at the far end of the canyon in low water. And marginal slickrock camps are occasionally usable just beyond mid-canyon on the right.

CANYON BY CANYON

HOLE-IN-THE-ROCK

Eighty-three wagons were driven down to the Colorado River through this cleft early in 1880. Two hundred and thirty Mormon men, women and children pioneered the route, built a ferryboat and crossed the half-frozen river here. Lake Powell covers about four hundred feet of their thousand-foot descent from rim to river.

Agile hikers can accomplish the six-hundred-foot climb in about an hour. In summer, the coolness of daybreak or the shade of late afternoon are best. Also, a loop hike is possible starting at shoreline about a mile-and-a-half north of Hole-in-the-Rock, ascending the remnants of the Jackass Bench Trail, using the miners' steps visible just above high-water mark, to the rim then heading southwest to the top of the Hole and down to the lake.

The head of Hole-in-the-Rock can also be attained by driving fifty miles of dirt road from Escalante, Utah.

CAMPING: No camps exist except for exposed talus sites.

HOWLAND CANYON

Howland Canyon is a tributary of West Canyon. The drainage extends for several miles, much of it sandy swale. But the abrupt end of Lake Powell marks the rim of a colossal amphitheater, once a favorite destination of West Canyon hikers coming from the Colorado. The name Howland comes from the two brothers who aided J.W. Powell on his first exploration of the Colorado River in 1869.

Howland Canyon is known to some hikers and backpackers simply as the dry arm of West Canyon.

Beware of strategically located surprise shallows just downstream of the Howland-West confluence.

CAMPING: Only at the highest lake levels does Howland Canyon afford camping, and even then a single sandy site is available.

Kayaking Lake Powell   *photo by Tom Bean*

ICEBERG CANYON

Before Lake Powell, Iceberg Canyon hikers gained entry by swimming a cold pool. The canyon's name grew out of rumors spread by the shivering explorers.

No less than six forks radiate from Iceberg Canyon. The first three are short; the last three are slightly longer.

Prime hiking awaits those who wish to explore on foot. All three of the longer forks allow entry. The left fork is longest at about a mile and is a fine hike. The middle fork is shortest at about a quarter mile and ends in an imposing amphitheater.

A natural dam and a small lake were once located in the right fork of the trio of longer forks. The dam was created by a rockfall and its crest rises to within fifteen feet of Lake Powell's full pool level. At lower water boaters must be alert for shoals or, at lake levels below about 3685, prepared for an abbreviated cruise. Use caution in this fork, snags often surprise unobservant boaters (perhaps this warning should be called the tip of the Iceberg).

In the early 1970s major rockfalls occurred on the main channel immediately upstream from Iceberg Canyon's entrance. They left the cliff fresh and clean much like a new canvas awaiting the brush and pigments of Mother Nature.

CAMPING: The first fork is normally hopeless. The second and third forks, branching to the left, sometimes offer marginal talus sites and, less commonly, small beaches. Of the three remaining longer forks, the left and center forks almost always contain sandy beaches. The right is most accommodating at high lake levels.

INDIAN CREEK CANYON

Sheer walls end in a bowl of rock. Sometimes a line of headwall seeps gently shower the final few feet of the lake.

CAMPING: A small talus slope is the only possibility.

KANE WASH CANYON

Kane Wash Canyon lies at the east end of Padre Bay. Its multiple forks surround an imposing blade of rock called "The Cookie Jar."

While Glen Canyon Dam was under construction, river runners pulled their boats out of the Colorado at the mouth of Kane Wash.

CAMPING: Two lobes of Kane Wash are located to the right of The Cookie Jar, a third lobe lies to the left. Each normally holds excellent camping beaches. And as is generally true of every northern tributary of Padre Bay, the beaches are concentrated on the west side of each embayment.

CANYON BY CANYON

KLONDIKE COVE

Not a canyon, Klondike Cove is more a shoreline recess. The tiny bay takes its name from the large gravel bar that edged the Colorado River just upstream.

CAMPING: Klondike Bay is an effective, if small, haven. Despite its minimal size, it usually provides one or two beaches, a ledgy site or two and several possible slick-rock camps.

KNOWLES CANYON

A trip into Knowles finds Kayenta Formation ledges ascending from lake level at mid-canyon. Small coves branch from the main course of the lake on both sides.

CAMPING: Knowles Canyon is beach stingy. Most of its sites are marginal talus slopes although ledgy campsites often dominate the end of the lake. Small sand pockets may appear at some lake levels.

LABYRINTH CANYON

Its twisting corridors led river-running hikers to call this canyon a labyrinth. The Arizona-Utah state line cuts through pointed Boundary Butte just east of mid-point of the canyon. The open views north across Padre Bay and south to Tower Butte are one of Labyrinth's charms.

At high lake elevations the end of the channel lies in a slot less than a boat-width wide. If hikers can swim or outflank this slot, a confined, tortuous passage lies beyond. In some places a kind of "staggering walk" is useful for negotiating Labyrinth's erratic course.

Hikers can also travel up-slope to circumnavigate Tower Butte beyond Labyrinth's south shore. Look for petroglyphs on a boulder on the butte's east side.

CAMPING: Good beach campsites can be found in Labyrinth's outer sections. The prominent bay just east of Labyrinth's entrance is lined with sand. In the canyon's main channel watch for the nifty beach at the end of an embayment to the right just before the canyon narrows. Nearer canyon's end slickrock sites are possible at some lake levels.

The Lake Canyon area was home for a large number of Anasazi Indians. Toehold routes, ruins and petroglyphs can still be found in the vicinity.

Not surprisingly, Lake Canyon once contained a lake. It was located several miles upstream from the deepest penetration of Lake Powell and was known as Lake Pagahrit or Hermit Lake. Its clear, fresh water stretched nearly half a mile cradled between sandstone walls. Lake Pagahrit was an unlikely oasis in harsh desert terrain and a welcome sight to the Mormon pioneers of 1879-1880. They rested and repaired equipment here after crossing the Colorado River at Hole-in-the-Rock and the subsequent difficult crossing of Grey Mesa. The far side of Lake Canyon was attained simply by crossing the crest of the dam.

Unfortunately, late in 1915 three days of heavy storms filled Lake Pagahrit to overflowing. The natural dam failed and the lake surged through the canyon to join the Colorado. The destruction of the Lake Pagahrit dam made the crossing of Lake Canyon difficult.

CAMPING: Although they are not plentiful, both slickrock sites and beaches are available in Lake Canyon.

The best camping beaches are to be found at the end of the main fork. Normally they are large enough to accommodate several boats. A sheltering alcove screened by trees lies immediately behind the strip of sand on the left side of the channel. Another strip of beach lies just beyond to the right. These beaches are at their best when the lake is just below full pool. They are also heavily used during the summer.

Two tributary arms of Lake Canyon enter from the left or north side. The first of these normally has a couple of slickrock campsites. The second tributary canyon on the left may have a couple of small sandy sites at or near its end when the lake level is several feet below full. This arm may also contain a small number of slickrock campsite possibilities.

Only one tributary enters Lake Powell from the south or right side of Lake Canyon. Here, too, one may find a slickrock campsite or two.

CANYON BY CANYON

LAST CHANCE CANYON

Last Chance Canyon stretches like a grand boulevard linking endless cross streets.

The west-side inlet opposite Little Valley and the two larger inlets immediately to the south, each contain hanging watercourses at their heads. In stormy weather these pouroffs may briefly spill torrents of water into the lake. Even in dry weather the chutes, especially the southern two, are worth a visit.

CAMPING: Tens of miles of rugged shoreline yield a minimum of campsites. Most are talus slopes that grudgingly reveal small beaches at low lake levels only. The branching tributaries beyond mid-canyon are the most likely to hold good camp spots. The highest concentration of campsites can be found in the major side canyon immediately southeast of Little Valley. Boaters usually have their choice of sand, shale, gravel and slickrock. The ends of Last Chance and Little Valley also provide some additional campsite possibilities, most of them talus.

LITTLE ARCH CANYON

A small arch of rock once perched near the mouth of this canyon. Lake Powell swallowed the span that prompted the name. Still another modest arch is located high on the right wall close to the canyon's entrance.

Little Arch Canyon is short but quite narrow in its upper reaches.

CAMPING: Although camps are unlikely, one or two slickrock sites may be possible immediately inside the entrance at some lake elevations.

Eroded sandstone in Rock Creek Bay   *photo by Tom Bean*

LLEWELLYN GULCH

Llewellyn Gulch carries the name of pioneer Llewellyn Harris.

A crystal-clear streamlet and petroglyphs tucked beneath the alcoves reward up-canyon hikers. A route up the north wall about three miles beyond the lake allows access to the Hole-In-the-Rock Road.

A rockfall of monstrous proportions occurred at the large beach at lake's end in January, 1988. Smaller falls during the preceding months hinted of instability; freezing temperatures finally brought on the cliff's collapse. About half the beach disappeared beneath the rubble and a tidal wave of lake water washed over the remainder, flattening a forest of tamarisks and willows. Fortunately, no campers were present.

Watch for prop-damaging rocks as you approach this beach.

CAMPING: A number of fine sandy sites lie within the canyon. Most are on the right shore nestled between the Kayenta Formation shelves. A small ledgy campsite or two at the mouth on the right can sometimes be utilized with the lake and boat traffic at minimal levels during the off-season. Probably the largest sandy beach lies just at the end of the lake. Alternative sandy campsites can be found outside and southwest of the entrance to Llewellyn. All of these locations are heavily used during peak season.

LONG CANYON

Long Canyon is short, or at least the section that includes Lake Powell is short. The unflooded portion can be hiked several miles to the north where it drops abruptly from a bench on the west flank of the Waterpocket Fold.

Lake level at Long Canyon lies near the top of the Wingate Sandstone. The purple ledges, blocks and balanced rocks of the Kayenta Formation rest just above with the Navajo Sandstone carrying the same themes on to the rim in orange and salmon colors.

Often the gooey, unstable silt deposits and large boulders at the end of the channel make access difficult to the upper reaches of Long Canyon.

CAMPING: Camping is limited to rough talus sites along the edge of the channel, sites probably useful only to houseboat campers.

CANYON BY CANYON

LOST EDEN CANYON

Three short fingers of lake water penetrate Lost Eden. The left fork holds no camps and ends in a crack. The middle fork is the longest, a straight corridor lined with sheer cliffs and flooded alcoves. The right fork is short and ends abruptly in a slot. The cliffs are composed of Navajo Sandstone.

During a nineteen day trip on the lake, rowing from Hite to Wahweap, I decided to swim the slot at the end of the right fork. It was hot and I had just rowed in from Halls Crossing Marina. With life jacket donned and dory tied to the cliffs, I swam the narrow crack to its flotsam-choked end. To my disappointment, hiking beyond the slot was not possible. On the return swim I noticed a peculiar piece of flotsam bobbing between the sheer walls. A couple more strokes put my eyes and nose within inches: it was my billfold. It had floated out of a pocket after I had neglected to put it in a safe place following an ice cream purchase at Halls Crossing. The marginal campsite described below was utilized to dry out the limp bills, soppy membership cards and smeared photos.

CAMPING: It is tempting to play it safe and say there are no campsites in Lost Eden. However, at some lake levels there is a marginal slickrock site in the right fork just before it pinches to an end.

MIDDLE ROCK CREEK CANYON

This is the middle fork of the trio of canyons called Rock Creek.

CAMPING: The sheer walls of Middle Rock's entrance don't spark confidence in finding campsites. But don't fret, the camps lie near the end of the waterway where the cliffs fall back and the canyon flares. A surprising number of sandy sites can be found here along with a few slickrock and shale possibilities.

MIKES CANYON

Monitor Mesa to the south and the vivid colors of the Chinle Formation dominate the setting of Mikes Canyon.

Watch for shoals — they can appear in cruelly devious places.

CAMPING: Numerous shaly beaches girdle the lake in Mikes Canyon. Most of these, however, are likely to be mushy at shoreline. Boaters have been known to sink in quicksand to their ankles and beyond. Use caution when stepping ashore.

MOQUI CANYON

The entrance to Moqui Canyon leads to five forks. Although the first three are short, the final two branches are major drainages. The most distant right fork penetrates farther into Moqui Canyon while the final left fork pushes into North Gulch.

Miles of hiking canyon extend beyond lake's end in both North Gulch and Moqui. Both contain streams and Anasazi ruins. Moqui Canyon is sandy and broad, North Gulch is narrower and thick with vegetation.

CAMPING: The two short forks to the left are sheer walled. The short fork to the right may allow talus or, sometimes, small beaches. Watch for snags near the end. North Gulch usually contains slickrock, ledgy sites or beaches. At high lake levels summer boaters often crowd the long sandy beach marking the end of the Moqui Canyon fork.

MOUNTAIN SHEEP CANYON

An ocean of slickrock waves roll into Mountain Sheep Canyon for most of its length. But at its upper end, the canyon walls steepen and converge to grip the lake in a long, narrow channel. The constricted canyon beyond lake's end is worth exploration. Wading is often necessary in the first few hundred feet. Although its walls do not tower, the twisting, sinuous, eccentric course of the canyon bed allows little time to look skyward.

Be alert for submerged domes of rock, most notably on the left a short distance into the canyon and again beyond the camping lobes at mid-canyon.

Because its mouth was mislocated on topographic maps, Mountain Sheep Canyon was once known as False Entrance Canyon. Cummings Mesa surrounds Mountain Sheep on three sides, its rim fifteen hundred feet above the lake.

CAMPING: Campsite possibilities are surprisingly limited. In mid-canyon, the best bets lie in the two largest lobes of the lake, one on the right, one on the left. Most are slickrock camps, some spots include sand pockets. Deeper in the canyon just before the lake narrows, two more possibilities appear on either side, again with more slickrock than sand.

CANYON BY CANYON

MUSIC TEMPLE CANYON

The lower reach of this watercourse was one of the gems of Glen Canyon. Powell described it as a vast chamber two hundred feet high and five hundred feet long with a narrow, twisting skylight. His brother's singing there moved Powell to write, "...we are pleased to find that this hollow in the rock is filled with sweet sounds. It was doubtless made for an academy of music by its storm-born architect; so we name it Music Temple." The chamber is now flooded by the waters of Lake Powell.

The deep, north-facing alcove walls just inside the entrance to Music Temple offer relief from the summer sun for floating lunches. Across the channel from the alcoves, a slickrock ramp allows agile hikers to ascend the steep slope, skirt the upper cliff to the left and continue beyond to gain a nifty view of the confluence area. It is a short but "sporting" hike.

CAMPING: Steep slickrock and overhanging alcove walls edge the water until the lake widens close to its end. Although beaches are absent, slickrock camping is often possible with pockets of sand present at some lake elevations.

MYSTERY CANYON

Mystery Canyon is aptly named — each of its three forks pinch into narrow, dim, high-walled canyons. Like several other side canyons of Glen Canyon, Mystery was given two names, one by the river runners who hiked up-canyon from the Colorado and another name by those who approached by land. The river men called it Mystery because of a series of beckoning but dangerously eroded Anasazi toeholds ascending a cliff. What lay beyond was a mystery. The land-based explorers named the main fork after the people whose structures and artifacts were plentiful there, the Anasazi.

Watch for prop-damaging rocks in this wider section — especially when the lake is just a few feet short of full.

The course of the canyon becomes confused at the far end of the wide section. There is an island here that, although not large, is not easily recognized as such because of its irregular shape and rugged terrain. Usually a slickrock camp can be established on this "Mystery Island" in a miniature inlet.

Beyond the island the waterway divides into tributary fingers. To the right is Moepitz Canyon — narrow and cool with high walls often cast in vermilion light reflected from the rock above. It ends in a flooded slot so narrow only swimmers can penetrate. It has no campsites.

A straight channel of water extends left from the entrance to Moepitz, passing south of the island and ending in a steep rock-filled ravine. A desperation slickrock camp is possible on the left about midway along this corridor when the lake is just a few feet below full.

Anasazi Canyon enters this straight channel from a narrow opening on the right. By keeping right one will follow Anasazi Canyon to its end through a series of twists and turns, red and blue light filtering down from the rocks and sky above. It, too, ends in a crack at high water and offers no campsites. Lehi Canyon comes into Anasazi from the left with walls not quite as high and sheer. But at the highest lake levels there can be a small slickrock camp at the end. This camp is vulnerable to flash floods, however. Use caution.

Once, while camped here in early November, my companion flung a rock at a persistent mouse with designs on our dinner. Although the rock was thrown only as a warning, a shard of shrapnel knocked the poor creature for a loop. The body came to rest belly up, limbs twitching. The atmosphere in Mystery Canyon instantly turned to gloom. Happily, after only a few words of remorse had been uttered, the little guy shook its head, regained its feet and staggered off into the darkness. No further discouragement to his advances was found necessary.

CAMPING: Usually only one or two marginal slickrock campsites are possible.

The entrance to Mystery Canyon is surprisingly narrow and twisting. But not far beyond, the walls fall back and the canyon widens. At some lake levels one might find a confined slickrock camp on the left along this wider section of canyon. Other small or marginal sites may be possible as described earlier.

NARROW CANYON AND CATARACT CANYON

A masterless watercourse lies upriver from the mouth of the Dirty Devil. In Narrow Canyon and lower Cataract Canyon the Colorado River fights to maintain its ancient ways; Lake Powell stubbornly refuses to allow it.

Be alert for driftwood, shoals and currents.

Dark Canyon is probably the most significant tributary. Backpackers often travel its depths in Dark Canyon Primitive Area.

River runners, finishing whitewater runs through Cataract Canyon, float Lake Powell's upper channel to their take-out point at Hite Marina. If you have an opportunity, ask them how they fared in Satan's Gut, Cataract's most unfriendly rapid.

CAMPING: A number of canyons join the main stem but none of them allow Lake Powell to enter far. Campsites can sometimes be found on talus slopes and sandbars at the side canyon entrances and along the main channel. But the rising silt deposits, fluctuating lake levels and changing river discharge make campsite locations uncertain.

CANYON BY CANYON

NASJA CANYON

Nasja takes its name from Nasja Begay, one of the Indian guides that led the Cummings-Douglass party to Rainbow Bridge. Surprise Valley, the remote, idyllic refuge in Zane Grey's *The Rainbow Trail* is located in upper Nasja Canyon about five miles beyond the lake.

When Nasja Creek flows it plummets free fall into the flooded amphitheater at the head of the lake. Hikers can explore the canyon above the waterfall by climbing the talus on the left and walking the Kayenta Formation ledge to the pouroff.

CAMPING: Near canyon's end a single strip of talus will allow houseboat anchorage. Alternative campsites are available outside and about one-half mile west of the mouth of Nasja Canyon—slickrock to the right and, a little farther on, sandy beach to the left.

NAVAJO CANYON

Boaters can follow Lake Powell fifteen miles and more up the canyon's meandering course. Look for an obvious arch, part of a triple alcove, on the left just beyond mid-canyon. Also, watch for miner's stairs that end about twenty feet above high lake level. They are located a few hundred feet beyond the arch.

Navajo Canyon heads fifty miles to the east on the highlands south of Navajo Mountain. Distant Inscription House Ruin, part of Navajo National Monument, is located in upper Navajo Canyon. Because of the size and nature of the country it drains, Navajo Canyon is destined to choke with silt rather rapidly. Lake Powell's end, therefore, changes location unpredictably. Watch for shallows. Also, because floods bring large quantities of driftwood into the lake here, Navajo Canyon has more than its share of bright campfires and broken propellers.

CAMPING: Considering its length, Navajo Canyon holds disappointingly few campsites. Its entrance offers a sand beach on the right and possible slickrock sites with sandy pockets nearby on both shores. Beyond the entrance, campsites are scarce until mid-canyon where the waterway suddenly widens and a large, popular, sandy hill edges the lake on the right. Slickrock sites are sometimes possible nearer lake's end.

NESKAHI WASH

Neskahi is a Navajo word that means "fatso." It may be that a person of generous proportions lived by the wash or ran sheep there.

Petrified wood can sometimes be found in the Chinle shales and conglomerates is this area. Please do not collect petrified wood, as it is illegal to do so without a permit.

CAMPING: Shaly beaches, Shinarump Conglomerate ledges and talus allow some camping.

CANYON BY CANYON

NOKAI CANYON

An entrance confined between low cliffs of Shin-arump Conglomerate leads to a small shallow-water bay. No Mans Mesa forms the eastern horizon, Piute Mesa the western horizon. Translated from the Navajo language Nokai means "Spanish" or "Mexican."

CAMPING: Long strips of shaly beach interlaced with pockets of sand make campsites common. More shaly sites can be found outside of Nokai to the west in Zahn Bay.

NORTH WASH

Along with Trachyte Canyon, North Wash was one of the original western approach routes to Glen Canyon.

CAMPING: Campsites are scarce. Only a few small shaly pockets and perhaps some ledgy spots lend themselves to camping.

OAK CANYON

The entrance to Oak is easy to miss — it lies on the tip of a slickrock point. Some maps mistakenly call this canyon Secret, probably because the entrance is obscure and its channel is confined and "secretive."

Before Lake Powell filled, despite its narrow nature, Oak Canyon could be hiked from the river to the Rainbow Bridge Trail, a distance of several miles. The unflooded portion of Oak Canyon can still be hiked today. It is narrow, twisting and much of it is shady even in mid-summer. Access to the upper part of the canyon is made difficult by scrub oak, hence the name.

CAMPING: Essentially none. One campsite might be established at the end of the lake if flash floods are not a worry and if the silt banks have dried out. A marginal slickrock site can sometimes be utilized on the left just inside the mouth — but don't count on it.

PADRE CANYON

The two Spanish priests, Dominguez and Escalante, and their entourage crossed the Colorado River close to the mouth of this canyon in November, 1776. They were on their way back to New Mexico after an unsuccessful attempt to reach Monterey, California — winter storms had made crossing mountain passes too dangerous. This Colorado River ford had been used for centuries by Indians, but after 1776 it was known as the "Crossing of the Fathers."

Look for a colorful bench of rock with interlaced red and white beds near canyon's end on the right shore. If you discover anyone carving their name in these beautiful formations, keep calm and, using a stage whisper, exclaim to a friend, "Look, a meathead!"

CAMPING: Numerous campsites are sheltered within Padre Canyon. Nearly all are on the west side. Most are sandy; a few, particularly near canyon's end are gravelly.

CANYON BY CANYON

PIUTE CANYON

Piute Canyon is a major watercourse draining the plateaus west of Navajo Mountain.

CAMPING: Pockets of shaly beach lie between the jumbled boulders of talus. More scattered pockets of shaly beach can be found outside the mouth of Piute to the east.

PIUTE FARMS

Native Americans, perhaps for centuries, used this area for agricultural purposes. Today, a temporary marina, accessible by road from Monument Valley, is located here.

Before Lake Powell, the San Juan River at Piute Farms spread wide but shallow. At minimal flows, river-running boaters were forced to get out and walk, dragging their craft over the sandbars in search of a navigable channel. Today's river runners ending their trip down the San Juan River take out at Clay Hills Crossing or Piute Farms.

CAMPING: Shaly beaches are numerous but the presence of the marina, deepening silt and murky water discourage camping.

QUAKING BOG CANYON

Quaking Bog Canyon is the short defile lying between the better known Driftwood and Cascade Canyons. Its name comes from a hungry pool of quicksand that once lay near its junction with the wild Colorado.

CAMPING: Chances are slim. However, at higher lake levels one or two marginal slickrock camps are possible. But don't pull out your tent just yet!

Rainbow Bridge   *photo by Gary Ladd*

68

RAINBOW BRIDGE CANYON

Rainbow Bridge represents, as well as any single feature can, the extraordinary landscape that surrounds Lake Powell. And although the bridge is not the longest natural span on earth it is perhaps the most sublime. A little stream, given enough time and aided by the elements has produced a masterpiece.

Check the short, nameless tributary canyon on the left about midway between the canyon's entrance and the bridge. In hot weather it offers shade for a floating lunch and in rainy weather it sports a waterfall plunging directly into the lake.

You may find your perception of size and distance is fooled by the scale of the canyons. As a reference, consider that the right wall adjacent to the courtesy docks is over eleven hundred feet high—twice the height of the Washington Monument.

Two old foot trails lead to Rainbow Bridge from the flanks of Navajo Mountain. The one-way distance using the shortest trail is thirteen miles. If backpackers arrive at the bridge during your visit ask them about their journey. If they act snooty, try to be tolerant.

If time allows, hike under the bridge and on up the trail an additional half mile to Echo Camp. It is sheltered in an alcove on the left where the canyon bends sharply right. A pool of crystal water and a tangle of vegetation make it a pleasant goal. Seldom used now, Echo Camp was once a kind of campers motel complete with permanent tents and kitchen. Outfitters from Navajo Mountain Trading Post brought their clients here on horseback before Lake Powell provided easier access to Rainbow Bridge.

Rainbow Bridge was officially discovered August 14, 1909 by Dean Byron Cummings, William Douglass, John Wetherill, Indian guides and others. Recent evidence supports claims that scores of people on numerous occasions saw the bridge before the 1909 expedition. Of course, Native Americans knew of it for centuries. More recently, miners stumbled upon the bridge but had little use for the amazing natural feature. Gold was interesting, a bridge was not.

Because of Rainbow Bridge's religious significance to Native Americans of the region, the National Park Service requests visitors to assist in maintaining a quiet atmosphere when entering the Monument.

No diving or swimming is permitted within the Monument site.

CAMPING: Bridge Canyon apparently devoted all of its talents to the creation of Rainbow Bridge. It provides no campsites and no camping is permitted within the bounds of the National Monument.

CANYON BY CANYON

RED CANYON

A landscape of intermixed colors and rough textures surrounds Red Canyon. Bert Loper constructed and lived for several years in a small cabin in Red Canyon. Loper was a miner and river boatman destined to die at the oars while running a Grand Canyon rapid in 1949. Lake Powell inundated the Loper Cabin site.

Castle Butte, near Red Canyon's mouth, not to be confused with Castle Rock in Wahweap Bay, towers nearly eight hundred feet above the lake at full pool.

Be wary of surprise shallows even far from shore.

CAMPING: Sites are numerous although sand is uncommon. Talus borders most of the lake's edge, sometimes interrupted by shaly pockets, gravel beaches and ledgy stretches.

REFLECTION CANYON

Walls of Navajo Sandstone rise sheer from lake's edge through out much of Reflection Canyon. But there are a few campsites.

Beyond the end of the lake the right fork is choked with annoyingly robust vegetation. But once beyond this barrier a hiker can connect with the Hole-In-The-Rock Road, crossing Llewellyn Gulch on the way.

The left fork also offers short hikes into rather narrow, steep, high-walled canyons. A rope hanging from one of its walls leads one to wonder who left it there and when.

CAMPING: Deep in the left fork, talus slopes offer anchorage to houseboaters while small beaches lie at lake's end. Be wary of submerged rocks on the approach to this area. In the right fork, look for several good beaches near the end.

Pleasure boat on the San Juan arm of Lake Powell   *photo by Tom Bean*

The high sandstone cliffs of Ribbon Canyon offer morning and afternoon protection from the summer sun to most of its campsites.

A small stream threads its way down the bed of Ribbon Canyon during the cooler months. Hiking the canyon beyond Lake Powell reveals abundant seeps and many alcoves watching from above. The Navajo Sandstone-Kayenta Formation contact lies just above lake level, a condition that almost always yields alcoves, seeps, and exceptional displays of desert varnish and hanging gardens.

Several years ago I made a series of solo rowing trips on Lake Powell. During one of these, eight days out of Wahweap, I approached the mouth of Ribbon Canyon. It was February and there were few boats to disturb the glassy surface and silent atmosphere of the lake. But looking over my shoulder I was shocked to discover a lone kayaker not three hundred feet away. This fellow from Aspen, Colorado, had started at Bullfrog and had been out for ten days with twenty days yet planned. Having explored and rowed for over a week myself, the effect was something like the Livingstone-Stanley meeting … in a small way.

Ribbon Canyon once followed a longer course before joining the Colorado. The evidence is clear: what appears to be the original mouth of the canyon is actually a breach of the north wall. The original Ribbon Canyon continued a mile or more through the now-flooded canyon just south of today's apparent mouth to join the Colorado River across and immediately downstream from Hole-in-the-Rock. The breach occurred because the meandering Colorado undermined and eroded the narrow ridge of rock that separated the drainages. Ribbon Creek broke through and spilled directly into the main stem. Lower Ribbon Canyon was abandoned and now lies nameless and largely unrecognized for what it once was. Today this detached canyon can be used at higher lake levels as a nifty short cut to the mouth of Cottonwood Canyon — but watch for submerged, prop-punishing shoals across from Hole-in-the-Rock.

CAMPING: There is an obvious and excellent beach on the left just where the canyon makes a dogleg to the left. Across the way from this corner beach are one or two marginal ledgy campsites probably best for houseboats. Father up-canyon are more marginal ledgy campsites on the left. Then close to the end of the lake at most higher pool levels is a narrow but nice strip of sand on the left. Across the channel from this beach one might find a pocket of usable sand at some lake levels.

CANYON BY CANYON

THE RINCON

Rincon in Spanish means "inside corner, nook." In the southwestern United States it refers to a small, secluded valley or a bend in a stream. All these meanings are appropriate for the Rincon, a topographic feature of Glen Canyon and Lake Powell.

Here the Colorado once looped far to the south, cutting deeply into the north face of Wilson Mesa before heading northwest to find Bowns and Long canyons. Where it swept most swiftly, along the cliffs on the outside of the bends, the Colorado also carved most vigorously. Attacked on both sides, the narrow neck of rock that separated the beginning and end of the loop gradually disintegrated. Then, many thousands of years ago, the snowmelt floods of a warm spring overtopped the crumbling ridge. The Colorado gushed through the gap and quickly enlarged the opening. Eventually the loop of river channel was abandoned. Left behind was a nook, a secluded valley surrounding a mesa where once there was a bend in a stream, the Rincon.

Cliffs of Wingate Sandstone stand above the slopes of the Chinle Formation; they offer some relief from both early morning sun and late afternoon sun.

Some locations offer a view of a jeep road descending the southeast cliff of the Rincon. The road joins the old Mormon Trail northwest of Hole-in-the-Rock. Miners constructed it during the uranium boom following World War II.

Logs and pieces of logs of petrified wood can be found embedded in the Chinle Formation in the abandoned channel of the Rincon. The same layer lies exposed in Petrified Forest National Park. Please remember, however, the collecting of natural objects within the Recreation Area is prohibited. This policy assures future visitors the opportunity to also see remnants of the great forests of 220 million years ago.

CAMPING: Lake Powell has invaded both ends of the former river channel loop, forming a pair of coves. Because lake level at the Rincon lies in the shales of the Chinle Formation, the shoreline is mostly steep talus. But toward the end of both coves the shoreline turns sandy and long strips of beach line the water's edge. The west cove is perhaps a little narrower than the east cove but both offer many campsites.

ROCK CREEK CANYON

This is the left fork of three canyons that merged just before joining the Colorado River. This lobe of Lake Powell is large enough to be termed a bay.

CAMPING: The far reaches of Rock Creek Canyon hold many campsites, including some long stretches of beach. Two stubby inlets on the left enclose smaller beaches. The largest sand strip is located on the left side of the main canyon close to lake's end. A couple more sandy sites can usually be found along the twisting channel just beyond. Normally some shaly beaches are located on the right before the lake pinches into a narrow channel.

The rock strata dip gently toward the mouth of Rock Creek Canyon. For this reason, all of the canyon's campsites are found at its far end where the softer, slope-forming, Carmel Formation ascends to Lake Powell's surface.

SAN JUAN RIVER ARM

The Navajo name for the San Juan River is "Pawhuska," which translates to "the mad river." The San Juan's muddiness and its propensity to suddenly rise or fall may account for the Navajo name. Even today the San Juan Arm of Lake Powell seems a bit different. Undulating rock strata along the length of the lake produce cycles of sheer-walled narrows followed by lengthy open bays. Side canyons are short. Because of its isolation, the San Juan Arm tends to be the least visited corner of Lake Powell.

SCORUP CANYON

Scorup Canyon honors the memory of John A. Scorup, co-owner of a cattle company which once operated in most of what is now Canyonlands National Park and all of what has become Natural Bridges National Monument.

CAMPING: Pockets of shaly beaches are most likely south of the mouth of the canyon rather than in Scorup Canyon.

CANYON BY CANYON

SECRET CANYON

Secret Canyon lies at the back of an ancient abandoned meander of the Colorado River. Today, Oak Bay covers the old channel and Secret Canyon, once perched above the river at the back of the meander, now occupies a prominent position.

Some maps label this canyon "Oak," confusing it with its neighbor to the west.

Before Lake Powell, Navajo shepherds brought their sheep down a trail into Secret Canyon. Steps, pecked and blasted from the slickrock, can still be followed on the northeast side of the canyon just beyond the overhanging walls of an alcove at water's edge. Also, hikers can follow Secret Creek to a quiet pool nestled beneath a four-hundred foot cliff. The hike is short, less than half a mile, but a small waterfall and a large poison ivy patch provide compensating challenges.

An unlikely route out of the canyon lies just beyond lake's end. A short series of Anasazi toeholds will lead daring hikers up the steepest pitch on a narrow nose of rock. It is important to remember that Moqui steps are easier to ascend than descend.

CAMPING: Secret is no secret; it holds an excellent stretch of beach that is often crowded in the summer. More campsites, mostly rocky, can be found on the perimeter of Oak Bay between Secret and Oak canyons.

SEVENMILE CANYON

Narrow and encircled by soaring walls, Sevenmile Canyon is dramatically different from its open, shale-shored neighbors to the north.

Beyond lake's end the left fork may be explored on foot along an intermittent streamlet.

CAMPING: Ledgy sites with possible sand pockets await in the right fork at most lake levels. At high lake elevations a beach may be feasible at the end of the fork. More potential sites, mostly ledgy, lie in the left fork. Also, small beaches may appear at some levels at lake's end. Splendid alcove walls streaked with desert varnish loom silently above these left fork camps.

SLICK ROCK CANYON

Slick Rock Canyon is named after the sandstone terrain that surrounds much of Lake Powell. The sandstone is not so much slick as smooth—rounded into domes with flowing curves and undulating surfaces.

Slick Rock Canyon had a large Anasazi population; ruins and petroglyphs were numerous before Lake Powell formed. Interestingly, unlike most other Glen Canyon side canyons, Slick Rock seems to have been spared the devastating flash floods that ripped through many Anasazi farming plots: the upper reaches of Slick Rock Canyon appear untouched by the gully-cutting torrents.

CAMPING: There are several campsite possibilities. Each shore offers a couple of sandy and widely separated sites. But near the lake's end a fine strip of sand begins on the left side. Several parties can share this stretch. It is a popular location, however; houseboaters often make this their headquarters for several days at a time. Just outside the mouth of Slick Rock Canyon are two or three more possible campsites. They lie a short distance north of the mouth on the east side of the channel. The first couple of possibilities are marginal slickrock sites. These are vulnerable to winds off the main channel, however. Another possibility, at some lake levels, lies hidden at the end of a short indentation in the eastern cliff about midway to the northwest bend in the main channel. On the western edge of the main channel, across from eastern cliff indentation, are another two or three slickrock and sand campsite candidates.

SMITH FORK CANYON

Sheer-walled and twisting, Smith Fork Canyon is similar to canyons common in the Navajo Mountain area. Sadly, an enormous Anasazi Indian petroglyph panel once located at canyon's mouth was lost as Lake Powell filled. Smith Fork takes its name from the Smith Brothers, miners who worked the Colorado River bars in this area.

CAMPING: Campsites are rare. The end of the lake may allow a sandy camp if flash floods are not likely. And a couple of slickrock sites might be possible in the lower half of the canyon at some lake levels.

STANTON CANYON

The small canyon is named after Robert B. Stanton, river-running engineer whose ineffective gold dredge lies beneath the lake near the mouth of the canyon.

CAMPING: Shaly beaches and ledges rim the lake. A dirt road originating near Bullfrog Marina reaches shoreline here to make lakeside camping possible.

CANYON BY CANYON

TICABOO CANYON

Prospector Cass Hite came to Glen Canyon in 1883. He built a house in the tributary he called Ticaboo, a Paiute Indian word meaning "friend" or "friendly."

In 1986 a landslide thundered into Lake Powell on Ticaboo's south shore. Portions of the Chinle Formation, lubricated by the lake's high waters, suddenly gave way, plunging tens of tons of Chinle and Wingate Sandstone into the depths.

CAMPING: Sites are scarce. At best, the Chinle talus allows shaly-pocket camps in the canyon's outer reaches. Farther on, Wingate Sandstone descends to lake level with its campsite-defying sheer walls.

TRACHYTE CANYON

Trachyte is a type of igneous rock found in the nearby Henry Mountains.

The tiny but important settlement of Hite, Utah, was located just upstream from the mouth of Trachyte Canyon.

The site was first called Dandy Crossing, largely because the river was easily approached from either direction. From 1946 to 1964 a ferry operated at Hite.

CAMPING: Campsites are usually plentiful. Many shaly beaches and gravel bars edge the lake.

TRAIL CANYON

Lake Powell has provoked many Chinle shale landslides. Recently such a slide wasted the old cross-canyon trail at Trail Canyon. The route once descended the steep slopes just west of the canyon's mouth, ran upstream along the San Juan River a short distance, then forded the river at Wilson Creek.

CAMPING: Campsites are rare. A small sandy beach sometimes appears on the right entrance. Others may be possible at some lake levels.

Hiker near Middle Rock Creek

photo by Tom Bean

TWILIGHT CANYON

Interlocking walls, a streambed littered with cobbles and shadowy corridors characterized this tributary of Glen Canyon. Hikers from the river often walked a short mile to an amphitheater of astonishing proportions. Twilight Canyon today features sheer, swerving cliffs gradually pinching the lake into flooded slots.

The right fork can be hiked for miles if lake silt levels allow access. Watch for places where landslides have forced the stream to abandon its old canyon and cut a new one beyond the landslide's margin. The left fork normally ends in a slot too narrow to admit boats.

CAMPING: The pickings are slim in Twilight; campers should be flexible, resourceful and prepared for disappointment. Depending on lake level two or three slickrock sites are conceivable in the right fork. In the left fork, another site, perhaps with sand, may be possible when Lake Powell is near full.

TWOMILE CANYON

Both Twomile and Fourmile canyons begin on the slopes of Mount Holmes, seen as the prominent mountain from Twomile's entrance.

CAMPING: The steep talus slopes leave room for only a few shale beach pockets.

WAHWEAP BAY

In the Paiute Indian language Wahweap means alkaline seeps or bitter water. Dogleg-shaped Wahweap Bay is studded with landmarks. Lone Rock stands as an island in the upper bay, rising over three hundred feet above Powell's high pool level. Castle Rock, across from Wahweap Marina, towers six hundred feet above the lake and marks the boundary between Wahweap Bay and Warm Creek Bay. Look for Wahweap Window, a natural arch forty feet wide, close to the lake across the bay and directly north of Wahweap Marina. Glen Canyon Dam is located a few miles to the south.

Be wary of shoals along the north side of the upper bay east and west of Lone Rock.

CAMPING: A myriad of sites are possible, especially in the upper bay. Coves and points on the north shore between the west end of the bay and Castle Rock offer numerous campsites, most of them beaches, some of them slickrock and gravel. The Lone Rock Beach, accessible by road and crawling with campers in summer, is located on the south shore of the upper bay. Antelope Island, east side of the lower bay, affords sand beaches, mostly along its southern end.

CANYON BY CANYON

WARM CREEK BAY

Warm Creek with its many beaches and proximity to Wahweap Marina is a popular Lake Powell destination.

A rough dirt road reaches Warm Creek Bay via Crosby Canyon, a northwest tributary of Warm Creek. When passable, this road is sometimes used by boaters wishing to avoid the congestion of the Wahweap area. It leaves the pavement at Big Water, Utah, northwest of Page, Arizona.

In 1911 Warm Creek was the site of a coal mining effort, part of a scheme to extract gold from the rocks and gravel at Lees Ferry, Arizona, twenty-eight miles downstream on the Colorado. Charles H. Spencer managed the operation and a steamboat christened with his name was constructed to carry coal from Warm Creek to Lees Ferry. The venture was unsuccessful but the half-buried ruins of the ninety-two-foot-long steamboat are still visible in the shoreline muds at the Arizona ferry site.

CAMPING: Like neighboring Wahweap Bay, Warm Creek Bay features excellent camping. Inlets and peninsulas in the upper bay contain numerous sandy beaches and a smaller number of gravel beaches. Miles of sandy beach edge the lake in the lobe of Warm Creek Bay extending north and east of the bay's mouth. Some of these, however, are of gentle slope sometimes making it difficult to reach shore by boat.

WARM SPRING CANYON

Warm Spring Canyon is simply straight and short. But its sheer Navajo Sandstone walls cast shade for summertime floating lunches.

CAMPING: Camping is not possible unless a modest heap of talus boulders is sufficient. Check the coves on the main channel upstream from canyon's entrance — ledgy sites with sand or shale pockets are likely.

WEST CANYON

West Canyon is long and diverse. Slickrock slopes cascade into Lake Powell near its entrance while high cliffs streaked with desert varnish edge the lake at its head. The high escarpment east of the canyon belongs to Cummings Mesa, whose opposite edge borders distant Forbidding Canyon.

Prior to Lake Powell's creation West Canyon's mouth lay at the eastern foot of Gregory Butte. Starting there, hikers could follow West Creek's idyllic course for miles. In its setting of red rock amphitheaters and sprawling cottonwoods, West Creek was a photographer's dream.

Watch for prop-eating submerged rocks lurking at the entrance to the canyon as well as immediately before the short fork to the right.

A magnificent canyon complete with sunless narrows and soaring cliffs lies upstream of Lake Powell's margin but quicksand, waterfalls and unpredictable silt levels contrive to make visitation interesting if not impossible.

CAMPING: Despite its length, West Canyon campsites are scarce. Where the canyon first contracts to a narrow channel, it forks. The right fork is short, and is called Howland Canyon. When the lake is at its highest level it offers a fine beach on the left. Prior to Lake Powell this sand slope lay on the rim of a colossal amphitheater sometimes visited by river runners. Back on the main fork a couple of beaches lie about mid-canyon, the second one by far the largest. It is just beyond an alcove wall overhanging the left shoreline. The beach is on the right where the canyon bends sharply left. Sometimes a slickrock, ledge, or talus camp can be established farther up-canyon near the end of an unusually straight stretch. And, finally, one or two sandy sites are possible near lake's end.

WETHERILL CANYON

A cascading slickrock wilderness surrounds Lake Powell in the canyon named after John Wetherill, co-discoverer of Rainbow Bridge. Like nearby Mountain Sheep and Cathedral, Wetherill Canyon slices deep into Cummings Mesa whose rims rise twelve hundred feet and more above the lake.

A tight canyon with modest cliffs lies beyond lake's end. Usually a swim is required to gain solid ground; the pinched canyon is reluctant to admit even small boats.

Some river runners knew this drainage as Catfish Canyon, in reference to the dark mass of fish seen loitering at its confluence.

CAMPING: Large beaches are lacking but a number of good sites, most with sandy pockets, can be found at mid-canyon. With hardly an exception these campsites are located on the left grouped in and near an embayment some maps mark as Cummings Cove. Farther on, also on the left, look for a larger site on ledgy rock with some sand at medium lake levels.

CANYON BY CANYON

WHITE CANYON

A loop of the Colorado River once followed the lower portion of White Canyon. It was part of a meander that has since been abandoned. Lower Farley Canyon was the upper half of the meander.

Before Lake Powell White Canyon was a major route to Dandy Crossing on the Colorado River.

In its distant upper reaches, White Canyon and its tributaries contain the spectacular rock spans of Natural Bridges National Monument.

CAMPING: The short left fork offers shale and gravel beaches. The narrow right fork is lined with gnarled and jagged crags. Farther on it widens and offers a few shaly pockets and shallow silt beds at its end.

WILLOW CANYON

Three major canyons from the north join Willow —two are visited by Lake Powell, the third lies beyond lake's reach.

Both the first two tributaries from the north can be hiked from lake's end. Hikers following the main stem of Willow will soon come to the third Willow Canyon fork. To the right is Fortymile Canyon—swimming may be required to penetrate its depths. Willow Canyon continues to the left. Broken Bow Arch, about two miles beyond the fork, is a common goal from this point. Be advised, the arch is not visible from a downstream position; hikers must pass beyond it before they can see it. Both Willow and Fortymile can be followed to the Hole-in-the-Rock Road.

CAMPING: In the first fork to the right, talus sites are available at nearly all lake levels. Some levels allow slick-rock camping. Sandy sites are sometimes possible close to lake's end. In the main stem of Willow, just beyond the fork, look for the deep alcove with a talus hill in the center; full-sized houseboats can enjoy this rain- and sun-sheltered camp. On the opposite side of the canyon a sandy niche normally awaits at most lake levels. Farther up-canyon talus slopes sometimes edge the water. The ends of the lake in both the main stem (to the left) and the canyon joining from the north (to the right) usually contain beaches.

WILSON CREEK CANYON

Wilson Creek cascades down a sloping face into Lake Powell when lake level is a few feet below maximum.

Wilson Canyon can be followed on foot to the mesa top where a rocky knob of unusual shape catches one's attention. The Mormon pioneers, building a road out of nearby Cottonwood Canyon, noted the rock's outline and named the saddle between the two canyons Aladdins Lamp Pass.

CAMPING: A few slickrock and ledge campsites are scattered along the length of the canyon at most lake levels. Also, a nameless tributary immediately east of the mouth of Wilson may offer talus, ledge and, perhaps, sand pocket sites at some lake levels. Beware of shallows just south of the entrance to this nameless canyon.

Navajo Canyon   *photo by Tom Bean*

CANYON BY CANYON

Aerial view of Dangling Rope Marina   photo by Tom Bean

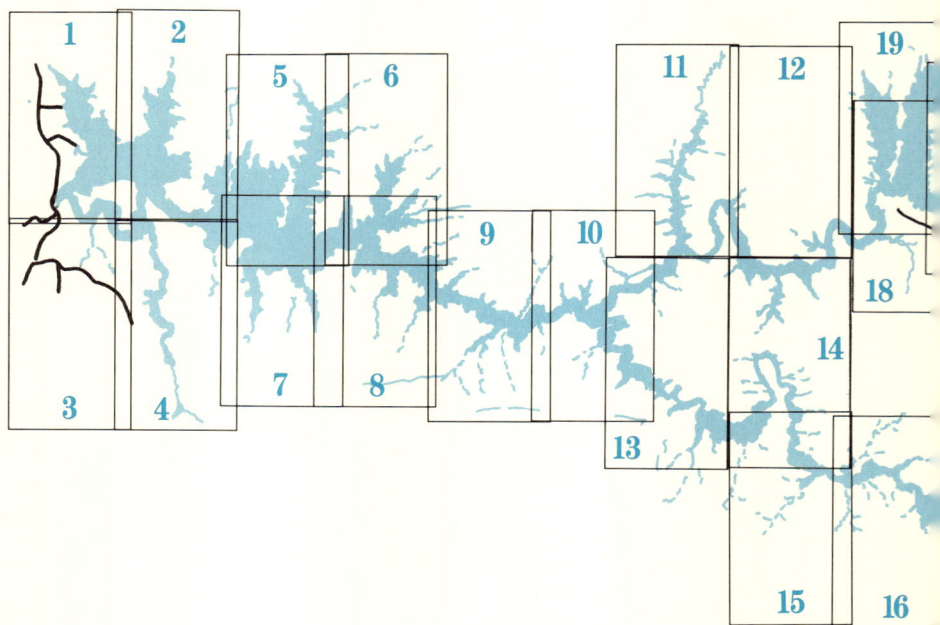

The map-grid below indicates areas which relate to the following pages of detailed maps. Detail-map numbers (not page numbers) correspond to the area numbers below, and are indicated in the upper right- or left-hand corner in blue. To further assist you in using the detail maps, a blue triangle points to the direction for continuation of a section of the map, and provides you with the appropriate map number.

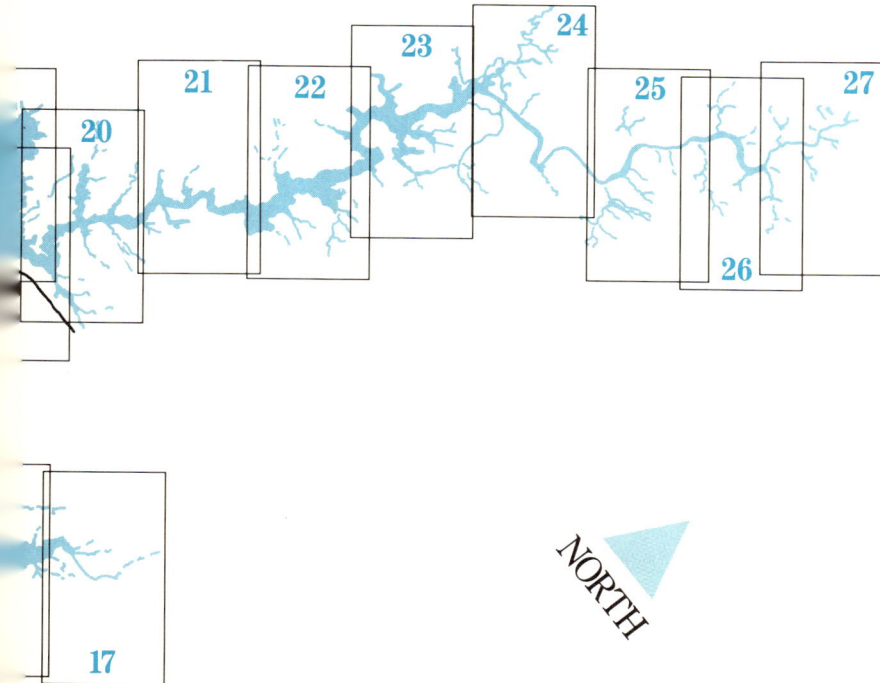

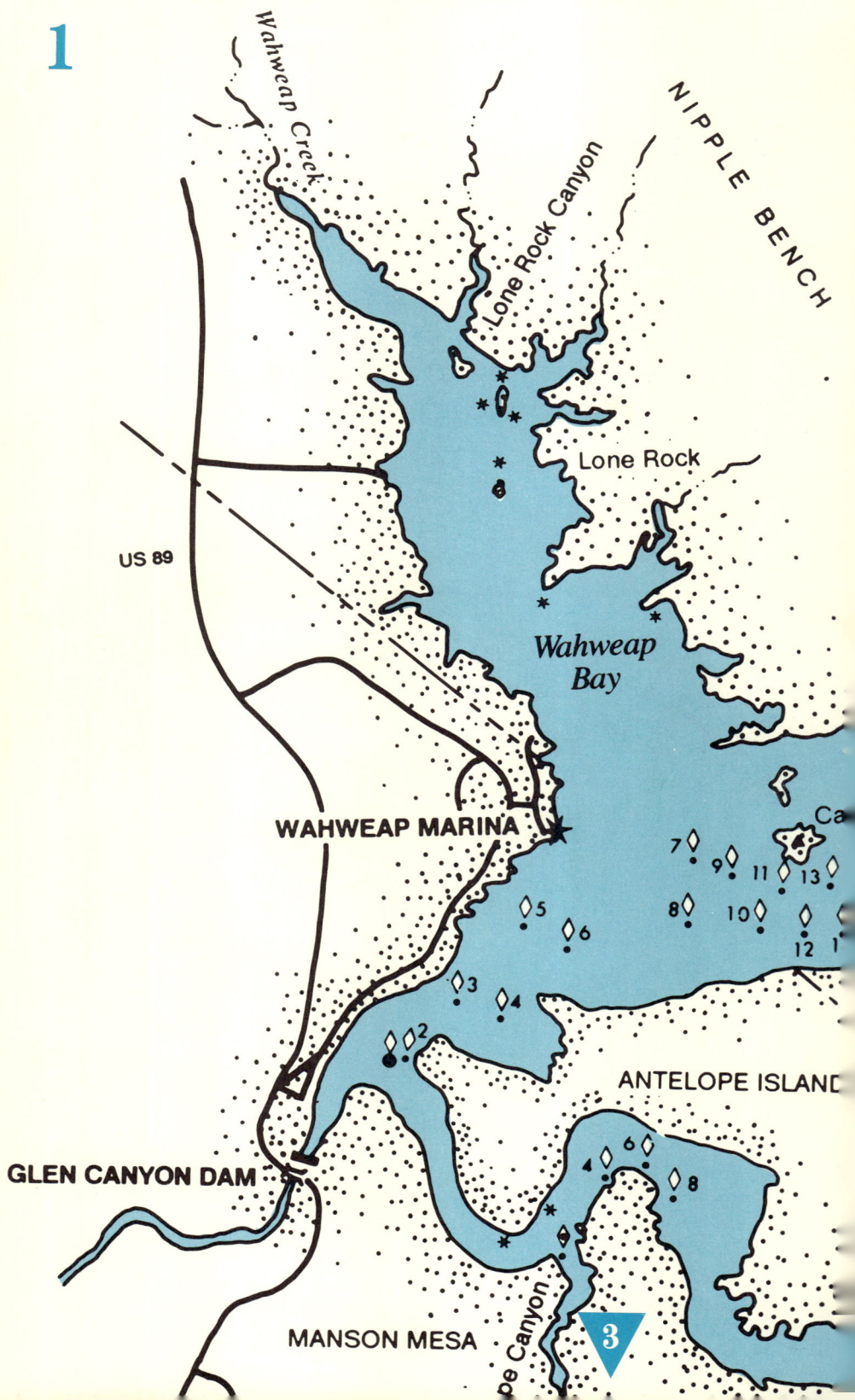

1

Wahweap Creek

NIPPLE BENCH

Lone Rock Canyon

Lone Rock

US 89

Wahweap Bay

WAHWEAP MARINA

Ca

7
9
11 13
8
10
5
6
12 1
3
4
2

ANTELOPE ISLAND

GLEN CANYON DAM

4 6
8

MANSON MESA

Canyon

3

LEGEND

* shoal
...·.. intermittent stream
⌒ road
! light (fixed structure)
◇ unlighted buoy
◇ lighted buoy
◈ mid-channel buoy
⬦ side canyon buoy

N↗

0   1   2   3

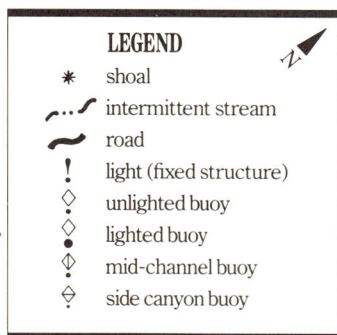

SCALE IN MILES

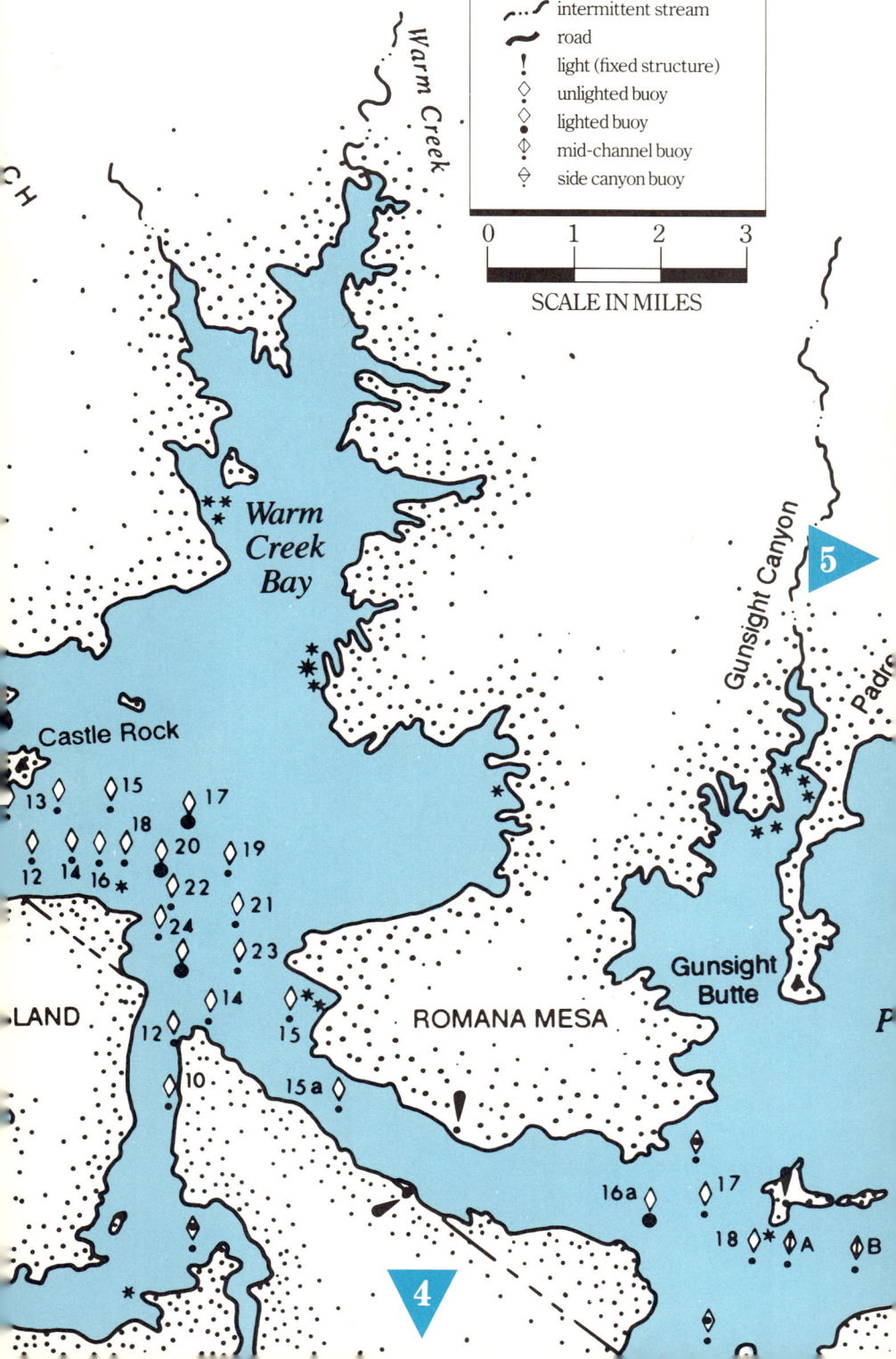

Warm Creek

Warm
Creek
Bay

CH

Gunsight Canyon

Padre

5

Castle Rock

13 ◇15
     ◇ 17
        18
◇ ◇ ◇ ◇20
12 14 16 22
        ◇19
      ◇21
   ◇24
      ◇23

Gunsight
Butte

LAND

◇14
12
◇15

◇10   15a ◇

ROMANA MESA

P

16a ◇   ◇17

18 ◇* ◇A   ◇B

4

3

MANSON MESA

Antelope Ca...

1

Page

US 89

AZ 98

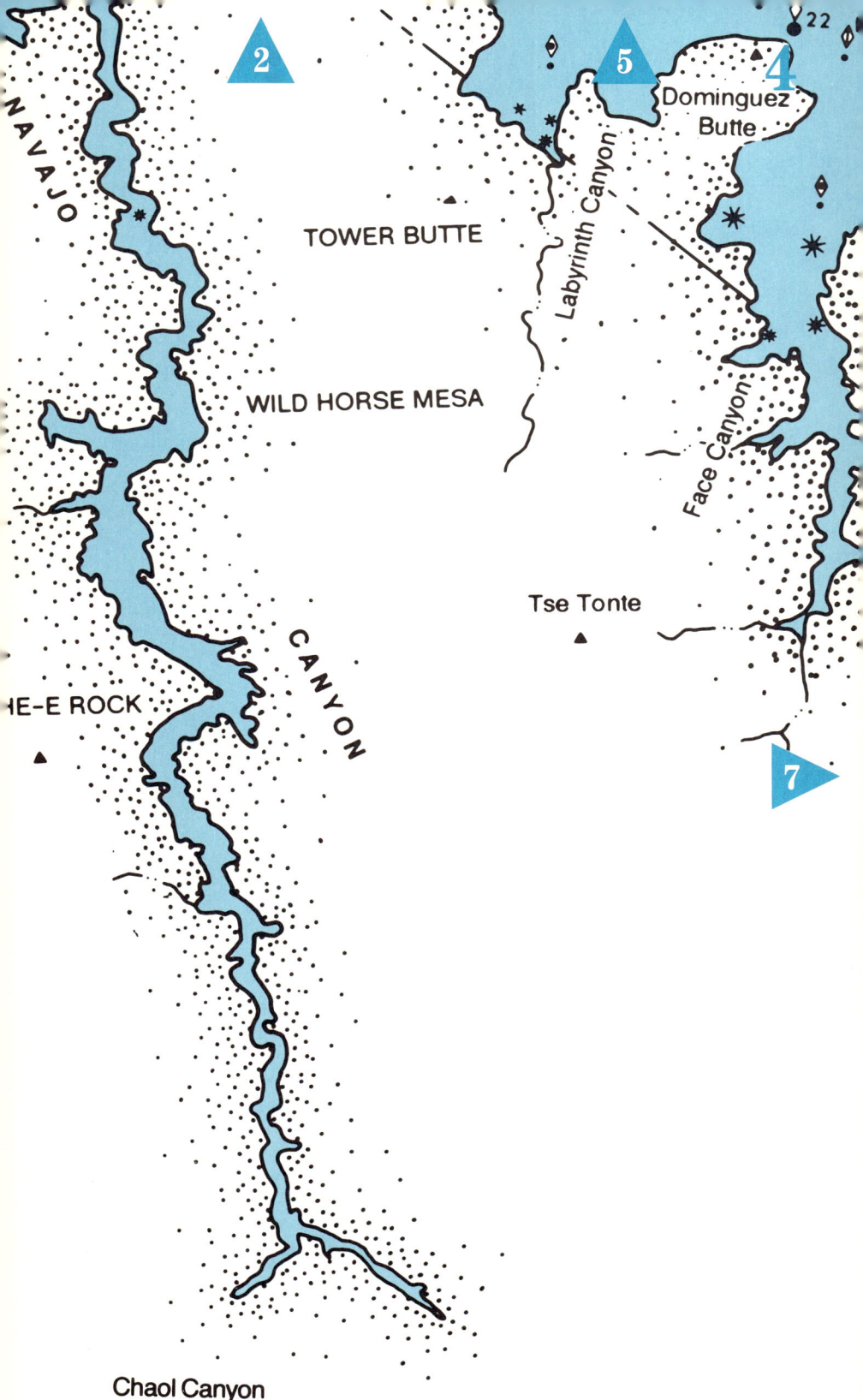

2

5

4

Dominguez
Butte

22

TOWER BUTTE

Labyrinth Canyon

WILD HORSE MESA

Face Canyon

Tse Tonte

C A N Y O N

HE-E ROCK

NAVAJO

7

Chaol Canyon

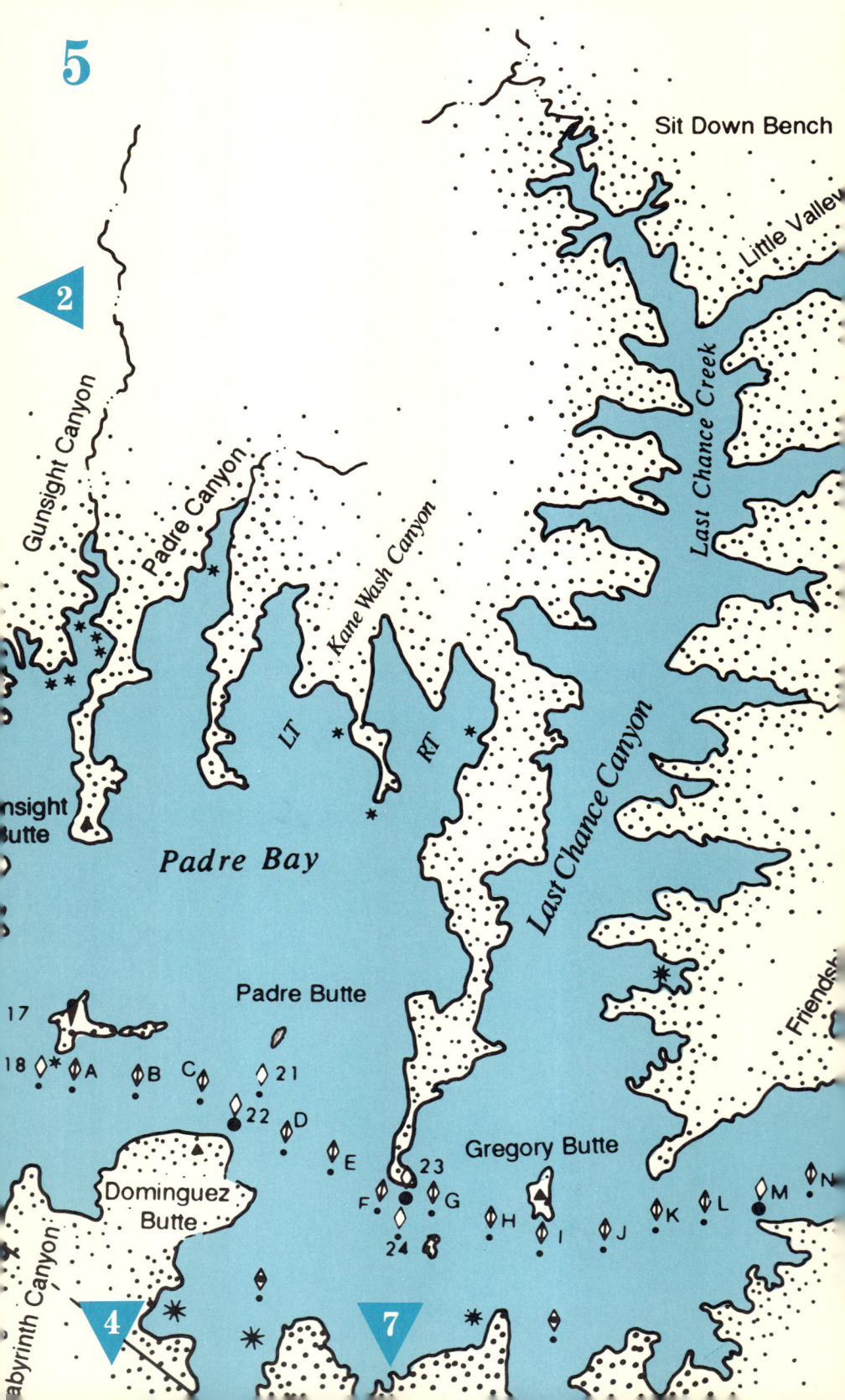

5

2

Sit Down Bench

Little Valley

Gunsight Canyon

Padre Canyon

Kane Wash Canyon

Last Chance Creek

LT

RT

Last Chance Canyon

nsight
utte

Padre Bay

Padre Butte

17

18

A

B

C

21

22

D

E

23

Gregory Butte

F

G

H

I

J

K

L

M

24

Dominguez
Butte

Friendsh

byrinth Canyon

4

7

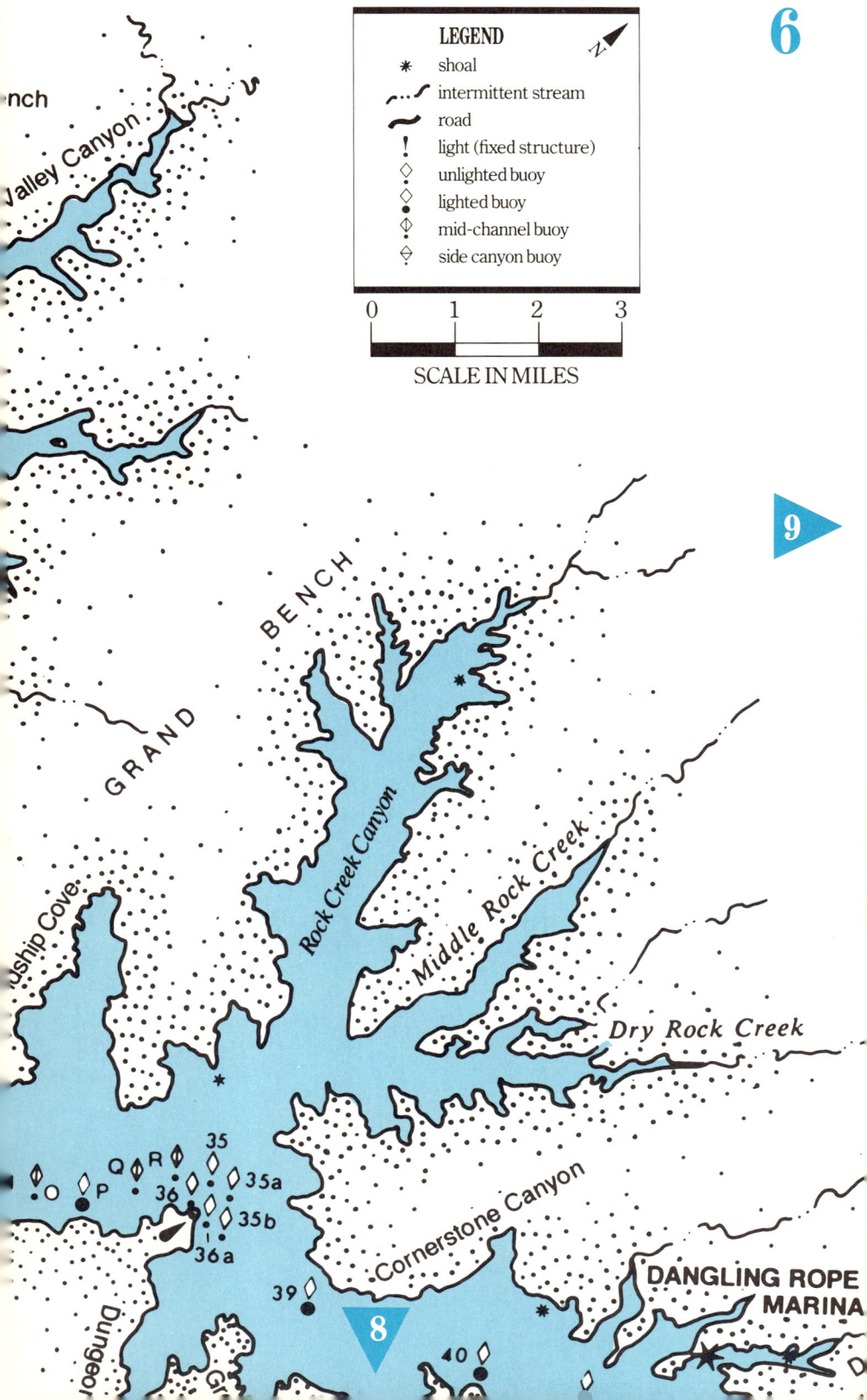

LEGEND

✳	shoal
⋯⌇	intermittent stream
⌇	road
!	light (fixed structure)
◇	unlighted buoy
◆	lighted buoy
⬙	mid-channel buoy
⬗	side canyon buoy

N

0   1   2   3

SCALE IN MILES

Valley Canyon

nch

9

B E N C H

G R A N D

ship Cove

Rock Creek Canyon

Middle Rock Creek

Dry Rock Creek

35
Q R
O P 36 35a
35b
36a

39

Cornerstone Canyon

8

40

Dungeo

DANGLING ROPE
MARINA

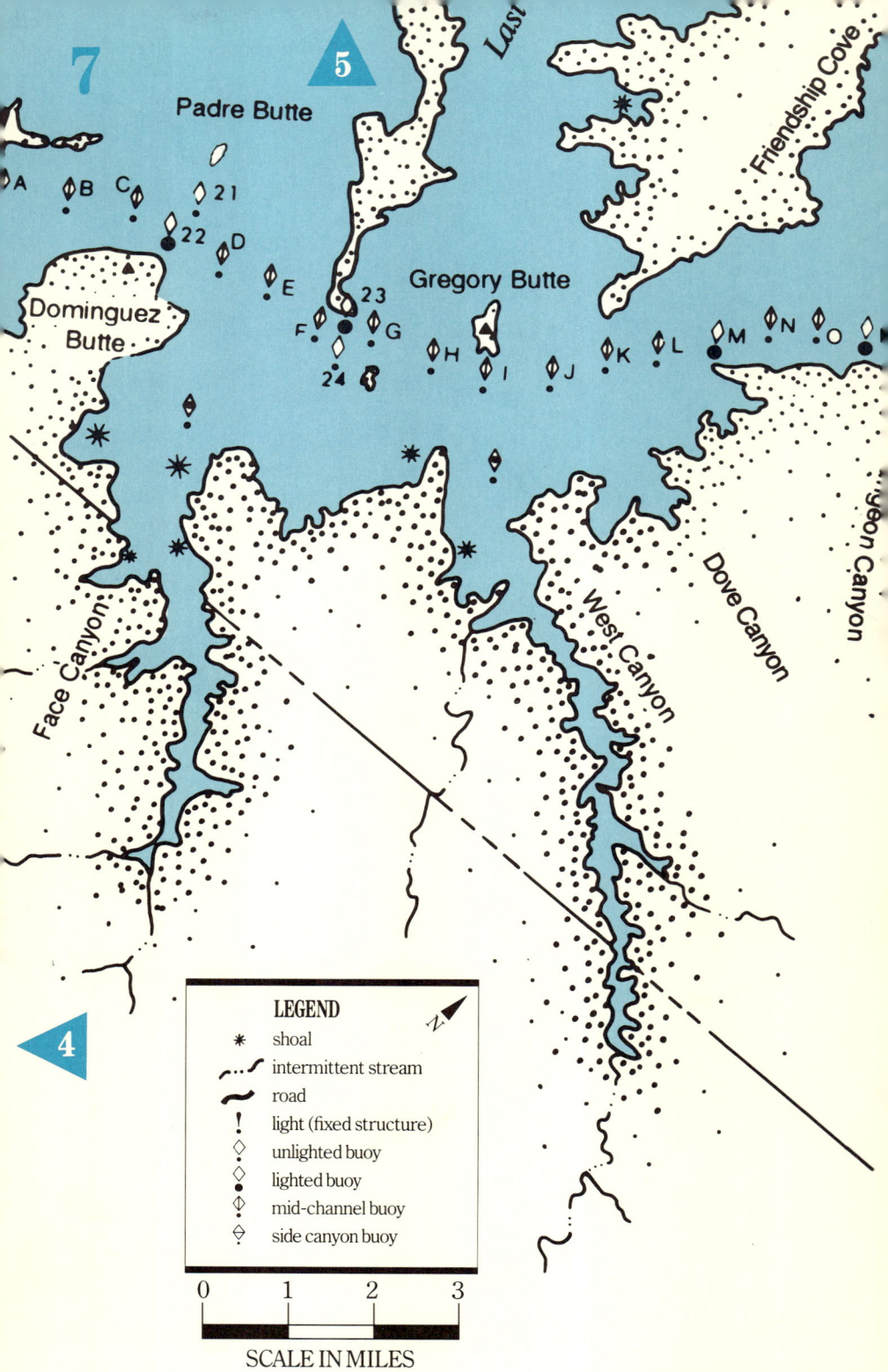

7

5

Padre Butte

A B C 21
22 D
E 23
Dominguez
Butte
F G
24 H I J K L M N O

Last

Friendship Cove

Gregory Butte

Face Canyon

West Canyon

Dove Canyon

...geon Canyon

4

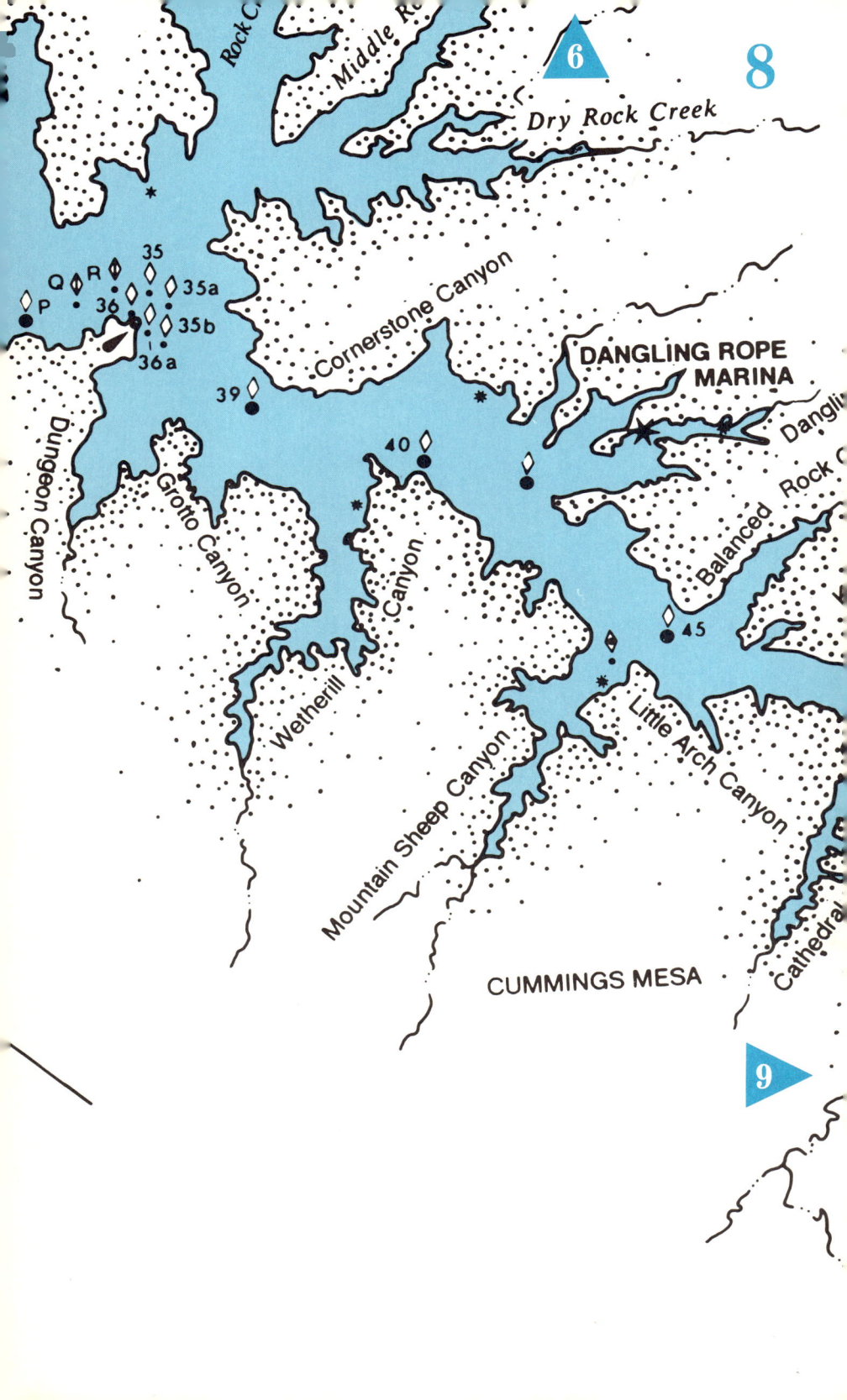

Rock C

Middle R

Dry Rock Creek

Cornerstone Canyon

35
Q R
P 35a
36
35b
36a

39

DANGLING ROPE MARINA

Dungeon Canyon

Grotto Canyon

40

Dangli

Balanced Rock C

45

Wetherill Canyon

Little Arch Canyon

Mountain Sheep Canyon

Cathedra

CUMMINGS MESA

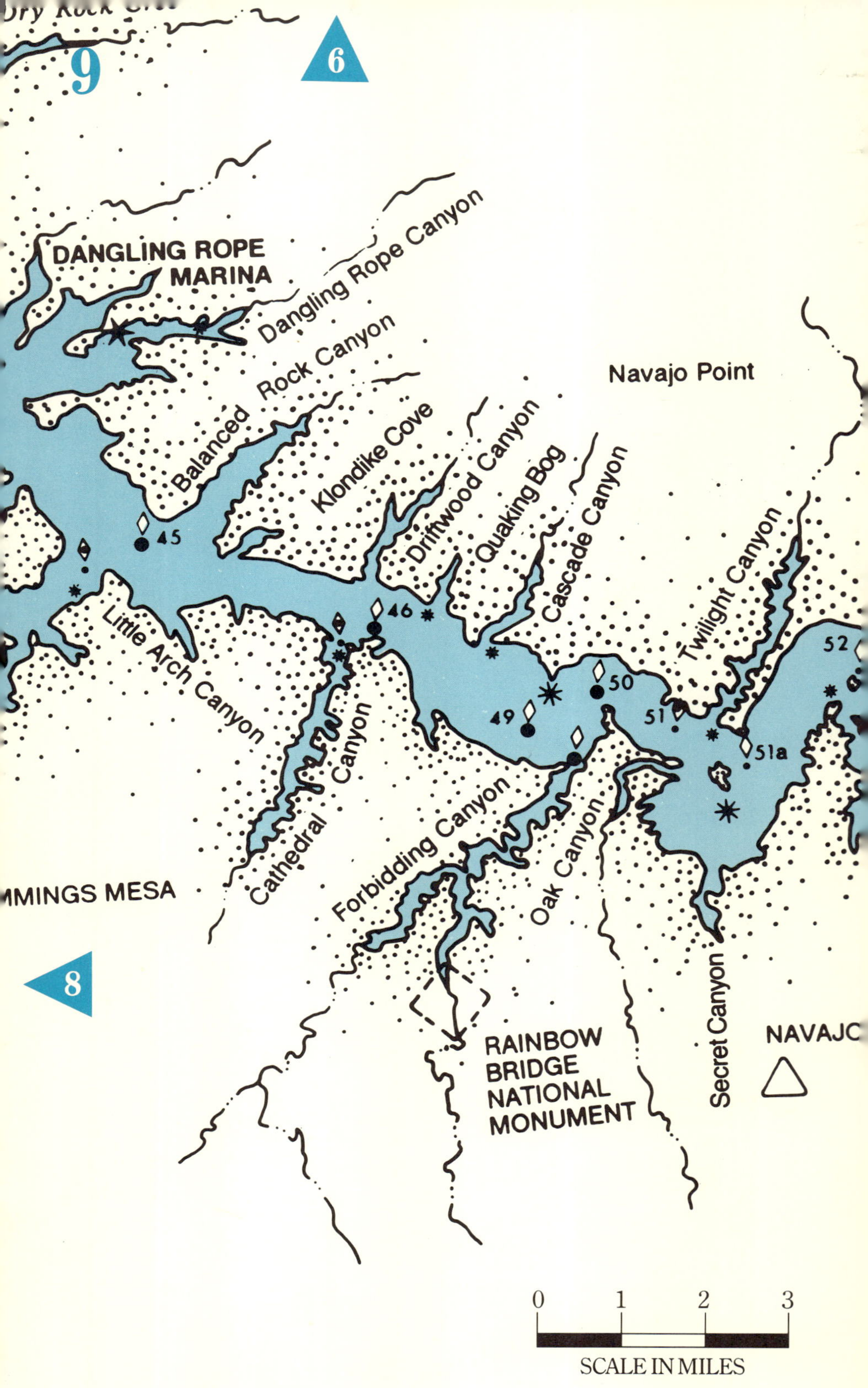

Dry Rock C...

6

DANGLING ROPE MARINA

Dangling Rope Canyon

Balanced Rock Canyon

Navajo Point

Klondike Cove

Driftwood Canyon

Quaking Bog

Cascade Canyon

Twilight Canyon

◊ 45
●

*

*

52

Little Arch Canyon

◊ 46
●

*

*

49
●

◊

50
●

51
◊

51a
◊

*

Cathedral Canyon

Forbidding Canyon

Oak Canyon

Secret Canyon

CUMMINGS MESA

8

RAINBOW
BRIDGE
NATIONAL
MONUMENT

NAVAJO

0   1   2   3

SCALE IN MILES

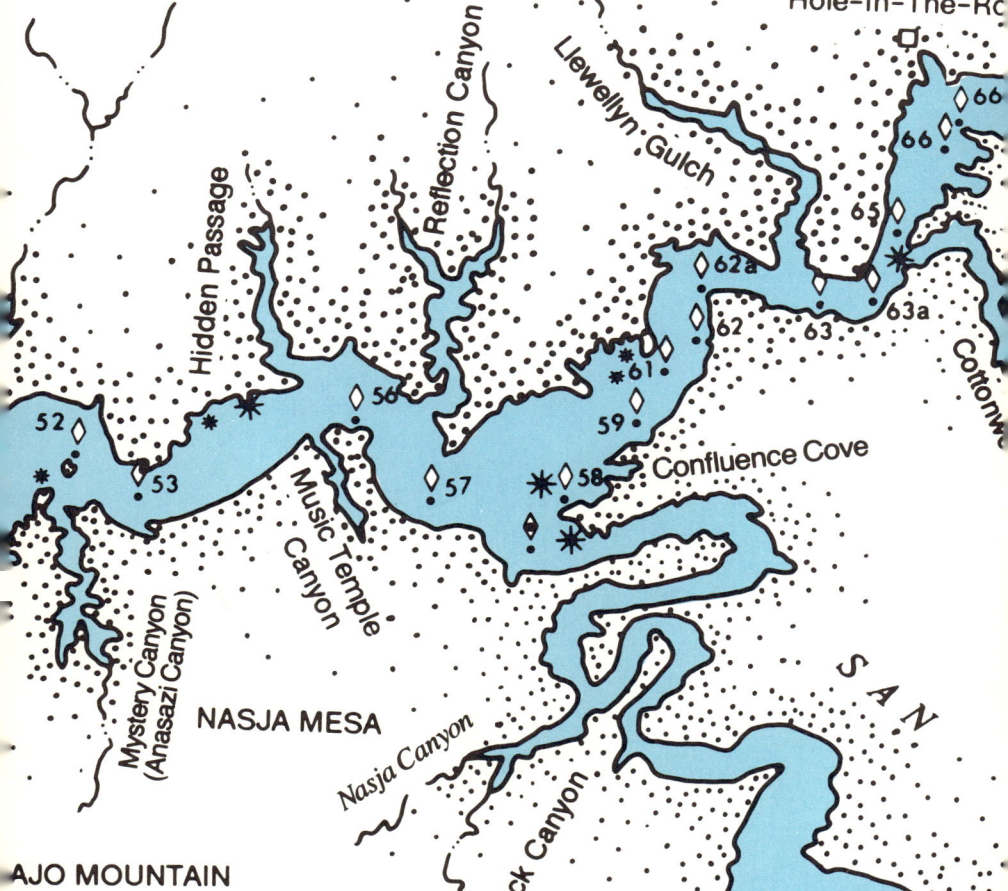

Map labels

11

10 Clear Cre

Indian Cre

11

Hole-In-The-Ro

Reflection Canyon

Llewellyn Gulch

66
66
66a

65

62a
62
63
63a

61
59

56

52
53

57 58

Confluence Cove

Hidden Passage

Music Temple Canyon

Mystery Canyon (Anasazi Canyon)

NASJA MESA

Nasja Canyon

Bald Rock Canyon

AJO MOUNTAIN

S A N

Cottonw

Cha Canyon

Trail Canyon

13

13

LEGEND

N

∗ shoal

⌒ intermittent stream

⌒ road

! light (fixed structure)

◇ unlighted buoy

◈ lighted buoy

⬦ mid-channel buoy

⬦ side canyon buoy

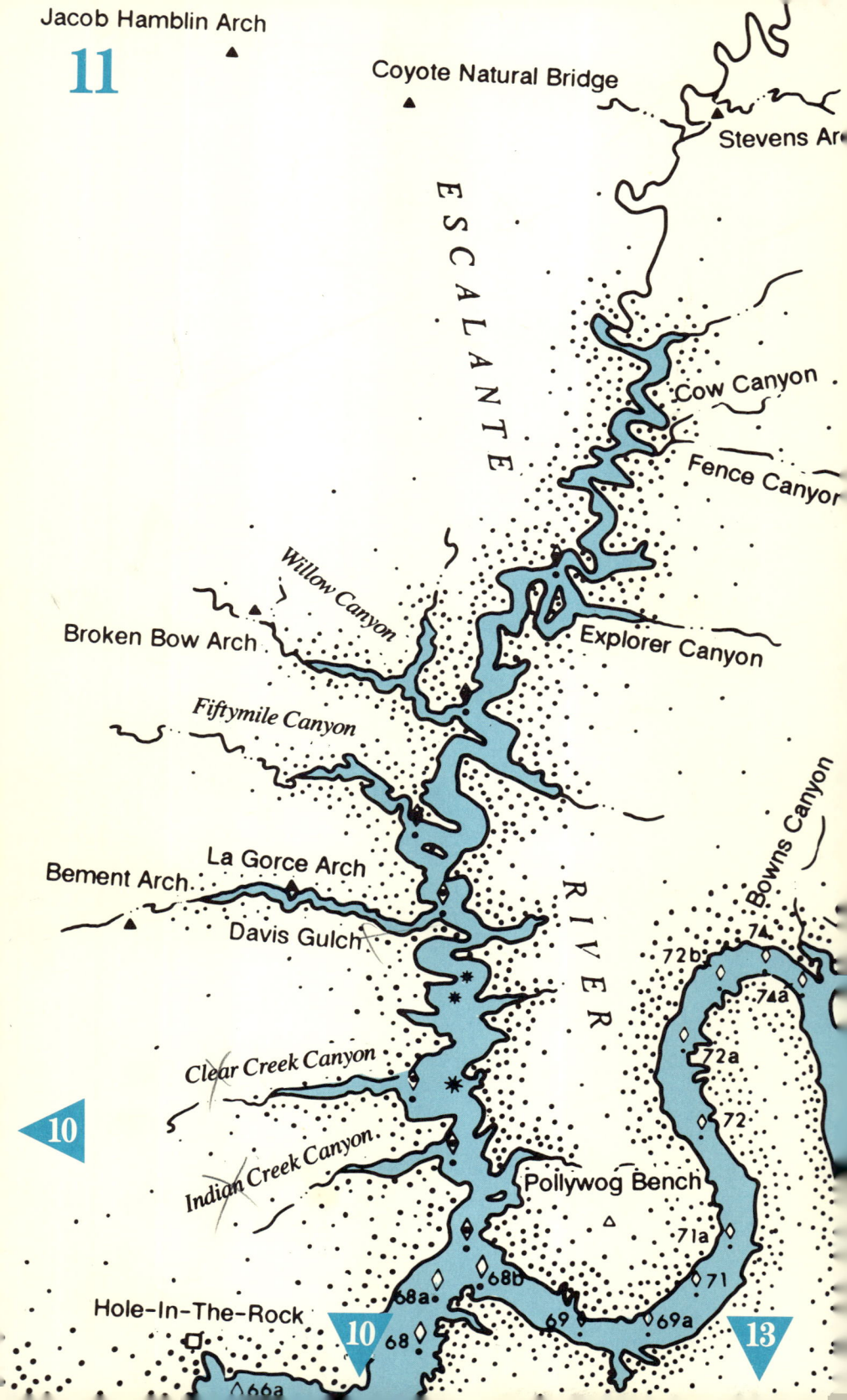

11

Jacob Hamblin Arch

Coyote Natural Bridge

Stevens Ar

E S C A L A N T E

Cow Canyon

Fence Canyon

Willow Canyon

Broken Bow Arch

Explorer Canyon

Fiftymile Canyon

Bowns Canyon

Bement Arch

La Gorce Arch

Davis Gulch

R I V E R

72b

74

72a

71a

72

Clear Creek Canyon

10

Indian Creek Canyon

Pollywog Bench

71a

71

Hole-In-The-Rock

68a

68b

68

69

69a

10

13

66a

LEGEND

✳	shoal
⋯⌇	intermittent stream
⌇	road
!	light (fixed structure)
◇	unlighted buoy
◈	lighted buoy
◈	mid-channel buoy
◈	side canyon buoy

0	1	2	3

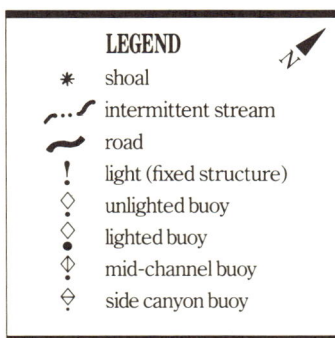

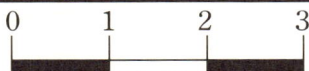

SCALE IN MILES

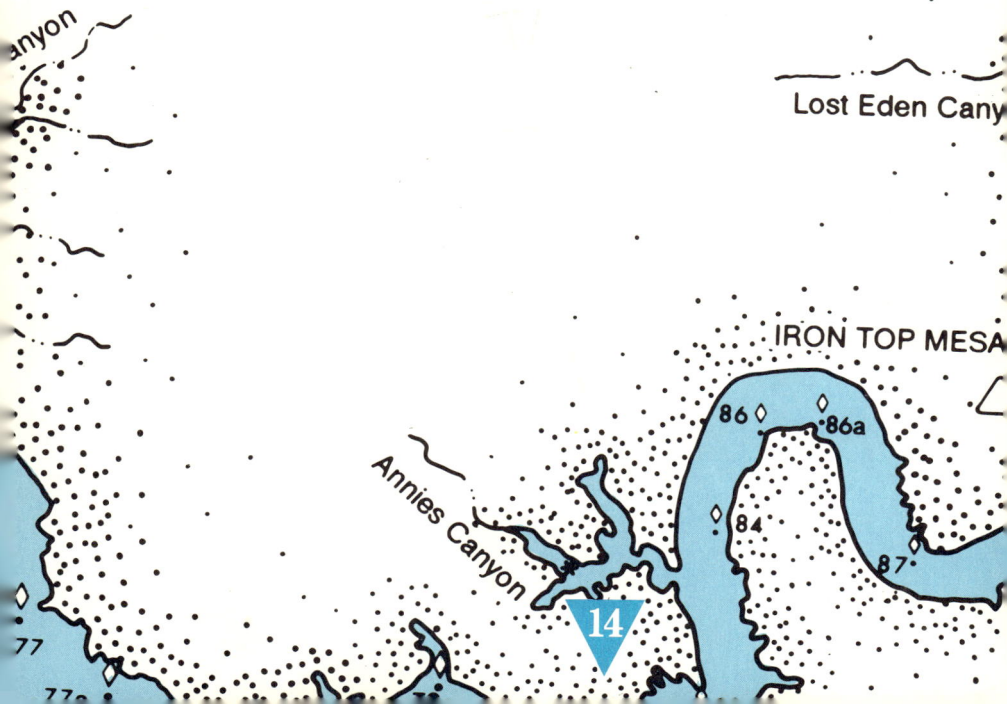

19

Lost Eden Cany

IRON TOP MESA

86 ◇   ◇ 86a

◇ 84

87

Annies Canyon

14

77

77a

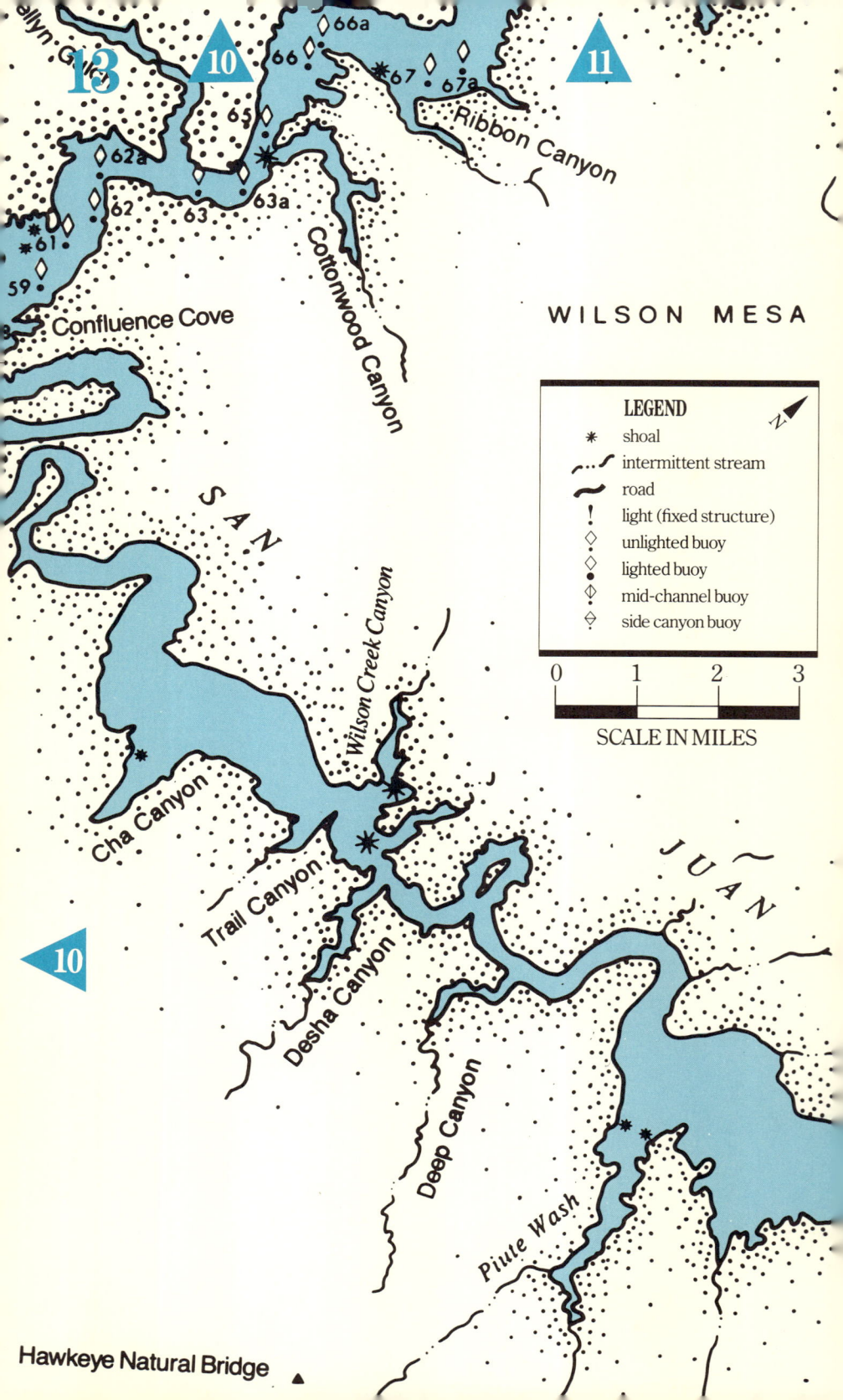

66a

66

67

67a

Ribbon Canyon

65

62a

62

63

63a

Cottonwood Canyon

61

59

Confluence Cove

WILSON MESA

13

10

11

LEGEND

N

* shoal
...⸝ intermittent stream
⌇ road
! light (fixed structure)
◊ unlighted buoy
◈ lighted buoy
◈ mid-channel buoy
◈ side canyon buoy

0   1   2   3

SCALE IN MILES

S A N

Wilson Creek Canyon

Cha Canyon

Trail Canyon

J U A N

10

Desha Canyon

Deep Canyon

Piute Wash

Hawkeye Natural Bridge

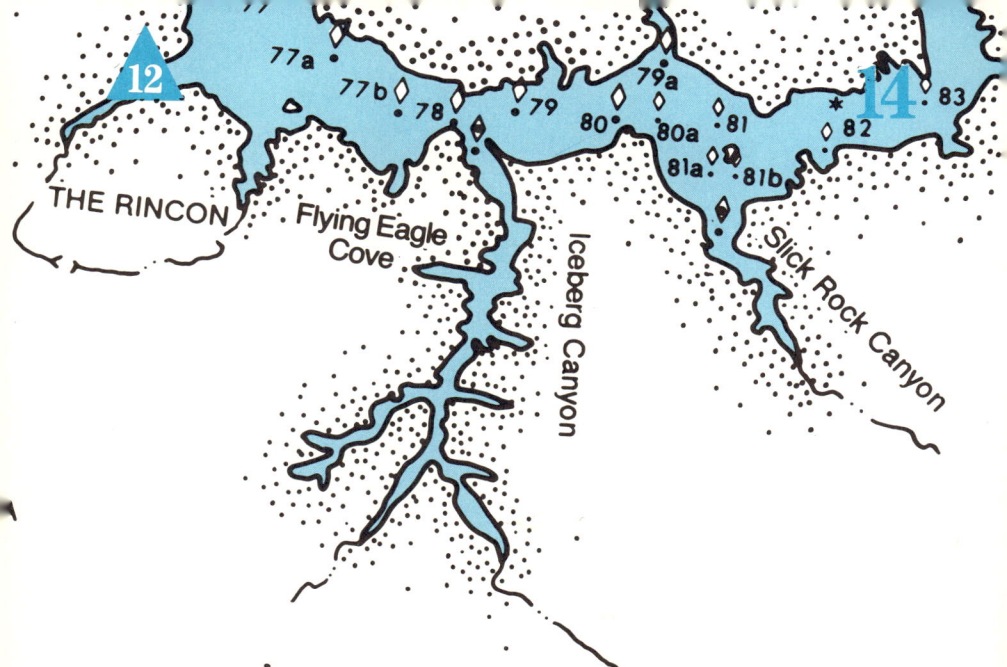

12

77a

77b   78

79a

79

80   80a   81

81a   81b

14
82   83

THE RINCON

Flying Eagle
Cove

Iceberg Canyon

Slick Rock Canyon

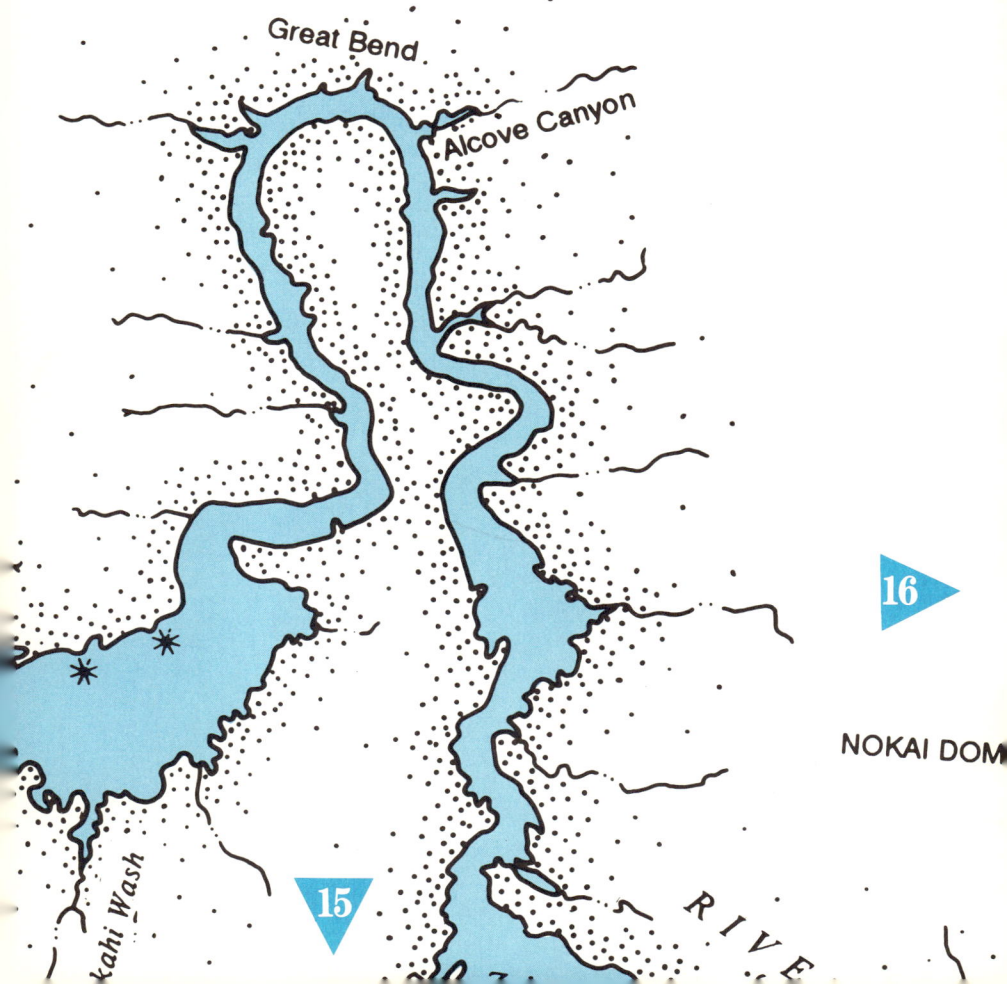

Great Bend

Alcove Canyon

16

NOKAI DOM

15

kahi Wash

R I V E

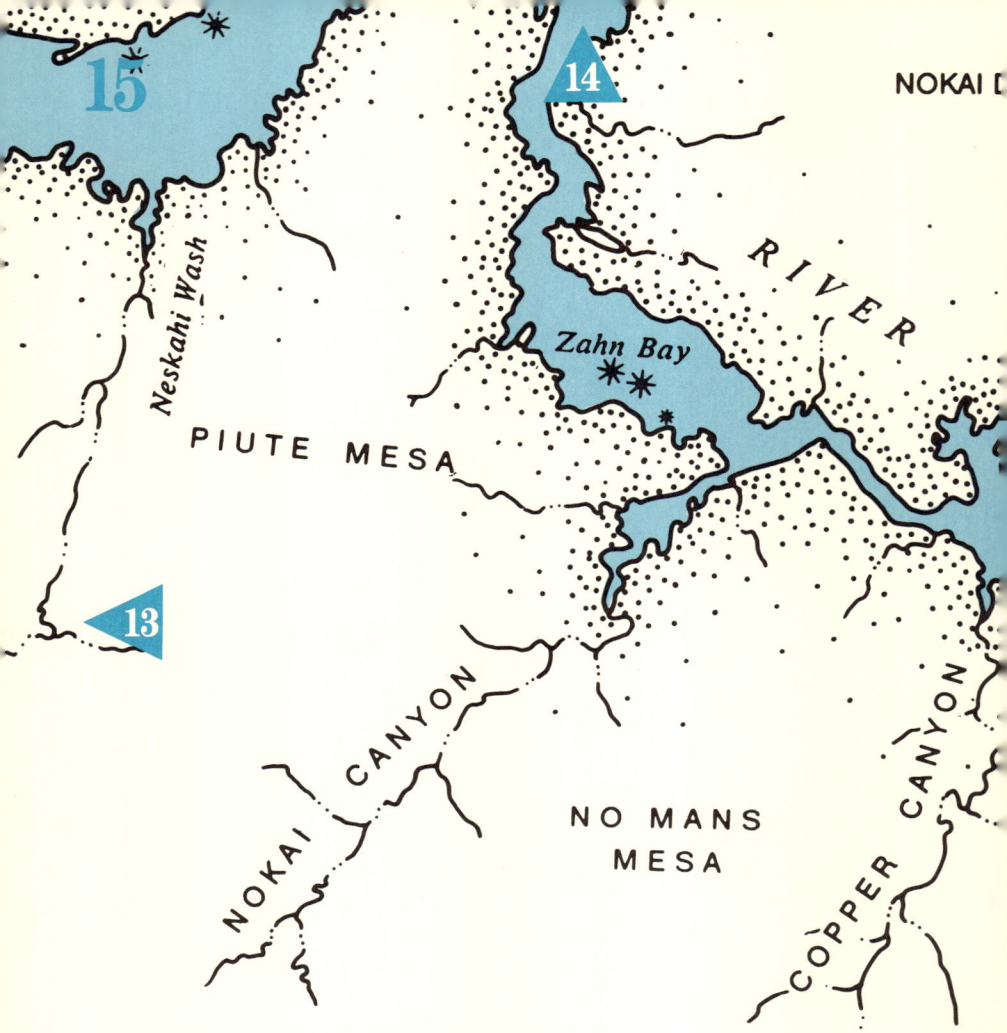

15

14

NOKAI

Neskahi Wash

R I V E R

PIUTE MESA

Zahn Bay

13

NOKAI CANYON

NO MANS MESA

COPPER CANYON

LEGEND

N

✳ shoal

intermittent stream

road

! light (fixed structure)

◇ unlighted buoy

◆ lighted buoy

⬦ mid-channel buoy

⬦ side canyon buoy

0   1   2   3

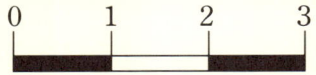

SCALE IN MILES

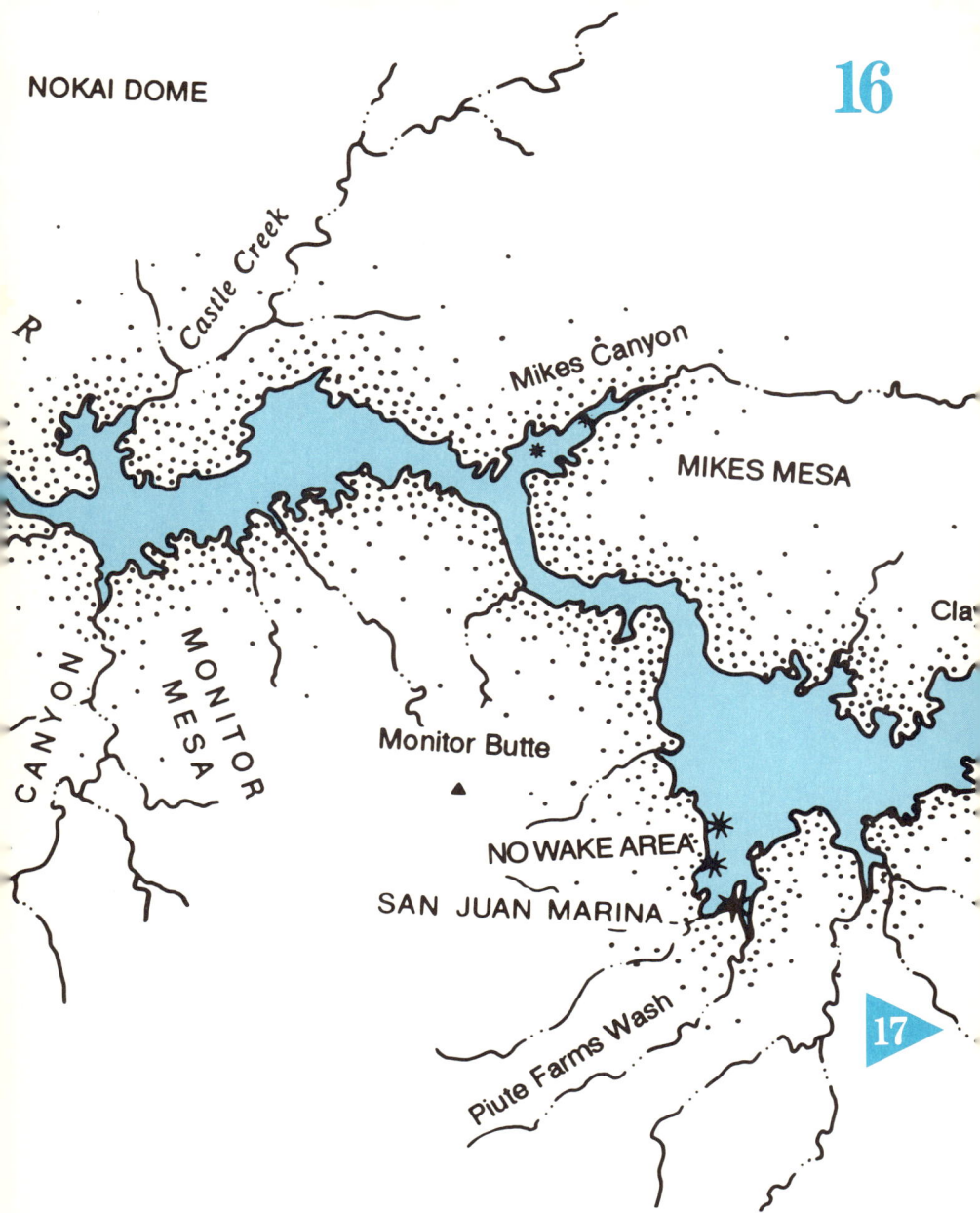

Casile Creek

Mikes Canyon

MIKES MESA

Cla

R

CANYON

MONITOR
MESA

Monitor Butte

NO WAKE AREA

SAN JUAN MARINA

Piute Farms Wash

17

17

Clay Hills Crossing

16

LEGEND

N

∗	shoal
⌁	intermittent stream
∿	road
!	light (fixed structure)
◇	unlighted buoy
◈	lighted buoy
◈	mid-channel buoy
◈	side canyon buoy

0   1   2   3

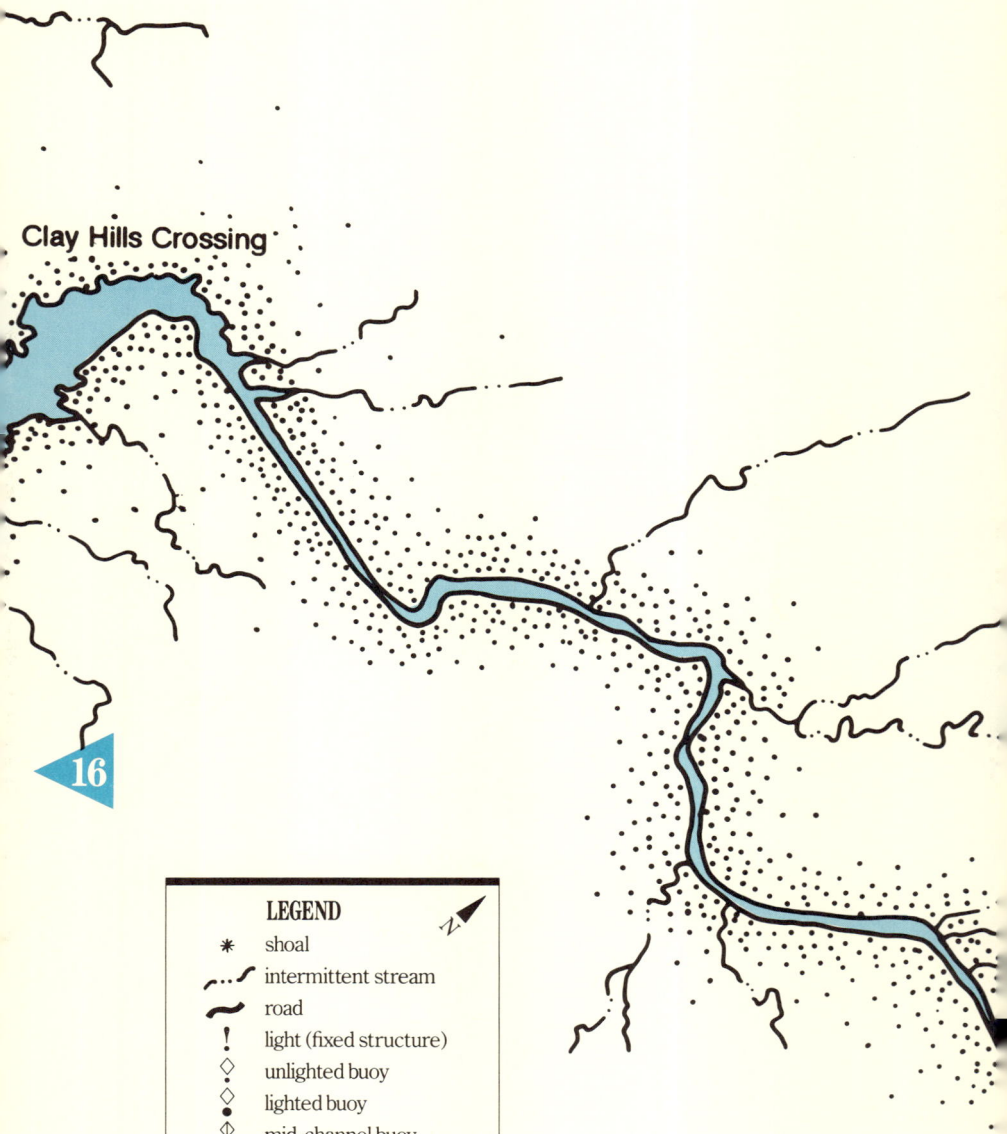

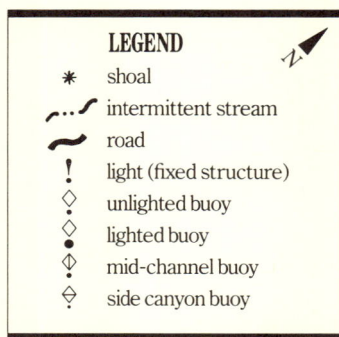

SCALE IN MILES

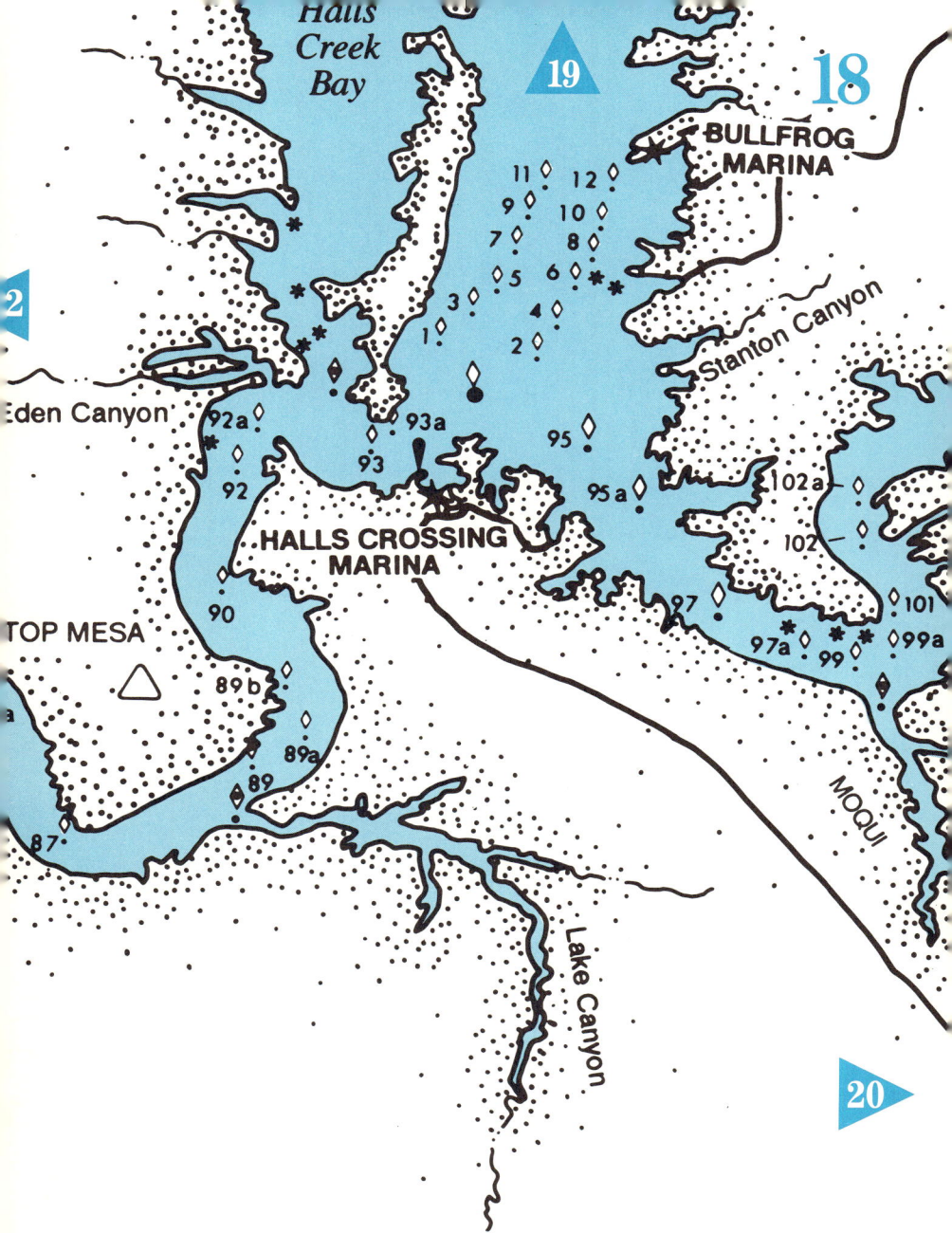

Halls
Creek
Bay

19

18

BULLFROG
MARINA

11 12
9   10
7   8
3 5 6
1 4
2

Stanton Canyon

2

Eden Canyon

92a   93a
93   95
92   95a   102a

HALLS CROSSING   102
MARINA

97
90   97a 99 99a

TOP MESA

89b
101

89a

89

87

MOQUI

Lake Canyon

20

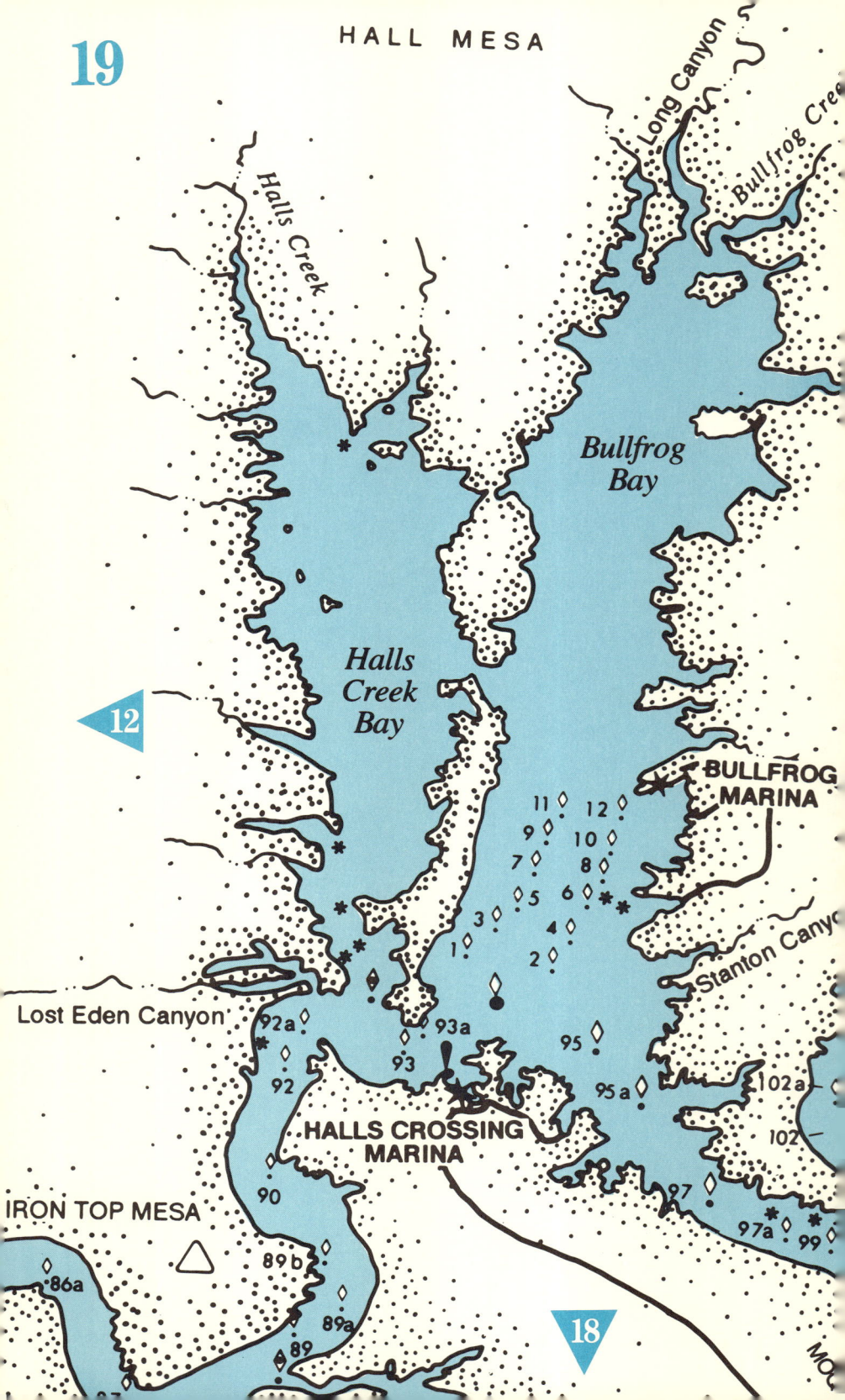

HALL MESA

Long Canyon

Bullfrog Creek

Halls Creek

Bullfrog Bay

Halls Creek Bay

12

BULLFROG MARINA

11 ◊   12 ◊
9 ◦   10 ◊
7 ◊   8 ◦
5 ◊   6 ◊
3 ◊   4 ◊
1 ◦   2 ◊

Stanton Canyon

Lost Eden Canyon

92a ◊
92 ◊

93a ◊
93 ◊

95 ◊
95 a ◊

102a ◊
102 ◊

HALLS CROSSING MARINA

IRON TOP MESA

90 ◊

97 ◊
97a ◊ 99 ◊

89 b ◊

86a ◊

89a ◊
89 ◊

18

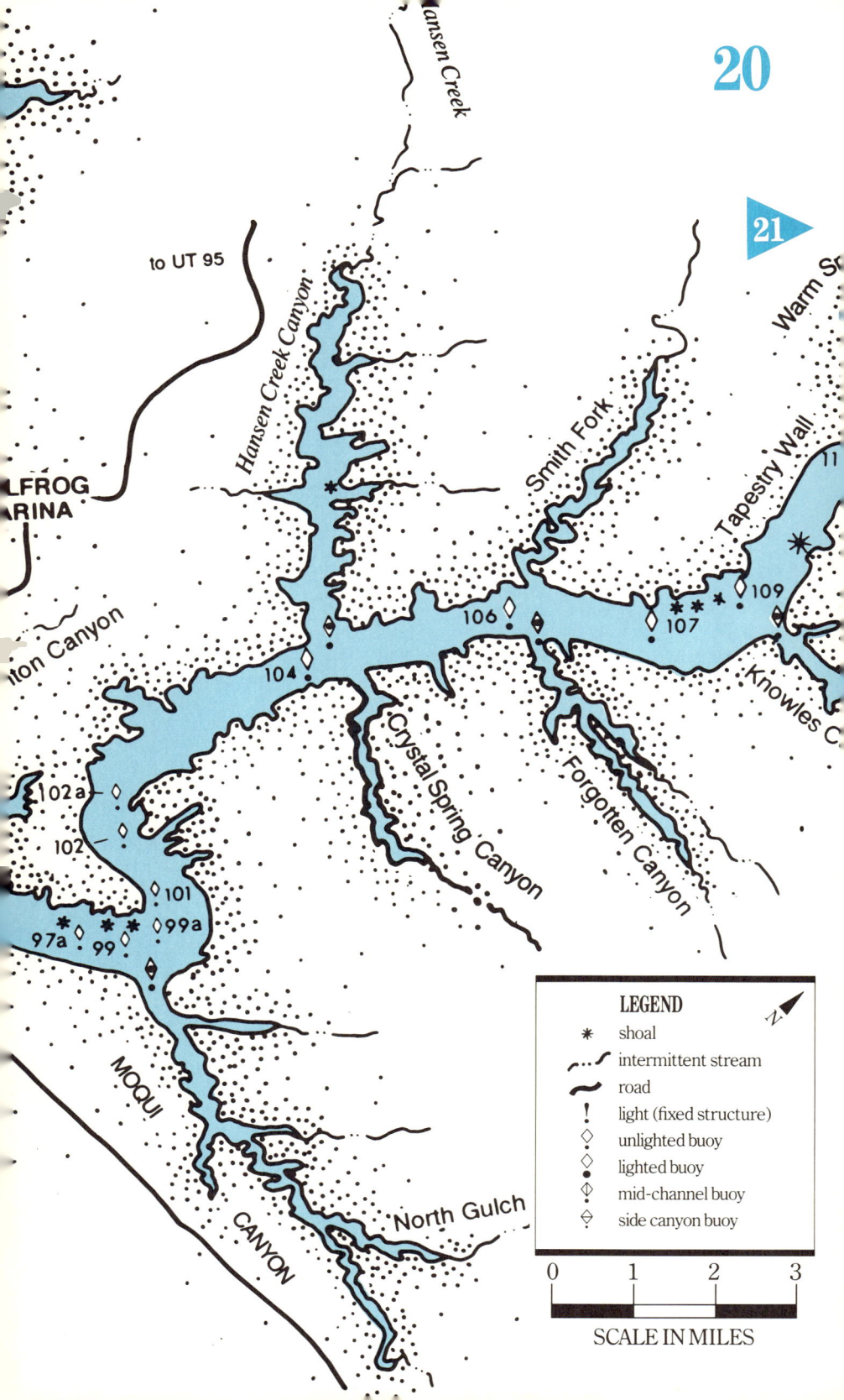

20

ansen Creek

Hansen Creek

to UT 95

Hansen Creek Canyon

Smith Fork

Warm S

Tapestry Wall

21

LFROG
RINA

11

*

ton Canyon

104

106

*

107

109

*

Knowles C

102a

102

101

99a

97a 99

Crystal Spring Canyon

Forgotten Canyon

MOQUI

North Gulch

CANYON

LEGEND

N

* shoal
intermittent stream
road
! light (fixed structure)
◇ unlighted buoy
◆ lighted buoy
◈ mid-channel buoy
⬡ side canyon buoy

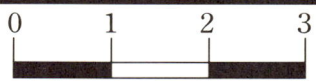

SCALE IN MILES

0   1   2   3

21

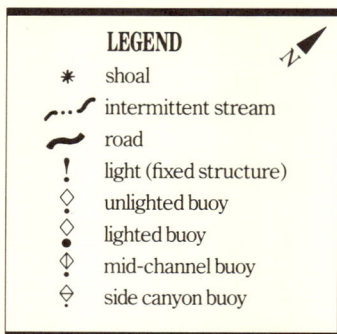

TICABOO MESA

20

Warm Spring Canyon

Sevenmile Creek

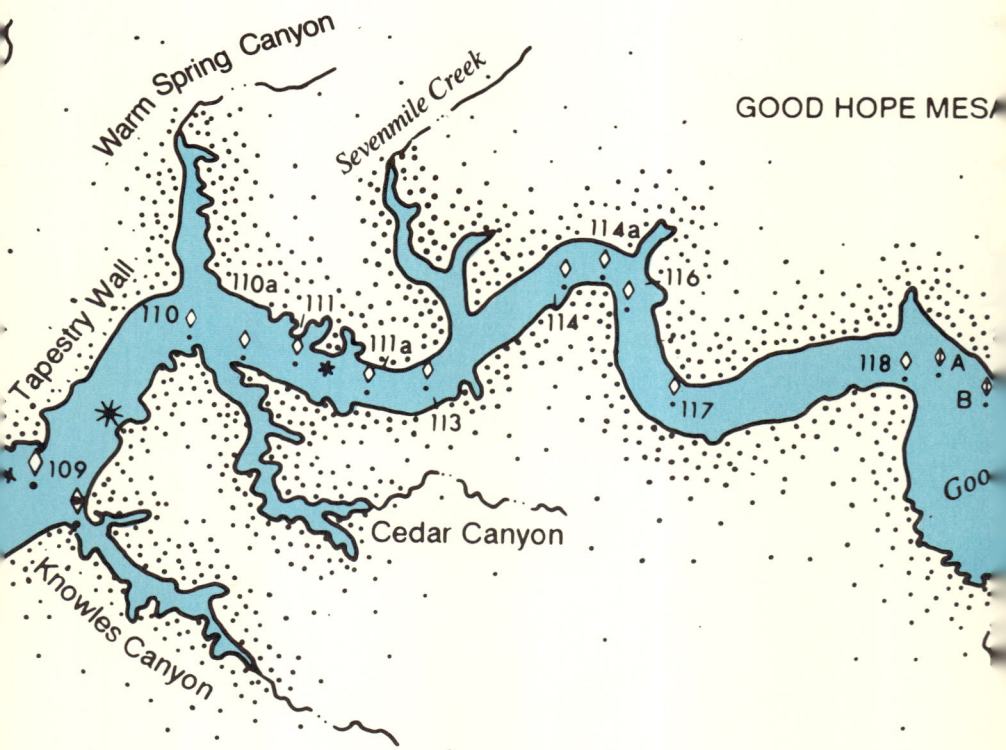

GOOD HOPE MESA

Tapestry Wall

110a

111

114a

116

110

111a

114

113

109

117

118

A

B

Cedar Canyon

Goo

Knowles Canyon

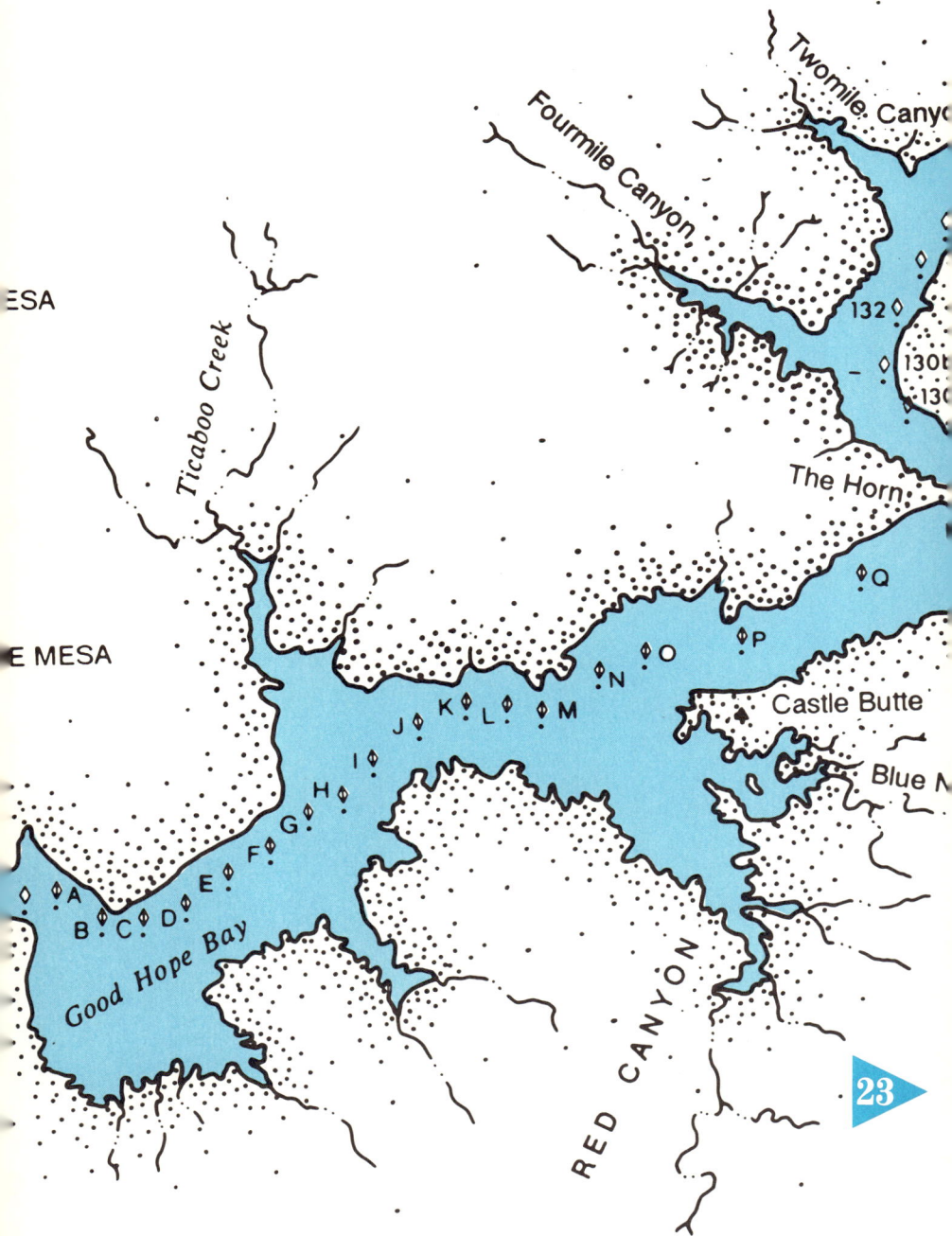

Twomile Canyo

Fourmile Canyon

Ticaboo Creek

ESA

E MESA

The Horn

132

130b
130

Q

P

O

N

J K L M

Castle Butte

Blue N

I

H

G

F

E

A

B C D

Good Hope Bay

RED CANYON

23

MANCOS MESA

23

LEGEND

✳	shoal
····	intermittent stream
⌒	road
!	light (fixed structure)
◇	unlighted buoy
◈	lighted buoy
⬦	mid-channel buoy
⬠	side canyon buoy

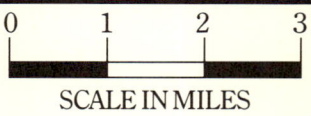

0   1   2   3

SCALE IN MILES

22

Trachyte Canyon

North Wash

Twomile Canyon

134   134a   136a   136b

◇139

132b   135   HITE MARINA

132a   135b   135b

132   135a   136

130b   Farley Canyon

130a

129c

WHITE

130   129b

R   129   129a   CANYON

Q

Horn

Scorup Canyon

UT 95

Butte

Blue Notch Canyon

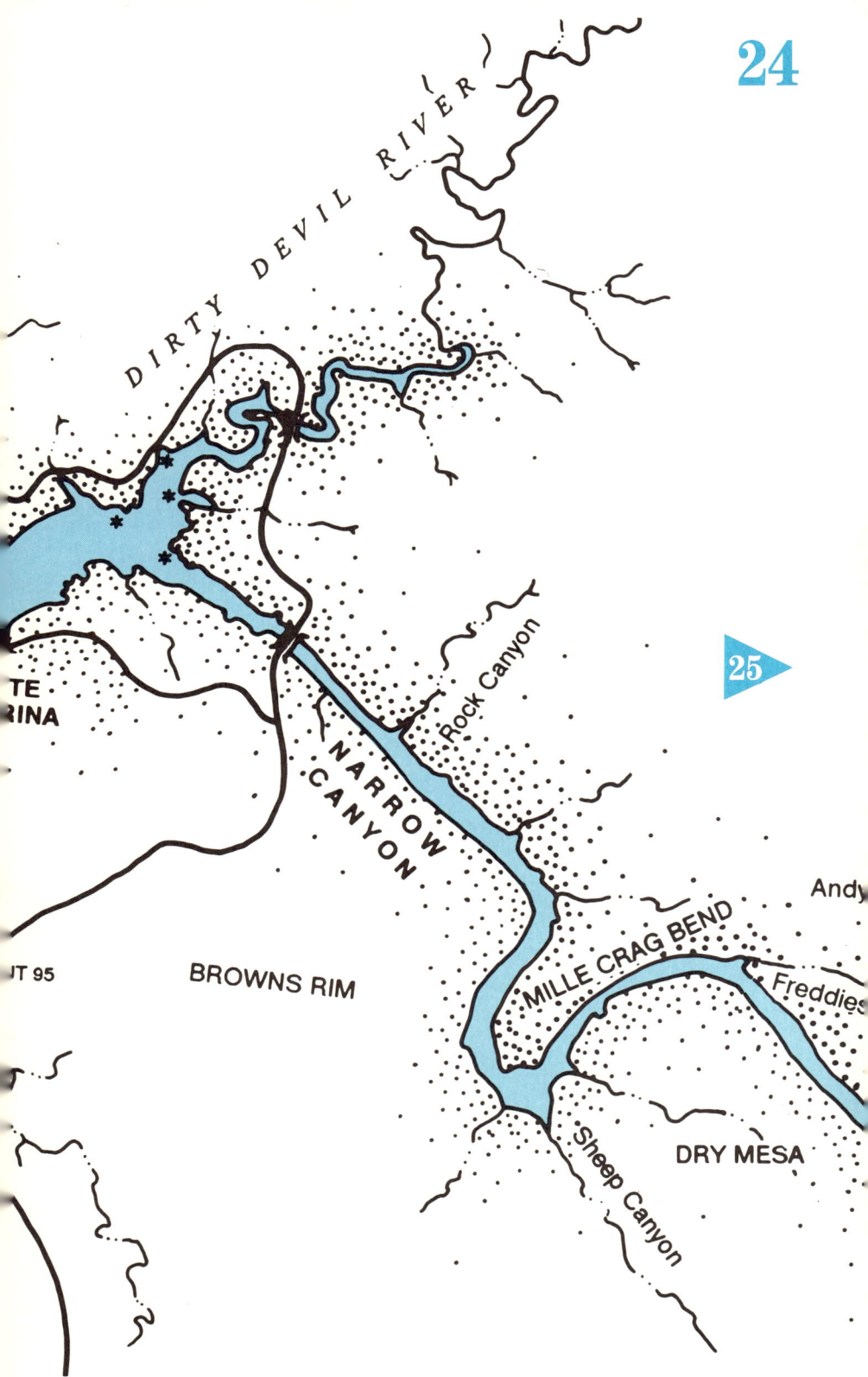

DIRTY DEVIL RIVER

25

Rock Canyon

TE
RINA

N
A
R
R
O
W
C
A
N
Y
O
N

JT 95

BROWNS RIM

MILLE CRAG BEND

Andy

Freddies

Sheep Canyon

DRY MESA

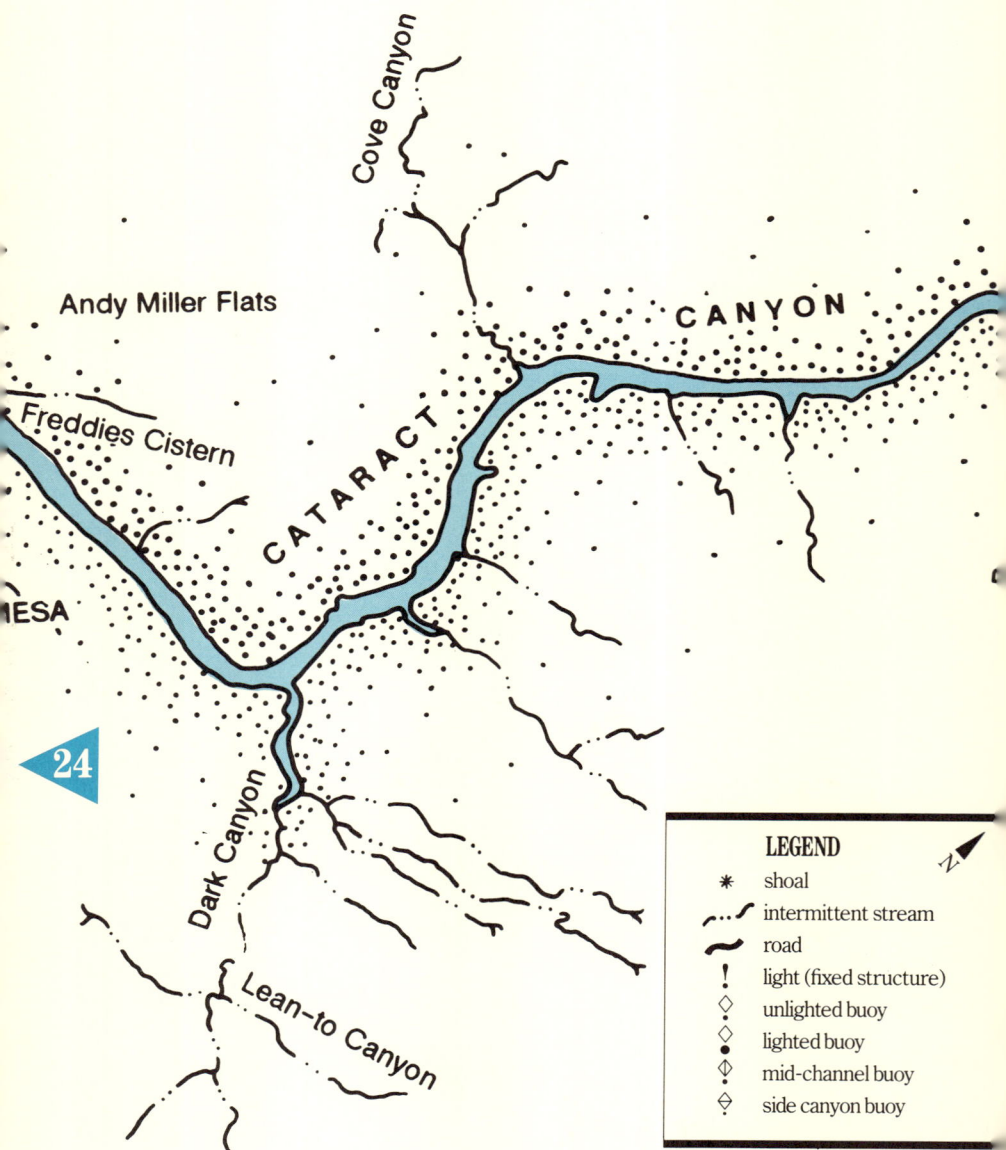

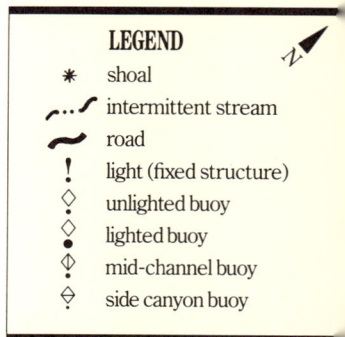

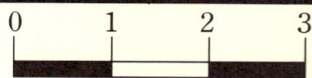

Clearwater Canyon

Bowdie Canyon

Gypsum Canyon

27

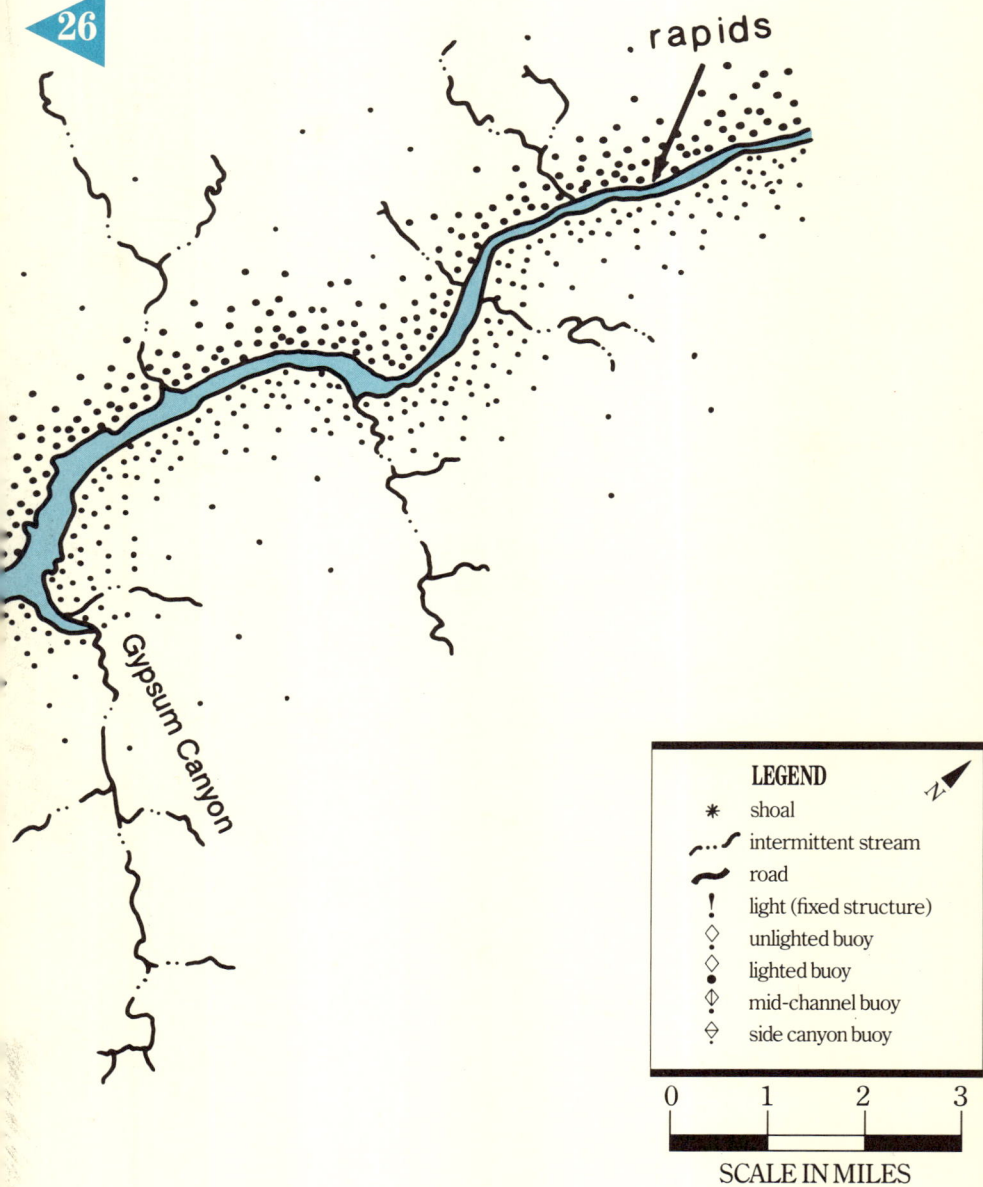

26

rapids

Gypsum Canyon

LEGEND

N

✳	shoal
⌐⌐⌐⌐	intermittent stream
⌐⌐	road
!	light (fixed structure)
◇	unlighted buoy
◈	lighted buoy
●	mid-channel buoy
⬦	side canyon buoy

0　　　1　　　2　　　3

SCALE IN MILES

T wo major rivers, the Colorado and the San Juan, meet in what is now the heart of Glen Canyon National Recreation Area. These two rivers have carved steep canyons into the otherwise flat upland known as the Colorado Plateau, a vast area that stretches from the Rocky Mountains to the western edge of Utah.

Although the Glen Canyon region may appear to be too arid to sustain much life, there is abundant evidence along the Colorado and San Juan rivers that people have lived here for thousands of years. These river corridors provided not only water, but everything people have needed to survive. Because of the considerable difference in elevation between the uplands and the canyons formed by the rivers, there was a rich variety of plants and animals which could be used for food, clothing, and tools.

This chapter is the story of people and events that were distant from one another in time and place, yet related to one another because of their common dependence on the resources of the Colorado and San Juan river canyons. Checked by Glen Canyon Dam, the Colorado and San Juan rivers have risen within their canyons to form the reservoir called Lake Powell. But we can still find the sites of past people and events that will be described in this chapter. To do so, use Glen Canyon Dam as a reference point. Locations of historic interest will be described by their approximate distance in miles from the dam.

THE PEOPLE

Prehistory

The human story of Glen Canyon before written records, or its prehistory, begins eleven thousand years ago. Much of North America was still in the grip of an ice age. In the Glen Canyon region, the climate was much cooler and wetter than it is presently. Instead of the shining lake you see here today, imagine deep canyons where huge mammoths, long-horned bison, horses, and camels grazed on lush grasses.

There were people here then, too. Pieces of stone blades made by cultures referred to as the Clovis and Folsom peoples have been found in Glen Canyon. Rock paintings which resemble mammoths have been discovered in Willow Creek Canyon, 9.5 miles up Escalante Canyon from mile 69 on the Colorado River.

Megafauna, enormous animals like the mammoths, disappeared not long after people began hunting them. By then, the climate was becoming warmer and drier, and so there may not have been enough grass for the animals to eat. However, some scientists believe that the megafauna were actually hunted to extinction.

With the demise of big game, archeological evidence indicates a change in the way people survived in the Glen Canyon area. New people may have arrived, or perhaps the big game hunters themselves developed what is called the Archaic culture. From radiocarbon-dated remains found in Bowns Canyon about mile 75, we know that the Archaic people of eight thousand years ago hunted small game. They also foraged over a maze of trails throughout the canyon, eating cactus fruits and the leaves of rabbitbrush as well as the seeds and flowers of many other plants. Archeologists have found Archaic collecting baskets, seed-grinding stones, storage bins filled with dried berries, and even the pits where they roasted the hearts of agave, also called century plants. The Archaic people made medicines, dyes, glues, sandals, and hunting snares from the plants and animals they gathered. Twigs they twisted into animal shapes have been found near Glen Canyon, and may represent prayer offerings or hunting magic.

Although the Archaic way of life may appear simple from our modern vantage point, these people were intimately familiar with a complex range of resources. Theirs was a highly successful way of life that endured for several thousand years.

However, there came a time when people began to grow food rather than only gather it. The earliest sample of corn from the Colorado Plateau, found in a cave just north of Glen Canyon, dates to 200 B.C. Because corn does not grow wild, this discovery indicates that people in this area had begun to farm. Corn had been cultivated farther south since a much earlier period, and so it may be that new people had migrated from that direction bringing agriculture with them. It is also possible that the first farmers of the Colorado

Plateau were Archaic people who were taught how to grow corn by their southern neighbors.

Archeologists refer to these first farmers as the Basketmakers, because many elaborate baskets have been found at their sites. Evidence of Basketmaker occupation that dates to A.D. 500 has been found in Moqui Canyon, about mile 99.

The beginning of farming in the region meant a dramatic change in the way people lived. In order to tend their crops, the Basketmakers lived in more permanent settlements, in rooms dug into the ground which archeologists call pithouses. Their society apparently became more complex than that of a wandering culture, as individuals became specialists within their communities. This is particularly evident from the fine work of different artisans of this period, although despite their skill in basketmaking, they fashioned only the crudest sort of pottery.

The Basketmakers cultivated corn, but still depended primarily on hunting and gathering for their food. As their way of life developed over the next several centuries, they began cultivating other plants as crops, including beans, squash, and cotton. Their communities grew larger, becoming clusters of above-ground stone apartments we call pueblos (from the Spanish word for villages). Their pottery became very fine, with painted designs that had evolved from the patterns of baskets.

Pottery from Anasazi burial grounds. Photo University of Utah, Anthropology Department. Photo courtesy of Utah State Historical Society.

The people of this more developed culture are called the Anasazi, a Navajo word meaning "ancient strangers." They are also referred to as Pueblo people, because of their distinctive kind of dwelling. To this day, people known as Pueblo live in similar stone villages in northern Arizona and New Mexico.

THE PEOPLE

At Glen Canyon, the Anasazi mostly lived in the side canyons rather than the main gorge. Today, it is not easy to see why they would have chosen these steep ravines of almost bare rock. However, studies suggest that during the Anasazi period, there were clear streams and patches of deep soil in these side canyons where crops could be grown. During droughts, the Anasazi lived nearer to the river's edge, wherever there were patches of land they could farm.

At Defiance House about mile 107, you can still picture the way Anasazi people lived from about A.D. 1050 to 1250. Not only did the Anasazi leave arrowshafts and corncobs here, but flutes, weaving tools, fine pottery, and jewelry as well. It appears that the Anasazi enjoyed music and appreciated beautiful things. Artifacts from this site also include gaming pieces, which suggests that they had the time for leisure and sport. And there is a kiva, an underground religious chamber, at Defiance House. All of these clues help us to imagine the vibrant culture of the Anasazi.

On the cliff above Defiance House, the Anasazi painted a picture of three warriors. Rock art at Glen Canyon dates back to at least 100 B.C. Early artists powdered min-

Dr. Angus M. Woodbury, Professor Emeritus of Zoology, University of Utah, inspects petroglyphs of Indian origin on the canyon wall below the mouth of Smith Canyon. September 7, 1957. Photo by Stan Rasmussen, Bureau of Reclamation. Courtesy of Utah State Historical Society.

erals to make the paint for pictographs or hammered one rock with another to strike petroglyphs into the dark "varnish" on cliff walls and on fallen slabs of sandstone. Many of the same symbols were used for centuries, but the meaning of most of these symbols has been lost.

The Anasazi were not alone in the Glen Canyon area. Escalante Canyon, at about mile 69, was a passageway between the Anasazi of Glen Canyon and the Fremont people to the north. The Fremont are so called because their culture centers around the Fremont River. Evidence of both Anasazi and Fremont people is found along Escalante Canyon, indicating that they mingled and traded.

The Fremont were distinct from the Anasazi in many ways, having developed their own cultural traits before they had contact with one another. The Fremont may have evolved from the same Archaic culture, or they may have been an entirely different people who entered the area from the north or east.

In either case, the Fremont lived mostly in pithouses long after the Anasazi began living in above-ground pueblos. Ceremonial kivas like those of the Anasazi were apparently not part of the Fremont culture. Archeologists believe the Fremont people depended more upon wild plants and game than the Anasazi did, although the Fremont did develop their own distinctive strain of corn known as "Fremont red dent." It is in their art that the most striking cultural difference is found. With elaborate clay figurines and in rock art, the Fremont portrayed people dressed in extravagant necklaces, earrings, loin cloths, and ornate headdresses utterly unlike anything the Anasazi pictured in their rock art or painted pottery.

The Anasazi and the Fremont traded and even intermingled their settlements. Yet both mysteriously disappeared from Glen Canyon by the end of the 1200s. They may have left because of drought, or perhaps other people encroaching on the area were threatening them.

Pottery of the nomadic Ute and Paiute cultures dating to around the end of the 1200s has been found in caves in the Glen Canyon area. Apart from this pottery and a certain kind of stone point, these Ute and Paiute newcomers from the Great Basin west of the Colorado Plateau left few traces. They moved constantly, unlike the more settled Anasazi and Fremont.

These early Ute and Paiute people camped in the abandoned homes of the Anasazi or lived in sagebrush huts or caves. Some families grew small patches of corn and squash in the summer, but they were primarily foragers. In historic times, they cultivated such places as Paiute Farms fifty miles up the San Juan River from its confluence with the Colorado. Today, there is a small Paiute Reservation seventy miles due west of Glen Canyon Dam and a Ute Reservation in southwestern Colorado and northwestern New Mexico.

All of these groups of people—from the Clovis and Folsom peoples on—lived entirely on the natural resources of the area. Because they had no written languages, our picture of them lacks detail. We can only imagine them making their way along the cliffs of Glen Canyon through the scratchy, tangled shrubs, watching for snakes, feeling the heat, hearing the hum of insects and the songs of birds.

The Dominguez-Escalante Expedition

However, the Spanish, who were the next to come to this area, kept extensive journals of their experiences here. We know exactly why they came and how they survived.

By the eighteenth century, the Spanish empire had outposts in much of southwestern North America. In July of 1776, the Spanish government sponsored an expedition of ten men to establish a route from Santa Fe, New Mexico to Monterey, California, to link these isolated outposts together. The expedition was led by Friars Dominguez and Escalante, who hoped to convert the Indians along their route to Christianity.

They chose a northern route through what is now Utah, because the various Indians they might encounter were they to go directly west from Santa Fe through present-day Arizona might be dangerous. In his journal, Escalante explained why: "[The Indians] fear ... that they will be abused and almost enslaved by the Spaniards ... A falsehood in which the demon succeeds in holding them by some sadly undeniable truths." Escalante was referring to Spanish slavers, who captured Indians and sold them as laborers to haciendas and mines in Mexico. The legacy of these slave raids was a guarded and often hostile relationship between native and non-native peoples throughout the history of the region.

The Dominguez-Escalante expedition was not a success. In October, when the party had gone only as far as what is now western Utah, an early winter storm forced them to turn back to Santa Fe. They decided to take the most direct route, which led them across the desolate country now known as the Arizona Strip, north of Grand Canyon.

Escalante wrote that the Paiutes they met along the way were terrified of them: "It pained us to see them frightened so much that they could not even speak ... We sent them away, telling them to notify their people that we came in peace, that we harmed no one, that we loved everybody."

Members of the expedition managed to learn from a Paiute man that they would soon reach a great river. He then described a ford, saying it was the only place where this river could be crossed.

The Dominguez-Escalante party reached the great river at its confluence with a smaller stream. (This place is now called Lees Ferry, and it is just below Glen Canyon Dam.) Today, the great river is known as the Colorado, the Spanish word for "reddish," because of the rusty colored sediment it carries. The smaller stream is called by the Paiute name, Paria. Where the canyons carved by the Colorado and Paria rivers meet, there is a small valley. This made it easy for the Spanish to reach the bank of the Colorado River. Although the opposite shore at this point is a steep cliff, they hoped this was the ford described to them by the Paiute.

Two men tried to swim the river, but they nearly drowned. The current was too strong and the river too deep to get the horses and supplies across. Clearly, the Spanish had not found the ford. Yet to the south, steep cliffs rose on both banks of the river, and they could see no place to cross in that direction either.

The expedition found a break in the cliffs to the north and decided to search in that direction for a crossing of the Colorado River. The steep and rocky cliffs, almost impassible with ledges, delayed them further. The weary Spanish finally made camp at Wahweap Creek, near where the Wahweap Lodge is now.

Below their camp, the Colorado River flowed through a steep-walled canyon. Surviving on cactus pads, berries, and horsemeat, the Spanish labored along the cliffs seeking a way down to the water. They became desperate as

a storm began blowing and raining, then hailing and thundering. They waited out the tempest, praying. Finally the storm ceased, and they continued their search for a route. They soon spotted a shallow place in the river below them. They cut steps in the rock so their animals could get down, and crossed the Colorado River at the place known to this day as the Crossing of the Fathers, at mile 18, fifteen miles east of their Wahweap camp. Eventually, the expedition returned safely to Santa Fe.

Crossing of the Fathers, Colorado River before Glen Canyon Dam. Photo courtesy Utah State Historical Society.

Coming down steps cut in solid rock by Dominguez/Escalante expedition in 1776. Photo courtesy Utah State Historical Society.

117

THE PEOPLE

The Spanish government did not make use of the expedition's maps and journals as planned. In time, the northern Spanish empire began to slip away from its rulers. Mexico won its independence from Spain in 1821, and the Glen Canyon area became Mexican territory. Mexican traders used the Crossing of the Fathers in 1829, but they preferred the "Old Spanish Trail" which crossed the Colorado River at an easier ford near where Moab, Utah, is today.

A Collision of Cultures

In 1848, Mexico ceded to the United States the territory that included what is now Arizona, Utah, and New Mexico. The U.S. Army set about establishing military dominance over the various groups of Indians living in the vast, mostly unexplored territory. The remote Glen Canyon area became a refuge for a few members of one of these groups, the Navajo.

Ancestors of the Navajo probably came to the Southwest in a great migration from the north around A.D. 1300. After the Spanish arrived from the south in the 1500s, there were many peaceful exchanges between the Navajo, the Spanish, and the indigenous Pueblo people. But there were also conflicts. Small bands of Navajo preyed on the Pueblo for food and on the Spanish in retaliation for slave raids. These marauding Navajo effectively discouraged Spanish, Mexican, and then American colonists from settling much of what is now northern Arizona and New Mexico.

Among the determined American colonists were the Mormons. After founding Salt Lake City in 1847, in the territory they called Deseret (now Utah), the Mormons sent out colonizing parties and missionaries throughout the region. Eventually, these Mormon pioneers reached the Navajo homeland.

A Mormon visionary named Jacob Hamblin believed himself to be divinely protected so that he could foster peaceful relations between his people and the Indians. Beginning in 1858, Hamblin and several other Mormons undertook a series of missionary trips to the Hopi ("peaceful") people, a Pueblo group in what is now northern Arizona. Sometimes his party rode in company with Navajo, and they camped with Spaneshanks, a Navajo leader. Nonetheless, they were robbed and one of the Mormons was fatally wounded by other, hostile Navajo on their third trip. This was only one of many skirmishes between the Navajo and the Mormons. The Mormons established prosperous farms in what is now southern Utah and the Navajo crossed the Colorado to raid them. The farmers retaliated, but not always against the actual culprits.

Jacob Hamblin. Photo courtesy Utah State Historical Society.

Such clashes were occurring throughout the new American territories. The U.S. Army was directed to put a stop to Navajo raiding, but as Captain John G. Walker wrote in 1859: "I am not prepared to say what would be the better line of policy towards them, but there is no doubt that a war made upon them now by us would fall the heaviest upon the least guilty, would transform a nation which has already made considerable progress in civilized arts into a race of beggars, vagabonds, and robbers."

Nevertheless, martial law was declared from 1861 to 1865 in order to deport all Navajo to a bleak reservation at Fort Sumner in eastern New Mexico territory. In command was Colonel Kit Carson, a former trapper and mountain man who knew the country and its people well. Carson was reluctant to punish all the Navajo for the depredations of a few, but he was obliged to obey orders.

In 1863, a tiny band of Navajo led by a man named Hoskaninni hid in the rugged country around Navajo Mountain due south of mile 53. Navajo stories relate that the supernatural being Monster Slayer was reborn there, armored in flint, to shield the Navajo from the Army. A prayer from that time goes in part:

> *I am spared! I am spared!*
> *Enemy has missed me! Enemy has missed me!*
> *Today it did not happen!*

Hoskaninni and his followers came out of hiding after an 1868 treaty allowed the Navajo to leave Fort Sumner. This was fortunate, because the Glen Canyon area was not to remain a remote refuge much longer.

Christopher (Kit) Carson. Photo courtesy Utah State Historical Society.

Major John Wesley Powell

Major John Wesley Powell made his first, epic voyage of discovery down the Colorado River in 1869. Powell hoped to prove that the Colorado could be navigated and to explore the unknown region through which the river flowed. A professor of geology, he wanted to study the canyons of the Colorado where he could see geology in cross-section.

Powell's expedition consisted of four boats and ten men. Only Powell himself could be considered a scientist, and he was mostly self-taught. He was a man of limitless energy, intelligence, and ambition. His spellbinding account of the adventure reveals his fascination with everything he encountered, including difficulty and danger. He did not just float along watching the scenery. He climbed cliffs, explored ruins, sketched and took notes and thought hard about what he was seeing, trying to understand the processes which had created the landscape.

THE PEOPLE

John Wesley Powell with Paiute Indian dressed to Eastern expectations, 1871. Hillers photo courtesy Utah State Historical Society.

Powell also appreciated the beauty of the landscape. His observations led to a number of the names used in the region today, including his name for the canyon itself: "So we have a curious ensemble of wonderful features — carved walls, royal arches, glens, alcove gulches, mounds, and monuments. From which of these features shall we select a name? We decide to call it Glen Canyon."

The trip through Glen Canyon was one of the few peaceful and uneventful parts of Powell's journey. Both above and below Glen Canyon, the rough river capsized Powell's boats over and over, soaking food and breaking and losing equipment. But from the Dirty Devil River at mile 141, which one of Powell's men named for its muddy and sulphurous-smelling water, the Colorado flowed relatively quietly until it erupted into the dangerous, uncharted rapids of the Grand Canyon. During the punishing trip through Grand Canyon, three men left the expedition. They intended to climb north out of the Canyon to Mormon settlements in southern Utah, but they were never seen again. Ironically, Powell and his remaining men reached calm water almost immediately after the others left them.

After completing this voyage successfully, Powell began making arrangements to repeat it. This time he asked the Mormon leader Brigham Young for help. Powell, Young, and Jacob Hamblin made a reconnaissance of the area together to find suitable places from which to supply Powell's next expedition. They also visited the Shivwits Indians who lived north of the Grand Canyon. The Shivwits apparently confessed to killing the three men who had left Powell's first voyage. An entry in Powell's journal about this incident reveals both his skill as an observer and the unusual qualities that made his friend Jacob Hamblin a central figure in the history of the area. "This man, Hamblin, speaks their language well, and has a great influence over all the Indians in the region round about. He is a silent, reserved man, and when he speaks, it is in a slow, quiet way, that inspires great awe. His talk is so low that they must listen attentively to hear, and they sit around him in deathlike silence."

After this meeting, Powell and Hamblin crossed the Colorado River at its confluence with the Paria in a rough boat their men knocked together. They went on to Fort Defiance in eastern Arizona Territory, where Powell helped to work out a peace treaty between the Mormons and the Navajo.

John Wesley Powell's second expedition down the Colorado began in May 1871. Arriving at the mouth of the Paria River in October, Powell and his men interrupted their journey until the following June. That winter, while he and his crew worked on data for a topographic map of the area, Powell also studied the language and stories of Kaibab Paiutes living nearby. He was already familiar with the language, having some years before studied the Utes, a related group of Indians. The Ute name for him was "Kapurats," meaning "arm off," because the intrepid Major Powell had lost his right arm in the Civil War.

Powell did not lose his interest in the region after finishing his second voyage. In 1873, he travelled through the canyon country studying the Indians as Special Commissioner for the Department of Indian Affairs. Thinking ahead to the commercial value of photographs taken on this trip, Powell dressed the Southern Paiute in feather warbonnets (which these people had never worn) so they would look like Easterners would expect Indians to look. Powell's anthropological studies were further funded by Congress in 1879, leading to the creation of the Bureau of Ethnology with Powell as its director. Powell also continued to study the area's geology, and in 1881 he was named director of the United States Geological Survey.

The Lee of Lees Ferry

Brigham Young believed that a ferry across the Colorado River at the mouth of the Paria would be useful in sending missionaries to the Hopi and in establishing Mormon colonies in Arizona. Such a ferry would require a ferryman. Conveniently, on the trip Young took with Powell had been a man who needed an obscure place to hide. His name was John D. Lee.

Lee had been accused of participation in the infamous Mountain Meadows Massacre. This tragedy had

THE PEOPLE

occurred at a time when the Mormon settlers in Utah Territory felt oppressed by the United States government. The Mormons had intended Utah to be their refuge from religious persecution, but there were inherent conflicts between the goals of Mormon religious leaders and those of secular government appointees. In 1857, in the midst of this tense situation, a wagon train of about 140 emigrants bound for California passed through southwestern Utah, belligerently taunting the Mormons and provoking further tension by such petty acts as robbing henhouses. Allegedly at the urging of the Mormons, Paiutes ambushed the wagon train in an isolated spot called Mountain Meadows. Then about fifty Mormons rode up and shot every one of the emigrants except for the smallest children. John D. Lee was said to have led the massacre.

Hearings on the incident took place many months afterwards. Facts were hazy, but a warrant was issued for Lee's arrest. He remained free, however, protected by his neighbors and possibly his church. Under pressure, the church finally excommunicated Lee just after his trip with Young and Powell in 1870.

Lee was an accomplished and intelligent man who had dedicated his life to his church. Brigham Young, still hoping to protect him, suggested that Lee become the ferryman at the Paria crossing. According to his diary, Lee replied: "I would want no greater punishment than to be Sent on a Mission to the Pahariere. I would turn out Indian at once & take no woman to such a place."

This was no idle consideration, as Lee had nineteen wives. Still, seeing no other way to protect him, Young assigned Lee to be the ferryman at the Paria. At the end of 1871, Lee arrived with part of his family at the place since known as Lees Ferry.

Lee eventually fled the Glen Canyon area, but was captured in Utah in 1874, and executed in 1877. His execution put the Mountain Meadows incident to rest in the minds of most people, but there are others who even now believe he was a scapegoat. In recent years, Lee was reinstated in the church.

In the late 1800s, hundreds of Mormon colonists used Lees Ferry, but a notable exception to this route was built in 1879. That year, a colonizing party set off from southwestern Utah to found a settlement on the San Juan River. They had planned a six-week journey, but it took them six months to reach their destination.

This adventure became known as the Hole-in-the-Rock expedition, and vividly illustrates the determination that made the Mormons so successful in settling the Colorado Plateau. They had already made the arduous journey to Utah from Illinois or Missouri, many of them on foot pulling everything they owned in handcarts. Now they bravely faced hundreds more miles of rough, rocky, gullied terrain.

In winter, less than one hundred miles from their destination, the colonists encountered Glen Canyon. To cross it, they built a road down a steep side canyon at mile 66, just above the Colorado's confluence with the San Juan.

First, they dynamited a narrow cleft at the head of the canyon to make the Hole-in-the-Rock, a passage wide enough for their wagons. Then they needed to get their wagons and stock down a thousand-foot cliff to the river. Day

The Hole-in-the-Rock Expedition

Looking down the Hole-in-the-Rock. Part of path is visible and river can be seen. Photo by E.L. Cooley courtesy of Utah State Historical Society.

after day for six weeks, they hammered and blasted the cliff face to gouge a rut for the wheels on one side of their wagons. At one point, the cliff was so sheer that they drilled holes into it, drove in oak posts, and piled poles, brush, and rocks on top to attach a road to it. A veteran of the expedition, C.I.

THE PEOPLE

Decker, recalled: "I don't think I ever seen a lot of men go to work with more of a will to do something than that crowd did. We were all young men; the way we did make dirt and rock fly was a *caution*." In the evenings after all their hard work, a fiddler played and the pioneers danced on the rocks above the canyon.

Forty Mile Dance Hall, used by pioneers who made the trip from Cedar City by way of Hole-in-the-Rock. Photo by H.J. Allen, courtesy of Utah State Historical Society.

Once the trail was completed, it took almost three weeks to ease the wagons down to the river. By the time everyone was at the Colorado's edge, the road was almost destroyed. Decker's wife, Lizzie, wrote her parents that night: "If you ever come this way it will scare you to death to look down it. It is about a mile from the top down to the river and it is almost straight down ... The first wagon I saw go down they put the brake on and rough locked the hind wheels and had a big rope fastened to the wagon and about ten men holding back on it and then they went down like they would smash everything. I'll never forget that day."

Crossing the river was a monumental undertaking, and then the terrain on the other side was as rough as the country already covered. The Mormons dug a roadway three hundred feet up Grey Mesa (which lies in the "V" between the Colorado and San Juan rivers.) It took two more months of road-building to reach the site where the pioneers founded the town of Bluff on the San Juan River.

A year later Charles Hall, ferryman for the Hole-in-the-Rock expedition, set up a new ferry at mile 94 where the river was easier to reach. This spot is still called Halls Crossing. Hall lived in a tiny cabin up the creek from the river. He would climb the rock slope above the creek bed to check for any sign of travellers camped at the crossing eight miles away. Once loaded, his clumsy ferryboat had to be towed upstream, then frantically rowed by two people while a third steered to reach the other side. There were few requests for this service. Hall stopped running the ferry after three years, just before the Glen Canyon gold rush would have kept him busy.

The Navajo leader Hoskaninni had been out of hiding for fourteen years when an eager young prospector named Cass Hite asked him where the Navajo found the silver for their jewelry. He was not the first to wonder. In 1880, just three years earlier, two prospectors searching for the "secret silver mine of the Navajo" had been killed in Monument Valley south of the San Juan River.

Hoskaninni kept quiet about the silver, but he took Hite down White Canyon to the south side of the Colorado River at about mile 135. Here, there was gold dust in the riverbanks, and the river could be crossed from either side fairly easily. Hite declared it a "Dandy Crossing" and began to pan for gold. Soon, prospectors mobbed Dandy Crossing, later known as Hite, Utah. By 1889, there was even a post office there.

The Glen Canyon Gold Rush

Cass Hite. Photo courtesy Utah State Historical Society.

Hite Ferry, 1938. Photo courtesy Utah State Historical Society.

The prospectors searched down the Colorado River and up the San Juan, and they kept finding gold. They made dozens of trails, even hacking steps for their pack animals into the cliffs with pickaxes. They pumped and sluiced and panned and sifted. Finally, they left their equipment to

Placer mining on San Juan River, 1894. Photo courtesy Utah State Historical Society.

THE PEOPLE

rust: pumps, picks, shovels, ore trucks, and sluice boxes. The silty waters of the Colorado River had worn out their gear as the frustration of separating the floury gold from mud had worn out their hearts.

Most Glen Canyon prospectors were individuals with a small grubstake and makeshift tools. However, there were two large-scale efforts to mine a fortune in gold from Glen Canyon.

The first was that of Robert B. Stanton, a mining engineer who first came to the area to survey a route for a railroad along the Colorado River. His first trip down the river in 1889 was a nightmare: the president of his company and two others drowned. When the railway's investors dropped that project, Stanton was ready with another scheme that inspired people to part with their money. He formed an enterprise to mine gold in Glen Canyon. It was called — of all things — the Hoskaninni Company.

Stanton's plan was to operate several large floating dredges, powered by damming tributaries of the Colorado. He began by building and improving trails, including the old Hole-in-the-Rock Trail. The steps you see there today were carved into the rock not by Mormon pioneers, but by Stanton's men.

An enormous dredge was hauled to Glen Canyon from the railway at Green River, over a hundred miles to the northeast. It was assembled and put to work in 1901. But this latest, most expensive technology could not separate the fine gold from its muddy source either. The Hoskaninni Company was a complete loss.

Remains of Hoskannini Company dredge near the Mouth of Bullfrog Creek. Photo courtesy Utah State Historical Society.

Then came Charles H. Spencer, who persuaded investors to finance a road to the San Juan River. In 1909, heavy machinery was set up to crush the sandstone of the Wingate Formation and refine the gold from it. Not much gold was recovered, but the underlying Chinle Formation looked more promising.

Spencer constructed a giant sluice at Lees Ferry, where the claylike Chinle Formation was well exposed. His crew built a twenty-eight-mile trail right over the cliffs to Warm Creek Canyon where they could mine coal to power the contraption. A steamboat was shipped in pieces from San Francisco to the Warm Creek mine. It was meant to carry coal to the sluice, but the little steamer could not deliver appreciably more coal than it burned in making the round-trip. Spencer's main problem, however, was with the Chinle itself. The sticky shale contained an element that interfered with the sluicing process. Spencer was compelled at length to admit defeat.

The Lees Ferry dredge. Photo courtesy Church Archives, The Church of Jesus Christ of Latter-day Saints.

The gold of Glen Canyon was a phantom. The miners could see it, but it was so fine that no known process could extract it. Hoskaninni had led Cass Hite, who had led hundreds of others, to gold they could see but never have. A few people continued to prospect in Glen Canyon, especially during the Great Depression of the 1930s. In 1949, uranium was found in White Canyon. A uranium mill was built there, as well as a post office and school. The mill lasted only a few years, because better sources of uranium were developed elsewhere in the world.

THE PEOPLE

The Cowboy Era

At the height of the Glen Canyon gold rush, a pony express route was initiated which ran north from Dandy Crossing up Trachyte Creek and on to Hanksville and Green River, Utah, over eighty miles away. A number of ranches were established in the area in the 1880s and 1890s that sold mules and food to the prospectors. Cass Hite himself had a little ranch at Ticaboo Canyon, mile 122, where he raised melons and grapes.

Most of the cattle and sheep camps were marginal outfits, but there were some larger ranches. The largest within what is now the Glen Canyon National Recreation Area was the Baker Ranch near Halls Crossing, where one hundred acres of alfalfa and corn were irrigated by Halls Creek and quite a few cattle were raised.

The rangeland of the area was in poor condition as early as the 1890s. Drought and overgrazing in the 1880s had reduced the grassy range to a scrubland. Because most of the land could support only one cow per one or two hundred acres, the range was seldom fenced. Ranchers would just build a cabin and corral, clear the water seeps, and let their branded cattle range free.

This led to a lively trade in rustled cattle. Rustlers would round up someone else's cattle or horses, drive them down to the Colorado River, and sell them on the other side in Arizona or Utah. The infamous "Outlaw Trail" ran from Montana to Mexico by way of Dandy Crossing. Some rustlers also found Lees Ferry convenient. Once three cattle rustlers made it to the ferry with the law hot on their heels but were rowed safely across just ahead of their pursuers. Then they tied up the ferryman, bathed, ate, and slept through the night while the frustrated lawmen paced on the other side of the Colorado.

Up the Dirty Devil not far from Hanksville was Robbers Roost, the scene of many a tale about outlaws,

Butch Cassidy. Photo courtesy Utah State Historical Society.

stolen livestock, and posses. During the 1890s, Robbers Roost was the lair of the Wild Bunch, a gang that robbed banks and trains and hid out in the canyon country. Between heists, members of the Wild Bunch sometimes worked on nearby ranches. The ringleader and most famous of the gang was Butch Cassidy. Cassidy (whose real name was Robert LeRoy Parker) is remembered as a cowboy Robin Hood. It is said that he once came upon a lady who was in tears because she had no money to pay her rent. He gallantly presented her with enough cash. A few hours later, he ambushed her landlord and stole the money back.

Ranching is still an important livelihood in the area. The rustling trade is all but forgotten.

Toward the end of the nineteenth century, Glen Canyon began an entirely new role as a destination for pleasure-seekers. The first people to float the Colorado River just for fun were George Flavell and Ramon Montez in 1896. Others who made the run in those early days included Julius Stone of the defunct Hoskaninni Company, who took the trip in 1909 with long-time Glen Canyon prospector Nathaniel Galloway.

In 1911, brothers Emery and Ellsworth Kolb, photographers of tourists at the Grand Canyon, rowed the Colorado River. They filmed their adventure, and Ellsworth published a book about it in 1914. This book documents the tremendous changes that had occurred in Glen Canyon in the brief forty-two years since John Wesley Powell's daring journey through its uncharted wilderness. On their trip, the Kolb brothers met prospectors and farmers who had read about them in the newspapers. Evidence of placer mining was everywhere, and they found Stanton's crew in the middle of assembling their steamboat at Warm Creek. The Kolbs even picked up mail addressed to themselves at Hite and Lees Ferry.

Recreation and Inspiration in Glen Canyon

Ellsworth and Emery Kolb, 1921. Photo courtesy Utah State Historical Society.

The Kolb brothers were also boatmen on a U.S. Geological Survey expedition that resulted in maps of Cataract, Narrow, Glen, and San Juan canyons. These maps encouraged more people to boat at least part of the Colorado River.

Norman Nevills began running the San Juan and Colorado rivers in the 1930s, entertaining his passengers with the kind of wild stories that have become a river-runners' tradition. Art Green ran noisy but popular trips upriver from Lees Ferry to Rainbow Bridge after 1940, using a boat with an aircraft propeller attached to the stern above the waterline. Half a dozen other commercial operators and hundreds of amateurs began to float the Colorado in all sorts of craft.

There were also adventurers who came on foot or horseback and wrote of their experiences. One of the most famous was Western writer Zane Grey, who first visited Lees Ferry in 1907 and used the setting in his writing. He and Theodore Roosevelt made the difficult overland trek to Rainbow Bridge in 1912, inspiring Roosevelt to publish an article about the trip.

Sharlot Hall, the first official territorial historian of Arizona, visited Lees Ferry during the mining boom in 1911. She wrote vividly of the perilous ferry crossing: "A wagon and team and two men were lost here in the spring by the tipping of the ferryboat. This wild river takes its toll every few months; the very waves as they pass look fierce and tameless and hungry ... It was this same wild current that Father Escalante feared to cross in 1776; he turned back after coming down and riding into the river twice. I don't blame him. Death sits mighty close to the bank here."

One very romantic character was a young artist named Everett Ruess, who explored the wilderness around Glen Canyon on foot in the early 1930s. He took long trips into the desert country alone and wrote about its beauty and wildness. Why? In his words: "I am roaring drunk with the lust of life and adventure and unbearable beauty ..." In 1934, when he was twenty years old, Ruess disappeared in Davis Canyon north of the confluence of the Colorado and San Juan rivers. Searchers found his boot prints in the dust and an inscription: "Nemo, 1934." No other trace of Everett Ruess could be found.

Not long after Ruess vanished, the beauty of the Glen Canyon region inspired a proposal to create "Escalante National Park." Although the area's resources were of national park caliber, other considerations defeated the proposal. In particular, the arid agricultural state of Utah was concerned about losing water and power rights to the Colorado River.

Rights to the Colorado River had become an issue early in the century. The U.S. Geological Survey's 1921 exploration of the river, which was actually the brainchild of Southern California Edison, investigated the Colorado's potential for generating hydroelectricity for southern California's growing population. The competing claims of seven states drained by the Colorado were resolved by the Colorado

The Transformation of Glen Canyon

The Colorado River before and after the building of Glen Canyon Dam. Note the "beehive" rock on the left of dam. Photos courtesy Utah State Historical Society.

131

River Compact of 1922. This compact divided the drainage into an upper and a lower basin at Lees Ferry. The Bureau of Reclamation recommended a series of dams to impound and distribute the water of the Upper Basin. The Colorado River Storage Project, which provided for four dams including one at Glen Canyon, was approved by Congress in 1956.

The dams along the Colorado River provide water and/or power to Wyoming, Colorado, Utah, New Mexico, Arizona, Nevada, California, the Navajo Nation, and Mexico, according to a specific allocation plan. Although all the partners do not take their full allocation, the water and power from the system have helped make possible the tremendous growth of cities in the Southwest. In addition, Glen Canyon has become a premier recreation spot in the Four Corners region. It was designated a National Recreation Area in 1972.

Concerns about Glen Canyon Dam's effects on the downstream environment have led to studies intended to set operating procedures that will minimize the harm done to Grand Canyon. The complexity of this research and political concerns about its results will take many years to resolve.

In its freeflowing state, the Colorado River carried several hundred thousand tons of sediment each day. Today, that sediment is settling where the river loses its momentum as it enters Lake Powell. Estimates vary as to how quickly the lake will fill with mud, but no reservoir lasts forever.

Recalling the History of Glen Canyon

From 1957 until the dam gates were closed to create Lake Powell in 1963, studies were made of Glen Canyon's natural and cultural resources. Researchers documented more than two hundred historic sites and two thousand prehistoric sites as well as other information.

The story of Glen Canyon's past was reconstructed using the expertise of many different specialists. An archeologist who found a broken arrowhead of a certain shape could recognize it as one that was made by a particular culture several thousand years ago. A palynologist (plant pollen scientist) could determine what plants grew here before agriculture and stockraising began. Biologists could learn what people ate to survive here centuries ago. By listening to the descendants of Paiute, Ute, Navajo, and white settlers, anthropologists were able to enrich our picture of how past generations lived here.

These studies confirmed that the Glen Canyon area is of major importance in understanding our heritage. Human history that goes back to the mammoth hunters is recorded here.

Now there is very little evidence left, and what remains is fragile. Each site and every artifact is important, because so much is lost forever under the lake.

THE PEOPLE

If you find a potsherd or other archeological evidence at Glen Canyon National Recreation Area, you have a chance — here in the solitude and stillness — to conjure up the past. Imagine what that broken piece of pottery tells you about the person who made and used it. Then leave it here — in the beautiful place its maker called home.

Broken Bow Arch in Willow Gulch, Escalante tributary, before Lake Powell. Photo courtesy Church Archives, The Church of Jesus Christ of Latter-day Saints.

On first impression the Glen Canyon National Recreation Area seems to be a barren rockscape supporting a few ravens and shrubs and little else. However, the varied canyon, plateau, water and river habitats of this area are home to an interesting variety of animals.

The best times to observe Glen Canyon animal life are evening, at night or near dawn. Most creatures are active at these cooler times, avoiding the heat of the desert day. The seasons of migration, spring and fall, are the best times to observe the larger and more mobile animals and the greatest variety of birds. A pair of good binoculars and perhaps a camera equipped with a telephoto lens are good aids to observation. Also helpful are ample patience and the ability to remain quiet.

Collared lizard

ANIMAL LIFE

here are about eighty mammal—fur-bearing, warm-blooded animals, which usually bear their young live—species known from the region of the Recreation Area. For the smaller animals unable to travel long distances, the Colorado River and its deep canyons have often been effective distributional barriers, resulting in an interesting display of geographic variation. Subspecies may differ on the two sides of the Colorado or San Juan. For instance, the white-throated wood rat lives on the east side of the Colorado River and the desert wood rat on the west.

One of the most exciting wildlife sightings possible in the Glen Canyon area is granted the observant visitor who spots a stately **desert bighorn sheep,** particularly the adult male with his majestic curved horns. These impressive animals are known for their rock-climbing ability. The relatively rare desert bighorn live in several small, widely scattered populations in the Recreation Area, and have been reintroduced recently in several locations under an cooperative state-federal game management program. Above Hite, a native population of desert bighorn still exists on the east side of the river where they are occasionally seen by river-running parties exiting Cataract Canyon or by boaters moving through upper Lake Powell. Bighorn are wary and alert, with acute vision. The sure-footed sheep take advantage of steep talus and broken cliffs for escape. Except for adult males, which may be solitary, bighorn move in small bands led by an older female. They subsist on a diet of shrubs and grass, and wander over ranges of many square miles. Early observers often described bighorn as being common, and the bighorn motif is one of the most prominent in Anasazi rock art. It is thought that a sharp decline in the bighorn population began during the 1870s as a result of disease imported with domestic cattle and widespread hunting by settlers and prospectors. Today, bighorn are protected and may be hunted in Utah only by special permit granted under a very limited lottery program operated by the state.

Mule deer are relatively common, a surprise for those who think of deer as mainly forest animals. Mule deer are found in watered canyons where there is woody vegetation such as buckthorn, hackberry or willow to supply cover. Hikers in narrow canyons may be startled by an explosion of brush and noise as deer bound updrainage seeking a route to bypass intruders. Flushing deer in this manner is not testament to silent hiking technique or stalking skills, for the mule deer's hearing is very keen. They prefer to hide and bolt for escape when approached too closely. Mule deer have large, wide ears much like their namesakes, and black-tipped tails. The distinctive heart-shaped tracks are plentiful in the moist soil of drainages. Deer are most active in the early morning and at dusk. In the Recreation Area deer may be seen in all months, although numbers may be higher in winter.

Coyotes, active during the day and widely distributed, may be the most frequently seen of the larger mammals. When not seen, coyotes may be heard instead, for they seem to take special delight in early evening vocal displays. The coyote's high-pitched, yelping song has held the contemplative attention of many a camper. An Indian term for the animal, "song dog," evokes both its dog-like appearance and the pleasure people have from listening to its night song. Coyotes are gray, dog-sized animals with rusty feet and backs of the ears. They run with tail down in contrast to the much smaller foxes, which run with the tail held straight out. Coyotes are found in all habitats of the Recreation Area, but are most likely to be observed in shrub-grassland or near riparian zones where rodent prey abound. Coyote pelts have had monetary value for two hundred years, resulting in the harvest of countless individuals. They have been widely persecuted by stockmen and the subjects of massive, expensive predator control campaigns for the supposed benefit of livestock and game. Coyotes have responded to these pressures by expanding their range and numbers and by persisting even in heavily settled environments, amply demonstrating their formidable adaptive ability. The coyote with its interesting family life and engaging personality, remains an important cog in the balance of southwestern ecosystems.

Gray fox are nocturnal, seldom-seen carnivores which prey heavily on small rodents and to a lesser extent, birds and insects. They also consume quantities of fruits and plants. Gray, with rust and white coloring beneath, foxes are more colorful than their larger cousin, the coyote. Foxes are found mainly in streamside habitats of the larger drainages, where they den on terraces.

Bobcat are tawny dark-spotted cats with long legs. Not abundant, they nevertheless occur throughout the area, especially at higher elevations and in drainages adjoining the higher plateaus. Bobcat are secretive, nocturnal rabbit-hunters that hide in dense cover or rocky areas by day.

Badger, striped skunk, and **long-tailed weasel** are the other important carnivores of Glen Canyon. All in the Mustelidae family, they share many features, including the use of dens. **Badgers** are vigorous burrowers and are said to disappear in seconds when surprised near a convenient area of soft soil. Their habitat includes terraces above the lake and its drainages, alluvial banks, and other spots with deep soil. **Skunks** are not such avid "do-it-yourselfers." They will use abandoned burrows, crevices, buildings, or other shelter. Many people think skunks are much bolder than they should be. They are one of the few animals that sometimes visit a camp at night.

Bats are among the most numerous of mammals, both in number of species and individuals. Little brown myotis, western pipistrelle, and Brazilian free-tailed bats are the most common varieties here. They are commonly seen in the evening flying over the lake shore. All of the desert bats are insect eaters and consume huge quantities, including the noxious mosquito, making them highly valued members of the animal community. They are highly specialized for a life on the wing, hunting flying food. They have the ability to echo-locate prey by emitting ultrasonic signals and precisely fixing an insect's position. Bats do not fly into people's hair. They will, on occasion, dip close after insects that swarm overhead, a service that is seldom appreciated. Bats are susceptible to rabies and should never be handled if found on the ground.

The more familiar desert animals include the **desert cottontail** and the **black-tailed jackrabbit.** Both desert cottontail and jackrabbits avoid the heat of the day, but can be seen foraging for greenery in the early morning or evening hours. Their list of enemies includes every carnivore and raptor of the desert, plus the snakes. Prodigious reproductive habits ensure both their survival and that of their predators. **Desert cottontail** are the local edition of "bunny," having a powderpuff tail. They hide in dense shrubbery or take over abandoned burrows. **Jackrabbits** are larger, leaner, and have improbably long ears. They can cover ten to twenty feet in a bound and run at top speeds over thirty miles per hour, which no predator can match. They seek the cover of dense shrubs.

Rodents are the most abundant and widespread of desert mammals, and the Recreation Area is home to several dozen species. Most rodents are active at night and spend considerable time below ground, thus are seldom seen except for tracks in the sandy soil of banks and terraces. An exception is the daytime-active **antelope ground squirrel,** a chipmunk-sized rodent with stripes down the sides. It carries its bushy white tail curled up over its back like a parasol reflecting the sun's heat and scampers about among shrubs foraging for seeds.

The **rock squirrel** is another common ground squirrel inhabiting rocky canyons. Rock squirrels have long bushy tails similar to that of the tree squirrel, but have the ground squirrel's habit of whistling loudly to warn of approaching danger, then ducking swiftly into a crevice or burrow.

Wood rats, also called pack rats or trade rats, are the inveterate nocturnal shoppers of the rodent world. Their habit of collecting curious objects for the nest sometimes causes them to drop whatever they are carrying in favor of some new, more attractive find, giving the appearance of having made a trade. Wood rats construct nests of sticks and clods in crevices. Such nests, also called middens, are apparently used for generations in some instances, and in sheltered environments may remain intact for centuries. Some middens contain kernels of corn, cobs, and other items scavenged from settlements or camps of paleo-Indians. The white-throated wood rat inhabits the east side of the canyon and the desert wood rat the west side.

Pocket mice and **kangaroo rats** are burrowing, nocturnal rodents with external cheek pouches for storing seeds while foraging. They have the habit of plugging their borrow entrances with soil during the day to conserve humidity and impede predators. These rodents have the ability to produce water metabolically from food, and rarely seek free water.

Kangaroo rats are well known for their long tail which they use to jump erratically, eluding pursuers. **Deer mice** and related species are numerous, being found in all habitats. These large-eyed, diminutive mice are frequent night camp visitors.

The largest members of the rodent order found in this area are **porcupine** and **beaver. Porcupine** live in pinyon-juniper woodlands and the moister canyons with oak. The flooding of Glen Canyon to form Lake Powell caused extensive loss of habitat for the **beaver,** but they seem to be recovering. They are found in various side canyons, especially where willow grows, and have even been seen along the lake near marinas. Colorado River beavers are bank dwellers, infrequently indulging in dam and lodge building.

There are approximately 205 species of birds in Glen Canyon, representing one-quarter of the species of North American breeding birds. This diversity is made possible by the varied topography and habitats of the Recreation Area and by the presentation of the river basin as both a north-south migration corridor and seasonal movement way between the high plateaus and low river canyons.

Lake Powell and the Colorado River are at least temporary wintering grounds for an impressive list of waterfowl. A recent one-day winter waterfowl survey covering parts of the lake and river yielded thirty species of waterfowl in the dabbling duck, pochard, sea duck, merganser, and grebe groups. Few waterfowl are resident, however. The fluctuating reservoir level and immature lakeshore plant communities offer little breeding habitat. **Coots** and the conspicuous **great blue heron** are perhaps the most commonly seen aquatic birds. **Gulls** are often seen on Lake Powell, particularly near marinas. The **California gull** (famous for saving grain crops in northern Utah during 1848-1850 by devouring hordes of crickets) is present in summer and fall, while the **ring-billed gull** is a winter transient.

Ravens are the most conspicuous land bird. They spend most of their time cruising at low altitudes in search of carrion. They nest in rock crevices and are responsible for most of the "whitewash" seen on cliffs along the lake. They are often confused with crows, which are smaller and uncommon here.

Red-tailed hawks are common, soaring at high altitudes or drifting in front of tall cliffs where they blend with the sandstone background. These heavy-set hawks have wide, rounded wings and sound a shrill, descending "keeeer" which often furnishes the wild sound effects for western movies.

White-throated swifts and **violet-green swallows** are common near cliffs where their acrobatic swoops and turns in pursuit of insects are entertaining. They are easy to spot at the Glen Canyon Dam.

A bird frequenting rocky areas near water is the **canyon wren.** This wren has a distinctive, delightful song—a loud, clear series of musical whistles sounded down the scale. The song echoes through the canyons, making it difficult to locate the bird.

Two birds of particular interest are the **bald eagle** and the **peregrine falcon,** both endangered species. **Bald eagles** are winter residents of Lake Powell, migrating south from the northern tier states and central Canada to fish in warmer climates for a few months. The National Park Service has been keeping track of eagle numbers in recent years and usually finds thirty to fifty birds in this area. Eagles prefer fish, but are opportunistic feeders and probably consume as much carrion and waterfowl.

The **peregrine falcon** may be a success story in the history of efforts to reverse environmental damage. Their numbers seem to be on the increase again in western states following years of decline due to the effects of pesticides. Decreases in spraying of the more damaging chemicals combined with release of captive-bred peregrines into the wild have raised the number of wild-breeding pairs. Falcons are the "top guns" of birds, soaring high and diving at great speed on their avian prey.

Other common land birds include **mourning dove, sparrow hawk, great horned owl, ash-throated flycatcher, horned lark, mountain chickadee, robin, loggerhead shrike, yellow warbler, house finch, house sparrow, chipping sparrow, and Brewer's sparrow.** In winter **dark-eyed juncos** and **white-crowned sparrows** are abundant.

Desert amphibians have adopted several strategies to survive their arid environment, including rapid life cycles to pass through the hatching, maturing, and breeding stages during the limited time vernal pools are in existence; and burrowing into moist mud or soil to estivate until future rains again create pools suited for reproduction. Near seeps or in rock crevices adjoining moist washes the small (one-to two-inch) **red-spotted toad** may be found. **Canyon tree frogs** may be found in waterpockets formed in slickrock or in wet niches. Their wide adhesive toepads enable them to cling to vertical rock surfaces.

Twenty-eight different reptiles can be found here, all of them interesting creatures with numerous adaptations to desert life. Iguanid lizards include the large **chuckwalla,** which may reach twenty inches in length, including the tail. This rock-dwelling lizard eats plants and likes to sun itself on boulders in suitable rocky habitat. **Collared lizards** are more common and almost as large, reaching fourteen inches, counting the tail. They are recognized by two black collar bands circling the shoulder and neck. These lizards will leap at and rush their prey, seizing insects and smaller lizards. They may run on their two hind legs, looking like miniature tyrannosaurs. They prefer rocky habitat with open reaches.

Other lizards of the area in the iguana family include several types of **spiny lizard** and the abundant **side-blotched lizard. Whiptails** are agile, slender lizards with colorful markings. **Western whiptails** are common and may be recognized by size (nine to twelve inches), and smooth dorsal skin with light mottling and stripes on a gray-brown or olive background. Whiptails occupy a variety of open habitats where they feed by chasing down insects.

The Recreation Area's snake fauna include thirteen species and various additional subspecies. The most common are the **gopher snake, desert striped whipsnake, kingsnake,** and **western patch-nosed snake. Western rattlesnakes** are the one venomous species, occurring in several varieties. One of these is the so-called **Hopi rattlesnake,** a subspecies used by Hopi Indians in snake dances. Rattlers feed mainly on small mammals and birds. Rattlesnakes are relatively common in the desert yet are seldom encountered because they avoid people. Most active in the evening and morning, they avoid the hottest or coldest parts of the day. They favor rocky areas and ledges. The best precaution to avoid snakebite when hiking and climbing in rocky country is to place your hands and feet only where you can see what is there.

The story of fish in the Recreation Area is an interesting one, testament to both the effects of human interference with the environment and the benefits of fishery programs to increase productivity. Of twenty-nine fish species known from Glen Canyon, only eight are natives, all the rest having been introduced. Three of the native species are endangered; the fourth is a candidate for the endangered list. The decline of native fish is directly attributable to competition from the introduced species and habitat modification by reservoirs, agricultural depletions, and other activities of mankind.

The **Colorado River squawfish,** one of the endangered species, was once the dominant fish of the river, found throughout the basin. It is the largest North American minnow, once exceeding eighty pounds and measuring up to six feet in length. Today, specimens of squawfish rarely exceed

ANIMAL LIFE

fifteen pounds and three feet. Squawfish were the dominant carnivore of the river, feeding on other fish and possibly aquatic birds. Apparently squawfish are tasty and were called Colorado River salmon. Squawfish are still occasionally found in the upper reservoir. Whether they maintain a small population based on upriver spawning is unknown, since squawfish may live over twenty years and the adults found in Lake Powell could be remnants. Any squawfish (for identification, the mouth extends past the eye) taken by an angler should be returned to the water unharmed, and the catch reported to the National Park Service.

Humpback chub and bonytail chub are medium-sized minnows (twelve to twenty inches) with dorsal humps that apparently stabilize the fish in swift current. Both are endangered and unlikely to be encountered in the lake. The bonytail is on the verge of extinction. **Razorback suckers** are large (up to three feet, fifteen pounds) native bottom-feeders now in decline through most of their former range. These fish are still found in the upper lake but it is unknown if they are successfully reproducing. Razorbacks have a sharp dorsal ridge and a fleshy mouth on the underside of the head. They are being considered for listing as threatened species and should be returned unharmed if caught.

Sportfishing on Lake Powell affords an exciting and popular recreational pastime that continues as one of the most rewarding year-round activities. Gamefish in Lake Powell include **striped bass, largemouth bass, smallmouth bass, black crappie, walleye, bluegill, channel catfish,** and an occasional **northern pike.**

Lake Powell's fishery is already famous, though still young and developing. It can be expected to improve over the years, with changes in the mix of species caught as fish populations equilibrate in their new environment.

Inquire locally for current conditions or purchase one of the several fishing guides sold at the marinas. All fishermen over twelve years old must be licensed, and there are bag limits. A Lake Powell stamp, which covers Arizona and Utah, is available.

Enjoyment of Lake Powell's fish and wildlife can be one of the most pleasurable aspects of your vacation in this wild and remote National Park Service area. Please remember not to disturb any of the animals unnecessarily and that collecting is not permitted except for the taking of game species under license.

Little brown bat

Antelope ground squirrel

Deer mouse

Rock squirrel

Kangaroo rat

Wood rat

Pocket mouse

ANIMAL LIFE

Badger

Black-tailed jackrabbit

Desert cottontail

Porcupine

Striped skunk

Beaver

Long-tailed weasel

Bobcat

Desert bighorn

Mule deer

Coyote

Gray fox

ANIMAL LIFE

Canyon wren

Dark-eyed junco

Great horned owl

California gull

Ash-throated flycatcher

Great blue heron

American coot

Bald eagle

Brewer's sparrow

House sparrow

White-crowned sparrow

Chipping sparrow

Mountain chickadee

Loggerhead shrike

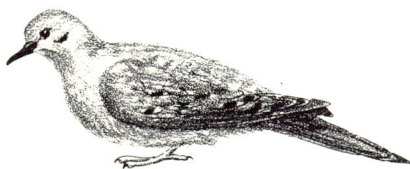

Mourning dove

Horned lark

House finch

ANIMAL LIFE

White-throated swift

Yellow warbler

Violet-green swallow

Robin

Raven

Peregrine falcon

Sparrow hawk

Red-tailed hawk

Chuckwalla

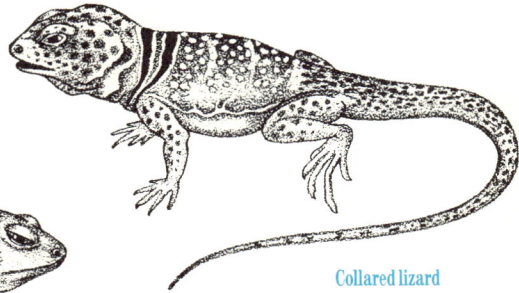

Collared lizard

Desert spiny lizard

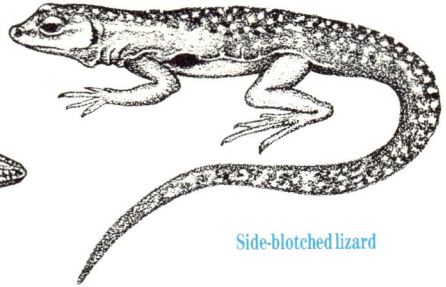

Side-blotched lizard

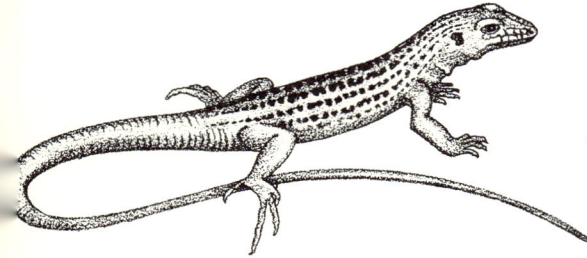

Western whiptail

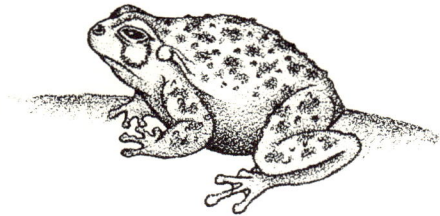

Canyon treefrog

Red-spotted toad

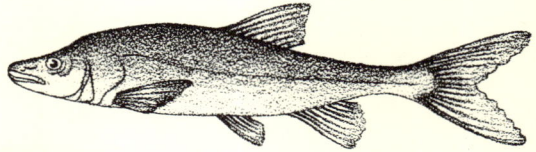

Colorado chub
(endangered)

Colorado River squawfish

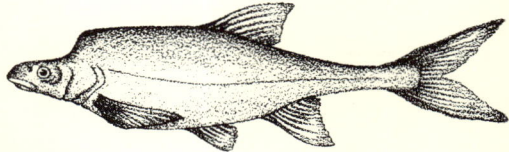

Humpback chub
(endangered)

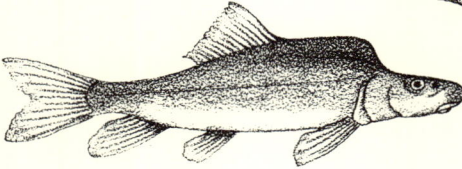

Razorback sucker

Gopher snake

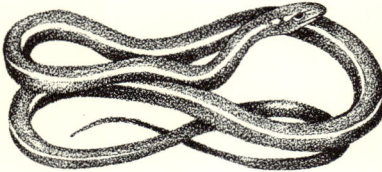

Desert striped whipsnake

Hopi rattlesnake

Kingsnake

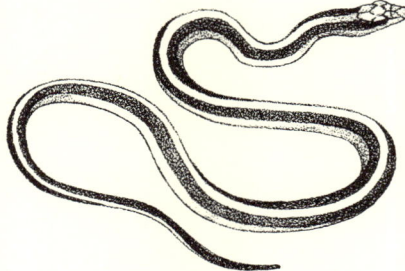

Western patch-nosed snake

Adesert might be described as a very warm place that receives less than twelve inches of precipitation a year, has extreme daily fluctuations in temperature, and where the evaporation rate exceeds the annual rainfall. Three of North America's deserts — the Chihuahuan, Sonoran, and Mojave — fit that description.

The fourth North American desert, the Great Basin which contains the Glen Canyon National Recreation Area, fits most of that description except that it is a cold desert instead of a warm one. Temperatures may be freezing or sub-freezing for a week or more, greatly influencing the distribution of its flowering plants.

A variety of interesting desert plants grow on the benchtops and mesas which make up the shoreline and areas surrounding Lake Powell. Plant communities will be presented from the lower elevations along the lakeshore up to the higher mesas and plateaus surrounding Lake Powell.

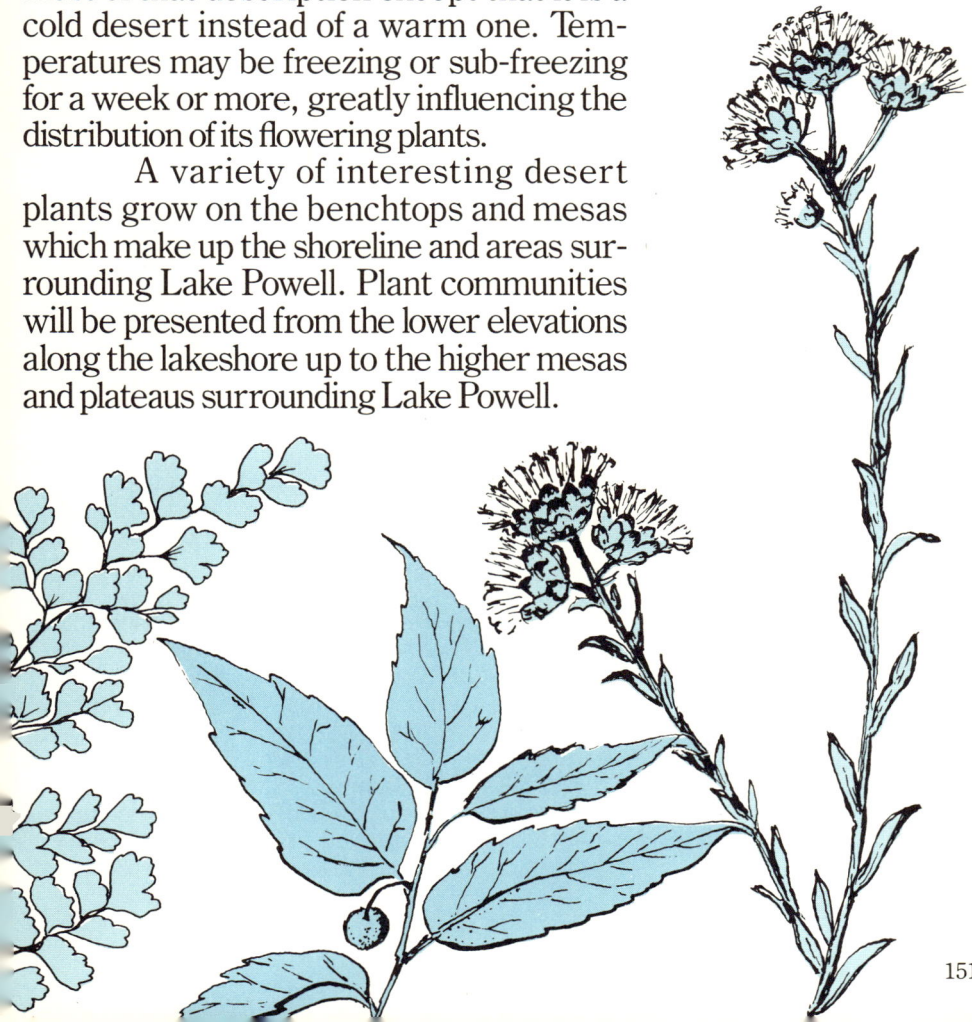

151

PLANT LIFE

The shoreline plant communities, or riparian areas, are now developing since Lake Powell reached full pool in 1983 at an elevation of 3,708 feet. Up until that time, the shoreline continued to rise each year as the giant reservoir filled behind Glen Canyon Dam. Since 1983 the shoreline vegetation, which is made up primarily of **saltcedar,** has begun developing on what was previously desert shrublands. Saltcedar, which was introduced into the Southwest in the mid-1800s as a windbreak around agricultural fields, has escaped from cultivation and is invading springs and riverways. Other species such as **cottonwood, willow, hackberry,** and **box elder** would grow on these newly inundated areas, but the saltcedar is much better equipped for the task with its millions of small hairy seeds which can be dispersed over thousands of square miles. It simply outcompetes the other species. Saltcedar quickly germinates in the moist sand or gravel, grows rapidly and uses a great deal of water, thus impacting plant development and producing an exotic habitat for wildlife. The United States Department of Agriculture is investigating use of a "biological control," the introduction of an insect that feeds only on saltcedar leaves, hoping to reduce the saltcedar infestation.

The floors of the canyons that drain into Lake Powell have plant communities that reflect that of the main canyon before inundation by Lake Powell. They are green with sedges, grasses, and willows with an occasional stand of cottonwood trees which can grow as tall as fifty feet. Within some of the narrow tributary canyons, **gamble oak** grow in such dense thickets that they are almost impenetrable.

In the large weathered alcoves formed along seeps and driplines in the sandstone grow hanging gardens. The broad, bright-green leaves of the plants in these moist gardens are a startling contrast with the silvery, inconspicuous leaves of the desert plants. They abound with gamble oak, **poison ivy, buckthorn,** and **maidenhair fern.** Among these greens are the red blossoms of the **crimson monkey flower** and the **scarlet cardinal flower,** and the white of the **mat forming spiraea** and the **New Mexico raspberry.** Some of the more rare plants represented are the **purple flowered primrose** which clings to the moist rock walls, **sawgrass** with its serrate leaf edges, **shooting star** and **death camas.** While no two hanging gardens are alike, they contain plants which reflect a cool, moist climate which was predominant throughout the Colorado Plateau ten thousand years ago.

The lower benches around Lake Powell support a variety of community types depending on soil depth and texture. On the benches below Nipple Bench and north of Wahweap, the soils are derived from the fine textured Tropic shales and support a sparse **mat saltbrush** community. These plants are less than a foot high and form large silver-grey mats. In some places the plants are widely spaced and appear to be the only living things in the area; but in the spring there will be a colorful display of **scorpion weed, evening primrose,** and **skeleton weed.**

Shadscale, closely related to mat saltbrush, is common throughout the Great Basin, forming pure stands in soils containing a high concentration of salt dissolved from sedimentary formations and concentrated in the valley floors. Commonly occurring with shadscale is the **Thompson indigobush** which produces spectacular purple-blue flowers, contrasting with its white bark. In the vicinity of Bullfrog Marina, the closely related **Fremont indigobush** produces an equally attractive blossom. Additional species associated with the shadscale community are **four-wing saltbrush, wire lettuce, Mormon tea,** and **goldenhead.**

Where sands accumulate and the soils are deep (twenty to thirty inches), **Indian rice grass, blackbrush, galleta, Mormon tea, globemallow,** and **yucca** grow. These plants are evident at Wahweap Marina, Lone Rock, and in the low areas surrounding Bullfrog Marina and Halls Crossing.

Within the Recreation Area, there are a number of isolated and inaccessible buttes and mesas. The National Park Service in cooperation with Utah State University and The Nature Conservancy visited some of these areas in 1987 for the purpose of collecting vegetation information for lands which had not been grazed by domestic livestock. Their preliminary findings show that **needle-and-thread grass,** a perennial bunchgrass with flowering stalks which stand three feet tall, is a predominant species. This is the grass which is believed to be the one described by early pioneers as growing "as high as a horse's belly" and which is now virtually absent from similar sites which are available for livestock use.

Benchtops and mesas with shallow soils are the most prevalent habitat type within the Recreation Area, and in these areas grow dense stands of **blackbrush.** The plants appear to be evenly spaced and provide a monotonous aspect to the already level landscape. Blackbrush is a member of the rose family but the yellow flowers lack petals and are hardly noticeable when compared to the showy garden varieties of roses.

Shrubs that occur with blackbrush are **rabbitbrush, hopsage, wolfberry,** and **yucca.** The **sego lily,** the Utah State flower, appears in both white and a sulfur yellow. **Blue larkspur, orange globemallow,** and numerous yellow mustards and sunflowers are common among the blackbrush shrubs. Antelope Island, the Hole-in-the-Rock Road west of the Escalante River, and the benchlands surrounding Bullfrog Marina are good examples of the blackbrush community.

The higher mesatops of the Orange Cliffs (north of Hite) and Kaiparowits Plateau at elevations of six thousand feet and above support **pinyon-juniper woodlands** with small, isolated sagebrush meadows. Both of these areas can be seen only in the distance from Lake Powell, but the vegetation is representative of the vast expanse of these types throughout the western United States. While the pinyon-juniper comprises less than ten percent of the vegetative cover of the Recreation Area, it was extremely important as wildlife habitat and for prehistoric human habitation. These woodlands receive as much as twelve inches of rain a year and can support agriculture. It was the fruit of the pinyon pine tree, the pine nut, which was widely used as food and may have provided some basis for human existence.

In protected sites of both the Orange Cliffs and the Waterpocket Fold, isolated stands of **Douglas fir** survive the hot summer temperatures because they grow in moist, north facing alcoves. The sun never reaches the soil at these sites, allowing the trees to survive two thousand feet lower than they commonly occur.

Barberry

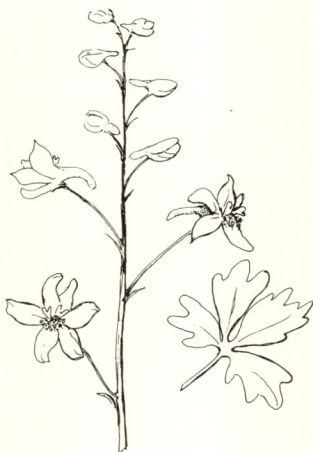

Blue larkspur

Blue gramma

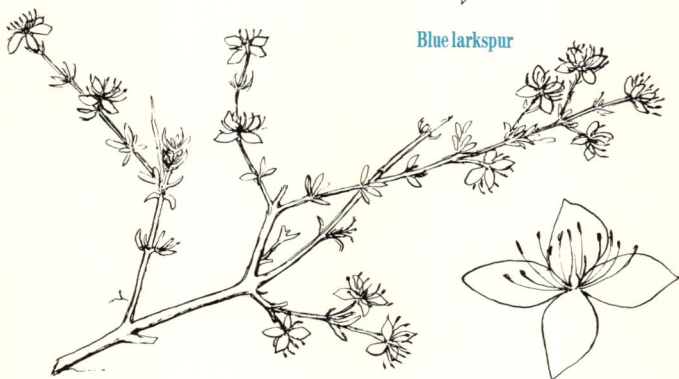

Blackbrush

Box elder

Buffaloberry

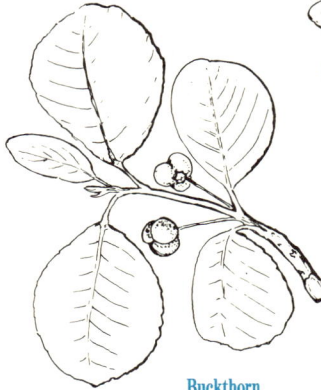

Buckthorn

Crimson monkey flower

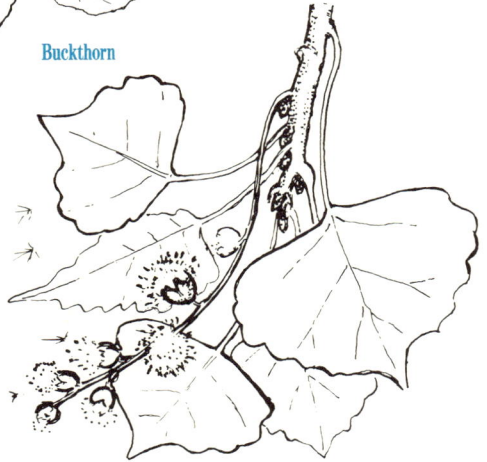

Cottonwood

Douglas fir

PLANT LIFE

Death camus

Evening primrose

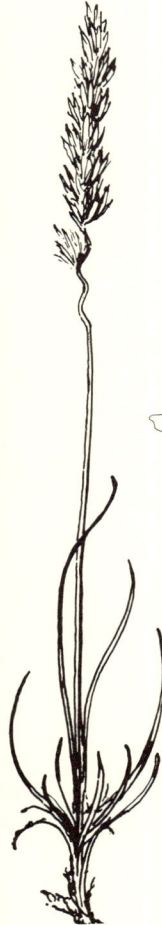

Gamble oak

Four-wing saltbrush

Galleta

Goldenhead

Hackberry

Hopsage

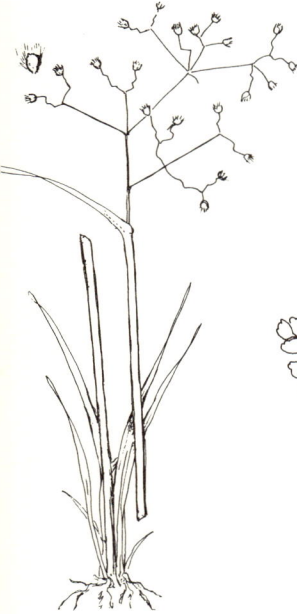

Indian rice grass

Maidenhair fern

Juniper

PLANT LIFE

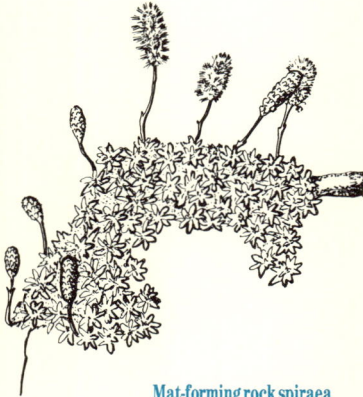

Mat-forming rock spiraea

Needle-and-thread grass

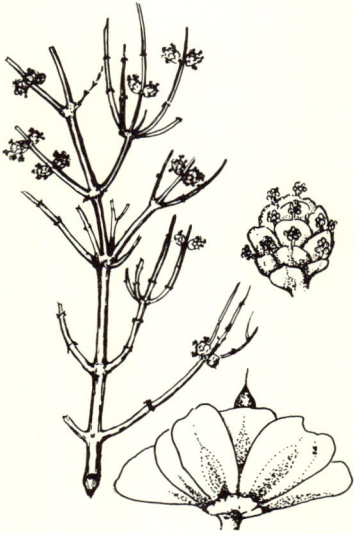

Mormon tea

Mat saltbrush

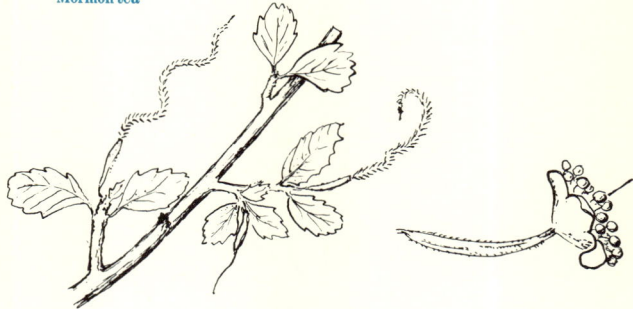

Mountain mahogany

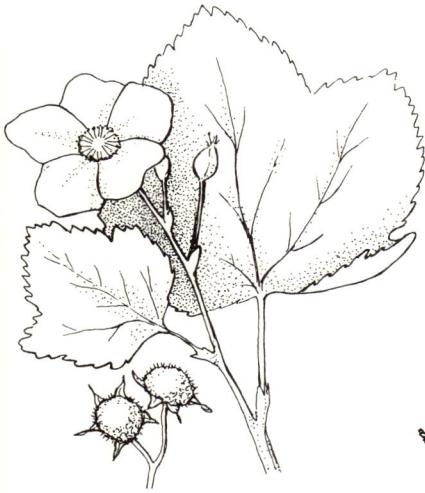

Orange globemallow

New Mexico raspberry

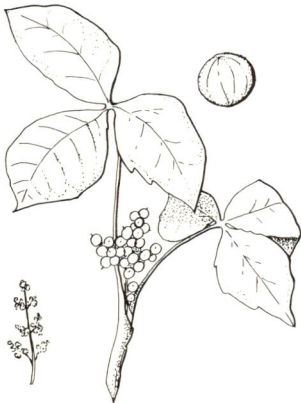

Pinyon

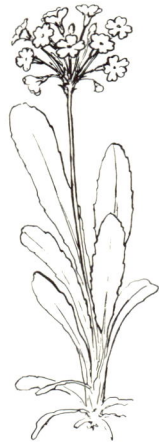

Poison ivy

Purple flowered primrose

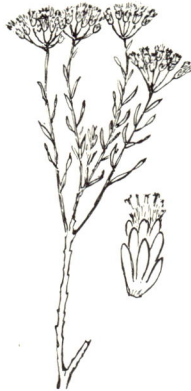

Rabbitbrush
Chrysothamnus Viscidflourus

Rabbitbrush
Chrysothamnus Nauseus

Sagebrush

Saltcedar

Scarlet gilia

Scarlet cardinal flower

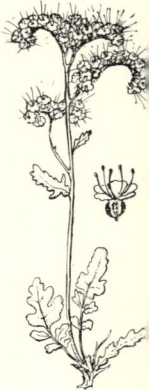

Scorpion weed

Shadscale

Shooting star

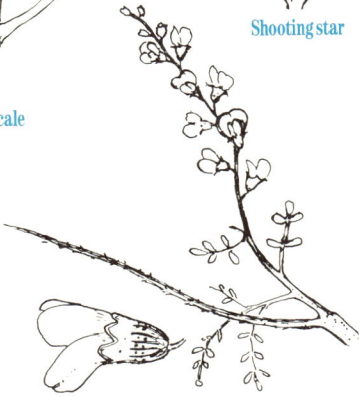

Thompson indigobush

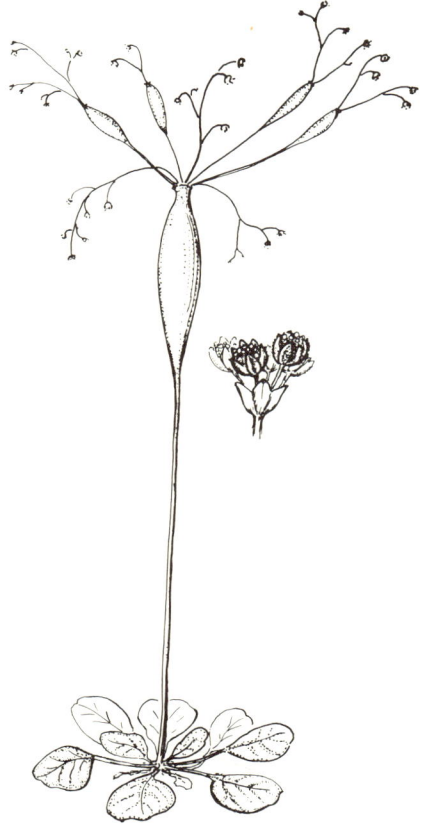

Skeleton weed

Stemless hymenoxys

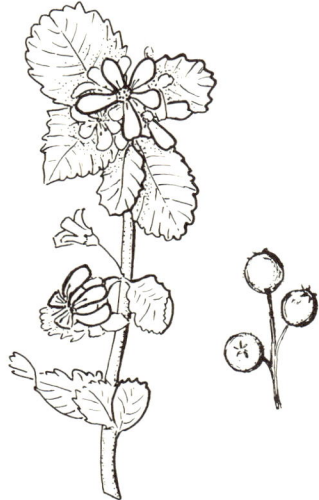

Utah serviceberry

White sego lily
Yellow sego lily

Willow

Wire lettuce

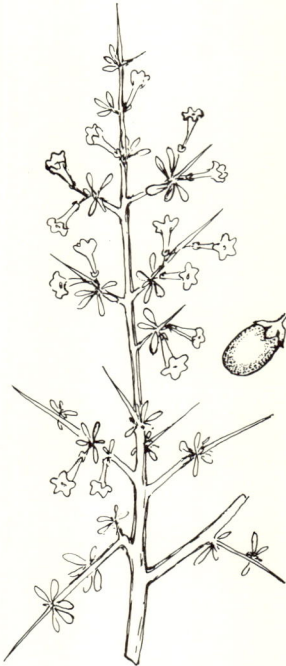

Wolfberry

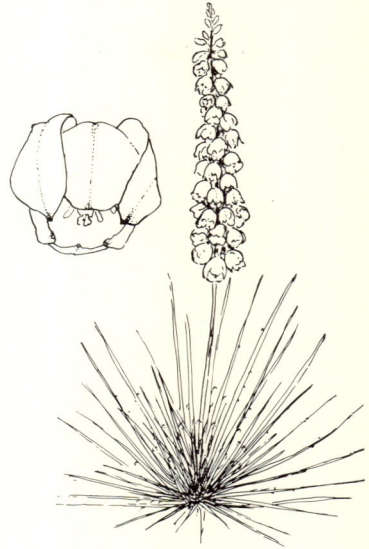

Yucca

Climate controls many aspects of landscape evolution. The rainfall of an area determines in part how much water is fed to the streams, and, therefore, affects the ability of the streams to do geologic work. In dry climates, many streams disappear completely when rainfall is scarce, then swell to capacity during brief flash floods. Weathering processes break down rocks into particles that can be transported by wind or water. These weathering processes, whether chemical or physical, are affected by climate. The rate of chemical reactions increases with temperature and moisture. Warm, moist climates will lead to speedy chemical decay of rocks and minerals; dry climates tend to slow down chemical weathering. The preservation of eight-hundred-year-old Indian pictographs and petroglyphs on the canyon walls in Glen Canyon National Recreation Area is an excellent illustration of the near lack of chemical decay in this area.

photo by Tom Bean

LAND SCULPTURE

Various processes, freezing and thawing for example, cause rocks to break apart into rubble. Without strong chemical weathering to round off the broken rock, the entire landscape tends to appear angular and jagged, similar to the landforms that characterize much of southeastern Utah (fig. 1).

arid   humid

fig. 1

When two or more rock types of different make-up are exposed to weathering and erosion, they will be sculpted at different rates and produce different forms — this is the principle of **differential weathering and erosion** and is basic to understanding the Recreation Area landscape. As the Colorado River cut through the rocks of the area, different layers were exposed, some with low resistance to erosion, others highly resistant. Sandstone and other resistant rocks tend to produce flat surfaces bounded by steep cliffs (fig. 2A).

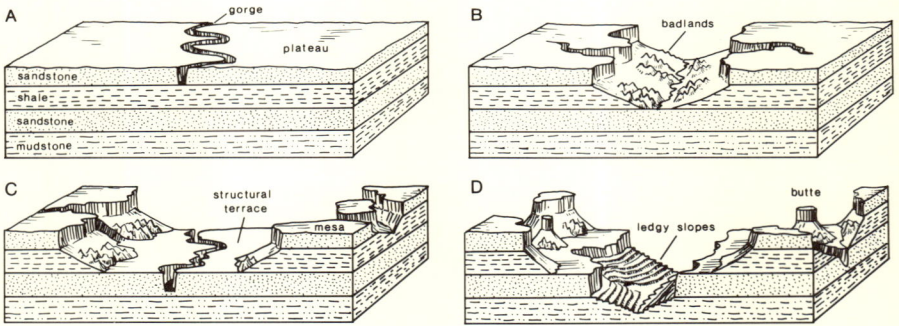

fig. 2

Away from the main gorge, the flat plane of the sandstone is practically unscathed by erosion because the water flow is not yet concentrated into well-organized channels. The thin veneer of water that flows over the rocky surface during heavy rains is laboriously slow in cutting away the resistant rock. The landscape that is created is one of monotonous flatness, interrupted by gorges that are so narrow that from a distance they may be hidden from view. Early travelers across the plateau were often dismayed after setting a course across a seemingly unbroken plain only to encounter an impassable canyon, forcing them to backtrack and begin again.

LAND SCULPTURE

Eventually the river breaks through the resistant sandstone and cuts into the non-resistant shale. The canyon continues to widen and deepen, but the shale cannot maintain steep slopes for any length of time, so its slopes become somewhat more gentle (fig. 2B). The shale, now beginning to show signs of an organized drainage network, may be carved into a series of closely-spaced rills and gullies called **badlands.** As a second resistant layer is encountered, the landscape pattern begins to repeat itself. A broad bench is created, bounded by a cliff on one side and the gentler upward-sloping surface on the other (fig. 2C). At this stage, tributary streams begin to take their toll on the landscape, isolating parts of the uppermost sandstone into tablelike landforms called **mesas.** Some of the mesas at this stage have been further isolated into small, flat-topped **buttes** — the last, dying remnants of what had been a vast plain in the initial stage of erosion. This stair-stepped landscape made of mesas, buttes, structural terraces and steep-walled canyons is a **plateau,** and the Colorado Plateau has long served as the stereotype for plateau landforms.

Most rock units are broken by a series of fractures or joints. Several of the prominent sandstone units in the Recreation Area are riddled with parallel joint sets that are often vertical or near vertical. The joints serve as avenues through which moisture can penetrate, and the moisture in turn accelerates the weathering of the rock along the joints. In time the joints are thus widened and deepened, and may later become the sites of small streams. The result is a regular pattern of parallel rock fins and gullies, a pattern that typifies many outcrops of the Navajo Sandstone (fig. 3)

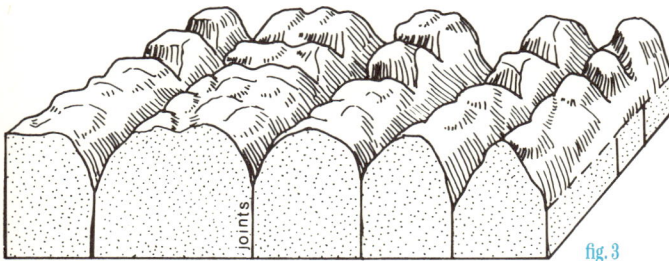

fig. 3

Joints are also important in the process of cliff retreat, because when the sandstone is undermined at the base of a cliff, it will tend to break off along existing weaknesses such as these vertical joints (fig. 4).

The downcutting of the Colorado River, the first and most critical process in overall canyon development, has triggered other processes that have had a great impact on the widening of the valleys as well as their form.

In porous rock, like sandstone, rainwater seeps in and makes its way downward through the rock until its move-

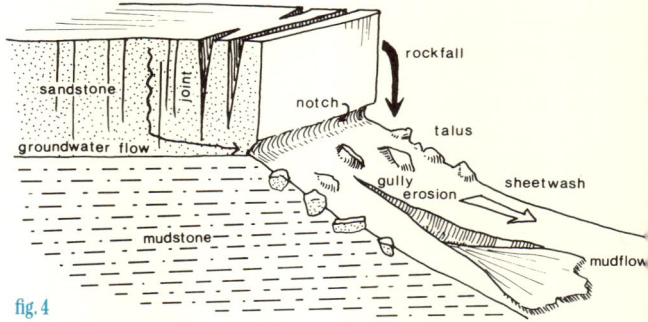

fig. 4

ment is stopped by a less porous rock layer such as shale or mudstone. The water then is forced laterally until it has an opportunity to exit at the cliff face, usually in the form of a seep or spring. The moisture concentrated here helps loosen the sand grains and binding cement and begins to form a recess at the base of the cliff (fig. 4). As the cavity enlarges, the cliff becomes less stable, and finally fails along one of the vertical joints. Slabs of sandstone, some of them massive, then break off and fall downslope. The fresh scars on the canyon walls around Lake Powell and the huge piles of talus at their bases are constant reminders of the importance of these processes, called **cliff retreat.**

Slumps also contribute to cliff retreat. This type of mass wasting involves the movement of large blocks of material downward along a curved slippage plane (fig. 5). Fresh slump scars occur in many sections of the San Juan Arm and from Good Hope Mesa to Trachyte Creek, where movement during the past few years has been initiated by high lake levels.

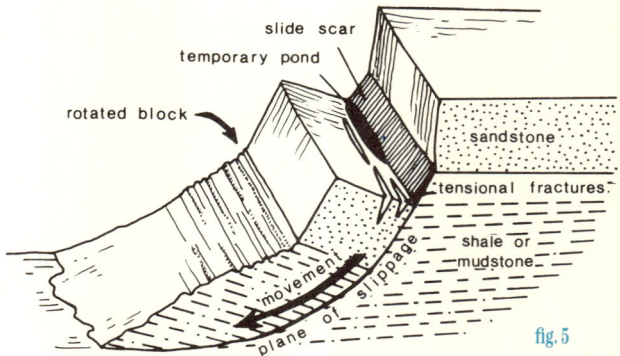

fig. 5

Streams that flow year round are also important sculptors. Those that have enough cutting power to keep pace with the Colorado River usually enter the main channel through spectacular narrow canyons. These intriguing side canyons with their precipitous sandstone walls are favorite places for Lake Powell boaters to explore, or in times of storm, to seek refuge. Other tributaries that were not capable of keeping up with the main stream's downcutting enter the canyon as **hanging valleys,** the sites of beautiful waterfalls after heavy thunderstorms. Variations in the rock resistance along these valleys may create a series of "jumps" as the water falls over the lip of a resistant unit and produce a plungepool below (fig. 6).

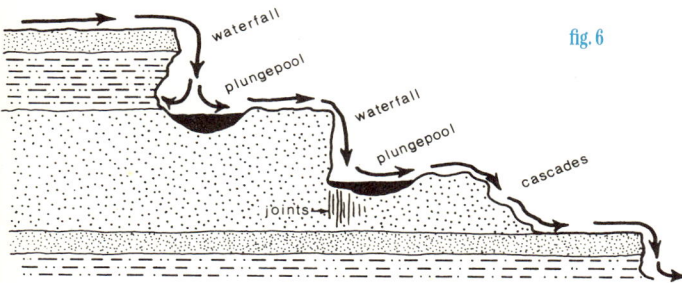

fig. 6

Many of the plungepool basins hold water long after the storm has passed and become interesting breeding grounds for a variety of insects and frogs as well as watering holes for larger animals.

Many tributary valleys of Glen Canyon end in ampitheaterlike valley heads, with high vertical and overhanging walls. Their development is often controlled by the dip of the rock units, which controls the flow of groundwater (fig. 7).

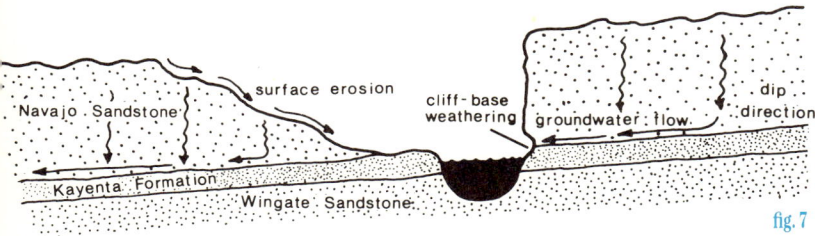

fig. 7

Another feature that is somewhat unique to the Colorado Plateau is the occurrence of valley-mouth alluvial fans. Where tributary streams carry an unusually high amount of coarse-grained, gravelly materials, the main channel of the river may not be able to transport the debris away. It is deposited at the junction of the two canyons in the form of a fan-shaped deposit, and often causes the main channel to be diverted in its course around the alluvial fan. Several of these can be found in Cataract Canyon near the head of Lake Powell.

Periodically, a stream may rise above its natural banks and flood the area, creating a floodplain. Prior to the filling of Lake Powell, there were narrow floodplains along stretches of Glen Canyon. Floodplains have always been important in the history of the river because of the availability of water for farming, and more recently, the placer gold mining activities of the late 1800s.

When conditions allow the stream to begin downcutting again, the floodplain will be abandoned and become a **stream terrace,** whose flattish form and gravelly mantle provide evidence of its origin (fig. 8).

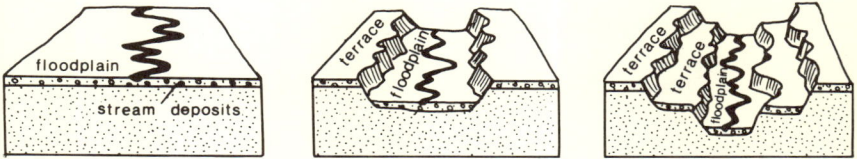

fig. 8

If floodplain development is interrupted by rapid downcutting in resistant rocks, the sinuous or meandering course of the river may persist, forming **incised meanders.** Some of the finest examples of incised meanders occur in the Colorado Plateau, such as the "Goosenecks of the San Juan" immediately east of Lake Powell. Those with steep and symmetrical walls on either side of their channel are called **entrenched meanders** (fig. 9).

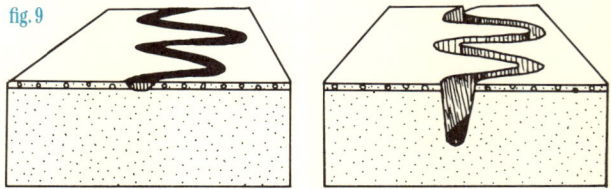

fig. 9

Most of the main channel of Glen Canyon from Halls Crossing to the mouth of the San Juan Arm displays **ingrown meanders,** which are formed if the meandering pattern continues to grow laterally as downcutting proceeds. Ingrown meanders are readily recognized by the steep cliffs on the outside of the meander loop where the stream is attempting to undercut the cliff (fig. 10).

fig. 10

The formation of incised meanders sets the stage for the development of two other distinctive landforms. One, formed where the stream undercuts the rock wall that separates the two sides of the meander loop leaving the former channel dry, is called a **meander core cutoff.** A curious mesa becomes isolated, surrounded by the old channel (fig. 11A). Excellent examples are seen along Lake Powell's shoreline at the Rincon and at the mouth of White Canyon.

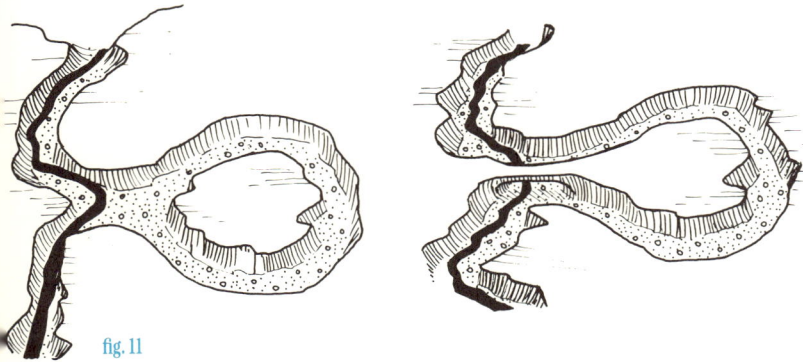

fig. 11

In the second case, the meander cutoff may occur under a resistant caprock such as sandstone, and the "roof" may remain as a natural bridge (fig. 11B). Several of the bridges in Natural Bridges National Monument about twenty-five miles southeast of Hite have formed in this manner. A few of the bridges in the Recreation Area landscape have a similar origin, including the world's largest natural rock span, Rainbow Bridge (fig. 12). The stippled pattern in fig. 12 represents the former course of Bridge Creek before the cutoff occurred. The bridge is of Navajo Sandstone and the base is anchored in the Kayenta Formation. The bridge has a span of 278 feet and rises nearly 300 feet above the waters of Lake Powell. The old channel gravels that once went around the meander loop can still be seen.

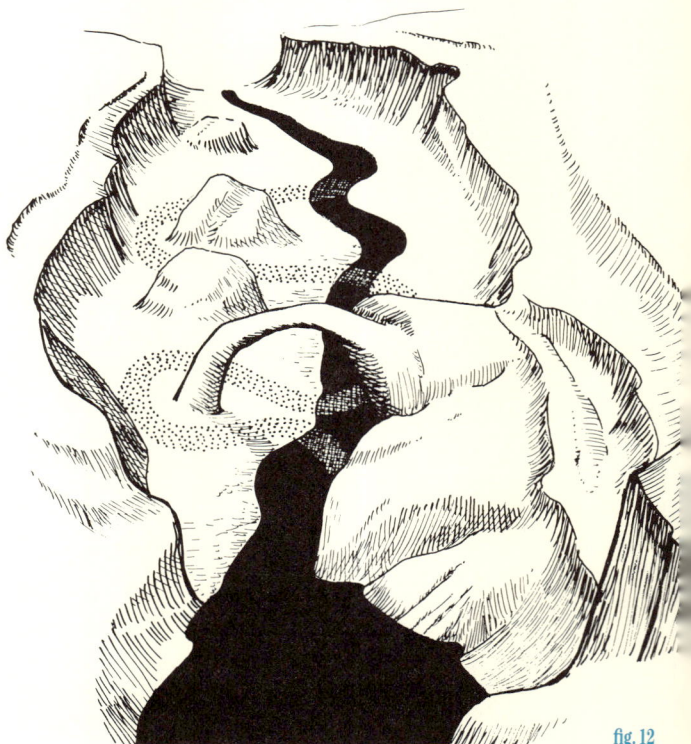

fig. 12

Landforms produced strictly by wind erosion are relatively rare. The lifting and removal by the wind of fine, loose particles from soil or weathered bedrock is at least partly responsible for two features found around the Recreation Area. In gravelly deposits, wind can remove only the smaller grains of sand, silt or clay, leaving behind a residue of coarser cobbles that become so closely packed that they are referred to as **desert pavement** (fig. 13). Recent research in the southwestern deserts of the United States indicates that other processes may contribute to the formation of desert pavement.

fig. 13

The other feature that may be wind-modified is a mushroom-shaped mass of bedrock called a **hoodoo rock.** Isolated bedrock knobs or spires are subject to the intense near-surface abrasion by sandblasting. Since sand transport is generally limited to the lowermost foot or so off the ground, the base of the rock outcrop is attacked most vigorously, producing the hoodoo form (fig. 14). Hoodoo rocks may also be formed by differential weathering of the softer shale beneath the resistant sandstone.

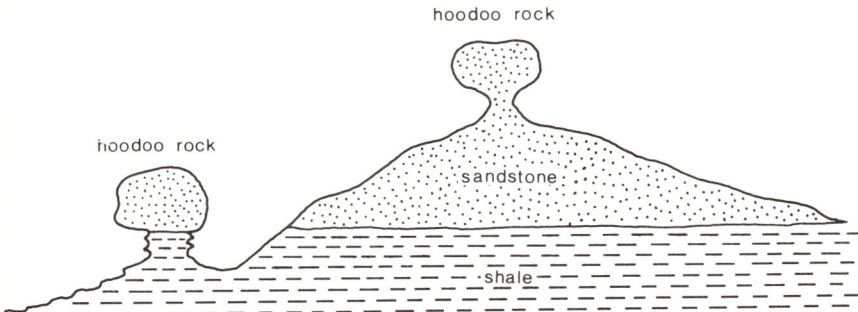

fig. 14

LAND SCULPTURE

Some of the most fascinating and colorful features of the Recreation Area landscape are not the result of the more notorious agents like wind, streams, and gravity, but rather the slow, often imperceptible weathering processes that leave a distinctive imprint on the land. **Rock color,** for example, may in some cases be inherited from the original pigments within the rock body, for instance the greens, maroons and grays of the various members of the Chinle Formation, or may be the result of a thin coating of surficial material resulting from prolonged exposure to surface weathering. The white coating on the underside of many stones in talus and terrace deposits is calcium carbonate, a relatively soluble mineral that is washed partially through the deposit then chemically deposited on stones and smaller soil particles as the water evaporates. Calcite also tends to accumulate in joints, and becomes obvious when slabs of bedrock break away from the canyon walls to leave a whitewashed surface.

The dark red, purple, and purple-black staining on many of the rock walls is a super-thin coating of **desert varnish.** In some places, the varnish is continuous and uniform, and in others it forms long, draping ribbons referred to as "tapestry." Its composition includes iron and manganese oxides, clay minerals, occasionally organic constituents and other compounds (fig. 15). The origin of desert varnish has

fig. 15

long been a matter of controversy. Many think that the rock glaze comes from within the rock, carried to the surface in solution by water and left as a chemical residue when the water evaporates. Some varnish undoubtedly comes from an external source, either from the atmosphere or from the rocks above. Much of the "tapestry" in the Lake Powell region is probably derived from red pigments from the overlying red formations (fig. 16). Black tapestry that forms ribbons down vertical cliffs and overhangs may have a strong organic

fig. 16

component, with the intermittent spillover of water nourishing algae and other hardy plants (fig. 17). Another origin of some forms of desert varnish is from the exposure of joints

fig. 17

that were impregnated with iron and manganese oxides by groundwater before surface exposure (fig. 18). Clearly, there are several possible origins of desert varnish, and it is likely that additional theories will be proposed in the future.

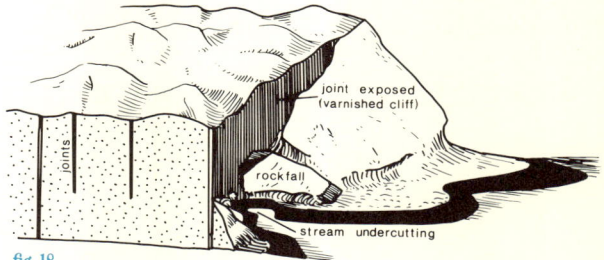

fig. 18

     A curious pattern of joints also results from weathering. Unlike other joints that form during lithification or from stresses accompanying folding and faulting, these joints parallel the modern surface of the rock outcrop. These **exfoliation joints** are caused by rock expansion. But what causes the rocks to expand? The answer lies in the fact that at some time in the past these rocks were buried by overlying rocks and were under high pressure, causing them to exist in a slightly compressed state. With the removal of overburden by erosion, the pressure was released, and the rock expanded, creating the stress to fracture the rock (fig. 19).

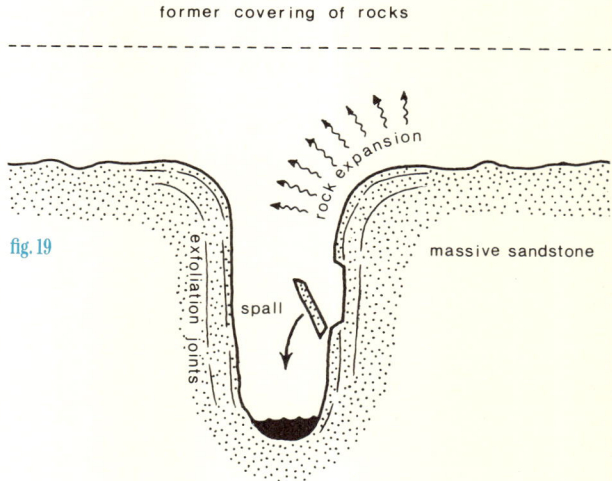

fig. 19

Massive sandstones in Glen Canyon such as the Navajo and Entrada formations commonly display exfoliation joints (fig. 20). Note the arched roof and the flat back wall, which help to distinguish cliff cavities produced by exfoliation from those due to other processes. During the construction of Glen Canyon Dam, exfoliation joints had to be bolted to the canyon walls to prevent spalling.

fig. 20

Flattish sandstone outcrops are frequently riddled with depressions ranging in size from a few inches across to tens of feet. These are **weathering pits** and are usually found at sites where moisture has hastened the disintegration of the rock and the loosened particles have then been carried away by the wind (fig. 21). Once the pit is large enough to pond water, airborne particles are trapped and

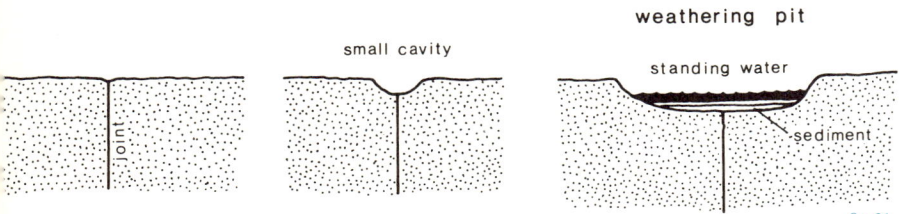

small cavity

weathering pit

standing water

joint

sediment

fig. 21

settle to the bottom to form a sediment layer, which can then support vegetation. These are commonly called "tanks" in the Southwest, and were of great historical significance because they pond water after rains and were a major source of drinking water for the Indians and early explorers. Many of the larger pits trap wind-blown sediment and become sites of interesting plant communities (fig. 22).

fig. 22

Cavities are also common on steep sandstone outcrops. Where dozens of small recesses pock-mark sandstone cliffs they are called **stone lattice, pitted sandstone,** or **honeycomb weathering.** Their alignment with joints or bedding planes suggest that they too are products of weathering processes that have been accentuated by moisture retention along these discontinuities (fig. 23).

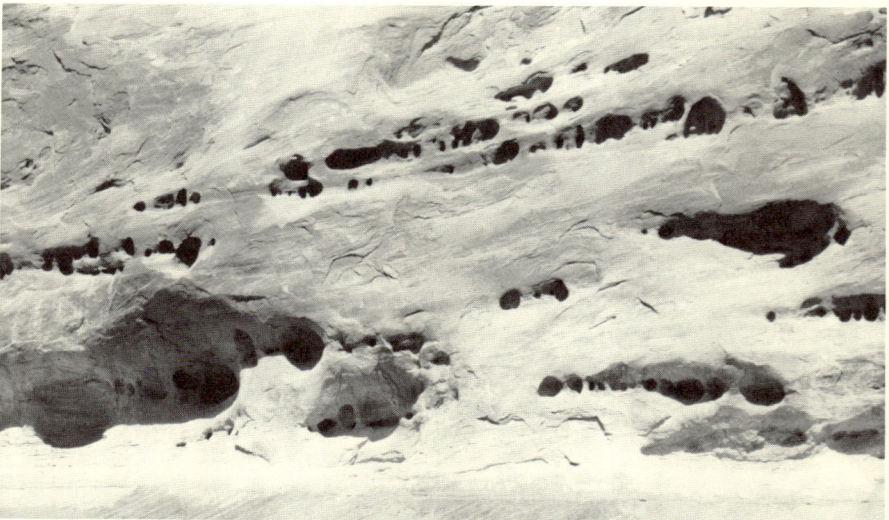

fig. 23

Cliff-base notches are formed in similar fashion, but are usually found where there is major contact between rock units (see fig. 24). Notches may become greatly enlarged along active seeps, forming **alcoves** or **rock shelters.** They differ from notches in that they are larger and more localized. These cool, shady sites were a favorite refuge for Indians that inhabited the area centuries ago. In some cases alcoves become so deeply recessed into the canyon walls that they intercept water that filters downward along vertical joints. Further enlargement of the alcove and the joint plane by weathering and stream erosion may join the two cavities together, forming a **natural bridge** (fig. 24).

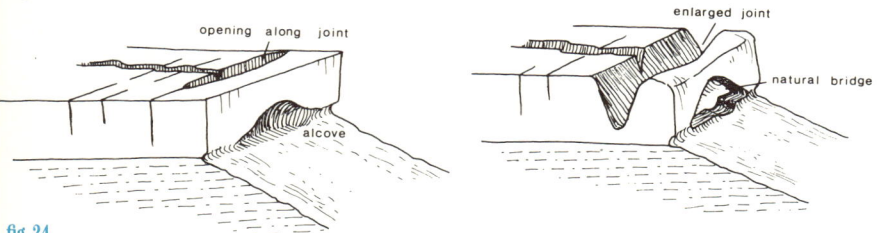

fig. 24

In a slightly different manner, the plunge pool erosion along jumps and waterfalls can similarly intercept a vertical joint, eventually diverting the flow of water into the joint and producing another type of natural bridge (fig. 25).

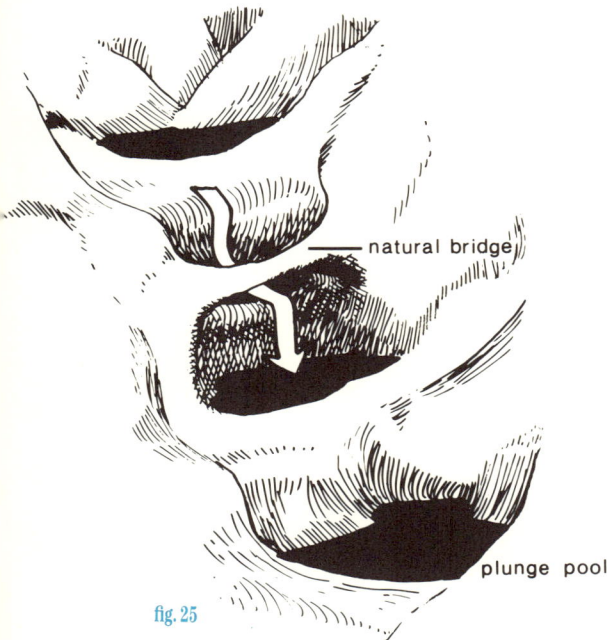

fig. 25

LAND
SCULPTURE

A third type of natural bridge is formed by the cut-off of an incised meander (see figs. 11 and 12).

Natural bridges have in common that running water was at least partially responsible for their development.

Although similar in appearance to natural bridges, **windows** and **natural arches** differ in that their origin is not tied to streams. Their development begins with the formation of a slender, vertical-standing slab of sandstone, often called a **fin,** like those that develop along closely spaced joints or at narrow meander necks (fig. 26). LaGorce Arch in Davis Gulch is actually a window formed in a meander neck.

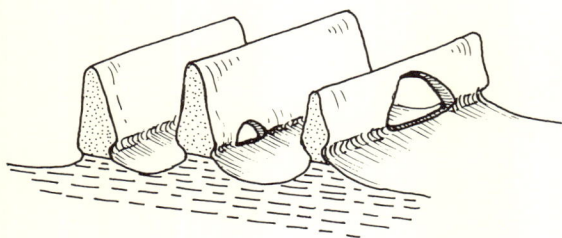

fig. 26

As windows become larger in size they grade into natural arches. The difference is one of scale—the window is a relatively small opening surrounded by an extensive slab of rock, whereas an arch is a larger opening with a more slender or delicate-looking roof.

FURTHER
READING

Baily, Paul
> *Jacob Hamblin, Buckskin Apostle*
> Westernlore Press, Los Angeles, 1961

Bolton, Herbert E.
> *Pageant in the Wilderness*
> Utah State Historical Society, Salt Lake City, date unknown

Comfort, Mary Apollini
> *Rainbow to Yesterday*
> Vantage Press, New York, 1980

Crampton, C. Gregory
> *Standing Up Country*
> Peregrine Smith Books, Layton, Utah, 1983

FURTHER READING

Durrant, Stephen D.
Mammals of Utah
University of Kansas, Lawrence, Kansas, 1952

Everhart, Ronald
Glen Canyon: The Story Behind the Scenery
KC Publications, Las Vegas, Nevada, 1983

Fradkin, Phili L.
A River No More
University of Arizona Press, Tucson, Arizona,
1981

Patraw, Pauline M.
Flowers of the Southwest Mesas
Southwest Parks and Monuments Assn., Tucson,
Arizona, 1964

Phillis, A. and M.; and Gale, J. and M.
Birds of Arizona
University of Arizona Press, Tucson, Arizona,
1964

Powell, J. W.
*Exploration of the Colorado River and Its
Canyons*
Dover Publications, Inc., New York, 1961

Robbins, Chamdler S., et al.
Birds of North America
Golden Press, New York, 1966

Rusho, W. L.; and Crampton, C. G.
Desert River Crossing
Peregrine Smith Books, Layton, Utah, 1975

Sigler, W. F.; and Miller, R. R.
Fishes of Utah
Utah State Department of Fish and Game, Salt
Lake City, Utah, 1963

Stegner, Wallace
Beyond the Hundredth Meridian
University of Nebraska Press, Omaha, Nebraska,
1956

University of Utah
*Upper Colorado Basin Salvage Program,
Anthropological Papers, 31 volumes*
University of Utah, Salt Lake City, Utah, 1966

Woodbury, Angus M.
The Reptiles of Utah
University of Utah, Salt Lake City, Utah, 1931.

MEMBERSHIP

Glen Canyon Natural History Association
P.O. Box 581
Page, Arizona 86040
(602) 645-2511

Glen Canyon Natural History Association is a non-profit organization authorized by Congress to work in co-operation with the National Park Service to assist the visiting public. Our goal is to increase public understanding of the Glen Canyon National Recreation Area and the surrounding Federal lands.

At visitor centers, our bookstores provide high quality publications and educational materials that enhance the visitor's understanding and enjoyment of this unique recreation area. Sale proceeds support educational, scientific, historical, and service programs.

Membership is open to the general public at the following dues rates:

Student (annual)	**$5.00**
Regular (annual)	**$10.00**
Life	**$150.00**
Patron	**$500.00**
Benefactor	**$1,000.00**

As an Association member you will enjoy:
- A 20% member's discount on items found in our sales outlets or through our mail order service
- Seasonal issues of the Association's newspaper "Reflections"
- A Norman Rockwell print depicting Glen Canyon Dam (new members only)
- Discounts at most other Cooperating Association bookstores, including Grand Canyon, Yosemite, Shenandoah, Yellowstone and Everglades
- The satisfaction of assisting educational, scientific, and service programs for the benefit of the visitor.

Your support as a member is appreciated. Please make your check payable to Glen Canyon Natural History Association and mail to P. O. Box 581, Page, AZ 86040.

GLEN CANYON
Natural History Association

ORDER FORM

Please send me additional copies of

THE **LAKE POWELL BOATER'S** GUIDE

NAME _____

ADDRESS _____

CITY _____

STATE _____ ZIP _____

Please include payment with order by check or money order payable to Glen Canyon Natural History Association.

MasterCard Number _____

Visa Card Number _____

Expiration Date _____

Signature: _____

If you are a member of the Glen Canyon Natural History Association, you are entitled to a 20% discount on your order!

Member Name _____

Exp. Date _____

Number of books _____ X $12.95 each = $ _____

Less membership discount _____

Subtotal _____

Postage and handling: First book $2.50 **2.50**

Each additional book $1.00 _____

Total $ _____

Make checks payable to: GLCNHA

Mail order and payment to: Glen Canyon Natural History Association
P.O. Box 581 • Page, AZ 86040